H Chamberlain

H Chamberlain

The African Adventure

Four hundred years of exploration in the 'Dangerous Continent'

Timothy Severin

The African Adventure

Picture research by Sarah Waters

E.P. Dutton & Co., Inc.
New York, 1973

This book was designed and produced by
George Rainbird Limited
Marble Arch House, 44 Edgware Road, London W.2., England
for E. P. Dutton & Co., Inc.
201 Park Avenue South, New York, N.Y. 10003
and first published in the U.S.A. in 1973

House Editor: Curigwen Lewis
Designer: George Sharp
Maps: Tom Stalker-Miller

SBN: 0-525-05110-4
Library of Congress Catalog Card Number: 72-96378

Text photoset by Jolly and Barber Ltd., Rugby, Warwickshire,
England
Printed and bound by Dai Nippon Printing Co., Tokyo, Japan

The illustrations which appear on the preliminary
pages are from *Wild Sports of Southern Africa*
by W. Cornwallis Harris

Contents

	List of color illustrations and maps	6
	Foreword	9
ONE	The Dangerous Continent	11
TWO	Knights of Prester John	25
THREE	Barbary and Guinea	53
FOUR	Agents from Soho	75
FIVE	The Social Spectrum	106
SIX	The Great Trek	134
SEVEN	A Naturalist's Paradise	165
EIGHT	Victorian Lions	190
NINE	Pride and Prejudice	216
TEN	Crisis in the Congo	244
ELEVEN	Conclusion	272
	Illustration acknowledgments	281
	Index	284

Color illustrations

The ruins of Lepcis Magna	17
Sixteenth century map of Africa	20–1
Prester John on his throne	24
Saint Tekla Haymanot in the company of angels and archangels	29
Above Ras Gedam from Massawa *Below* The pass of Rah Eesa	32
Painted wooden panel from Ethiopia	49
Sidy Hassan, Bey of Tripoli	52
The new settlement on the river at Sierra Leone *Inset* Benin bronze plaque	56–7
First day of the Yam Ceremony	60
Torture scene in Barbary	64
Mungo Park	97
Sandwind in the desert	100–1
The Castle of Mourzouk	104
Sir Joseph Banks	105
Two portraits of James Bruce	109
Sketching ruins in Tripoli	112
Hugh Clapperton	114
Dixon Denham	115
Consul Hanmer Warrington's country house	118
Camel conveying a bride to her husband	122
Tuaregs	126
Boers resting after a day's trek	146
Dancing dress of Dingaan's harem and a Zulu woman of rank	150
Dingaan in his ordinary and dancing dress	151
Bechuana hunting the lion	154

A pair of gnus 155

The Battle of Blauwkrantz 158–9

Lingap, a Matabele warrior 163

Geranium, Nova Species 166

The sassaby and hartebeest 170

Hunting at Meritsane 171

Above Driving in an eland
Below Return from the chase 174

Andries Africander 175

The *Lady Alice* in sections 209

Above Livingstone almost sunk by a hippo
Below Missionary support party resting on the
river bank 213

Speke, Grant and Bombay in 1863 217

Feasting on 'the choice bits' of an elephant 221

Richard Burton in fencing dress 224

Stanley in the uniform of the Belgian Free State 258

Above The house at Vivi Station
Below Novice explorers celebrate on a dead hippo 262

Stanley directing a boat to be carried to the river 267

Phalanx dance by Mazamboni warriors 270–1

Maps

North-east Africa 35

North and West Africa 67

South Africa 154–5

Central Africa 212

Foreword

It would be rash for a writer to assume that he can satisfactorily compress the entire story of Africa and her explorers into a single volume. Yet so vivid a subject should not be skirted merely because it is massive. This book sets out only to identify and trace some of the major themes within the mainstream of events and show how the African adventure, as I have called it, had a certain cohesion while it progressed from the first timid contacts to the hectic scramble of the late nineteenth century. Even so, the scenario is daunting enough, and would have been even more difficult but for the chance to support the text with contemporary pictures. Fortunately Africa's splendours lured many explorer-artists to record their impressions (and reveal their own attitudes) with paint brush and pencil, and several of their portfolios can still be found, sometimes published in bygone travel books and memoirs, occasionally as unpublished manuscripts tied up in brown wrappers and tucked away in mahogany cabinet drawers. This book has been planned with such illustrations very much in mind, and my first thanks are due to Sarah Waters for her ingenuity and perseverence in delving out the best examples of such work. Secondly, it follows, I am indebted to those librarians who very kindly let me use material in their possession, notably the Royal Geographical Society who are the custodians of an outstanding collection of Victorian Africana; the Royal Commonwealth Society where the librarian Mr Simpson is himself a well-known authority on Africa; and of course the British Museum's departments of Printed Books, Manuscripts, and Maps.

One of the happier discoveries of doing research on African exploration is to find that some of the great explorer families still take an interest in the subject. Two of them in particular were very kind: Dorothy Middleton, whose great uncle by marriage was Francis Galton, pioneer in South-west Africa and author of the indispensable *The Art of Travel*, herself read this typescript and gave me valuable advice from her wide knowledge of the subject; and Richard Stanley, grandson of the redoubtable H.M., generously allowed permission for some of his grandfather's unique pictures on glass to be reproduced here. I should like to thank them both very much.

TIMOTHY SEVERIN

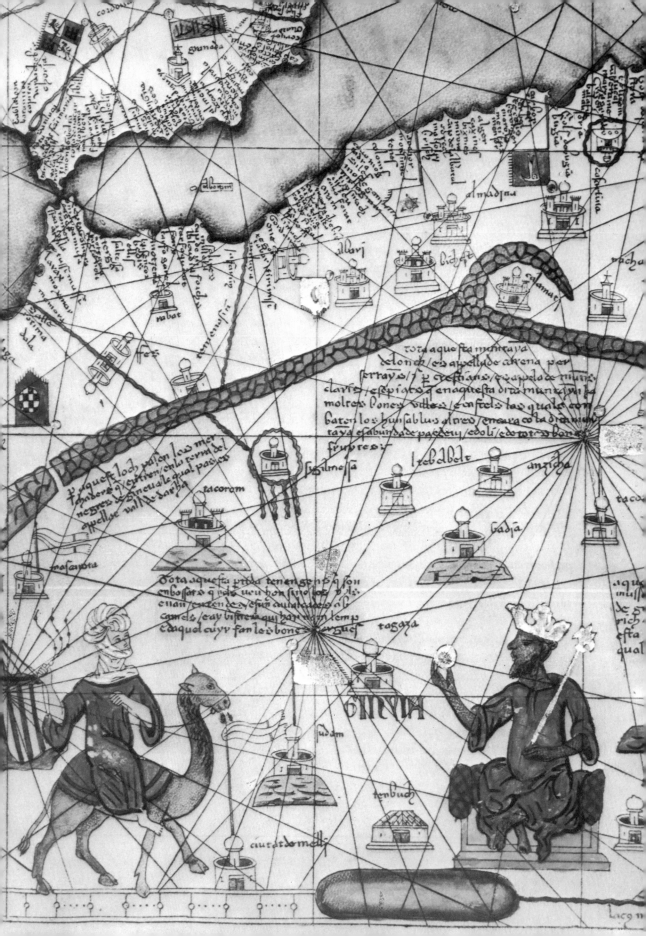

The Dangerous Continent

CHAPTER ONE

The citizens of Cairo had never seen any prince quite like him. Seven and a quarter centuries after the Prophet's Hejira – 1347 AD by Christian count – this African potentate entered their city as a pilgrim on his way to Mecca. His entourage glittered with barbaric splendour. In front marched five hundred slaves, each bearing a ceremonial staff of solid gold, sixty pounds in weight. Next, mounted on a fine charger, rode their master Mansa Musa, Lord of Mali in Negroland. Behind him came woolly haired Negroes from across the desert, veiled camelmen and guides, swarthy Berbers from El Maghrib or 'The West', and a motley gaggle of hangers-on. There were servants and bondsmen and fellow-pilgrims, who cooked strange foods, used outlandish customs amongst themselves, and spoke a weird collection of tongues which baffled comprehension. The *pièce de résistance*, however, was Mansa Musa's private purse for expenses *en route*. He turned up with eighty to a hundred camels loaded only with gold, a travelling exchequer of nearly fifteen tons of raw bullion.

True to her traditions, Cairo was impressed but not overwhelmed. The city's merchants fell joyously on the caravan. They sold the gawking pilgrims lengths of gaudy cloth at five times the usual price. Petty Egyptian functionaries asked, and received, outrageous bribes for their alleged assistance over trifling matters. Slave dealers in particular did well. The foreigners had an apparently insatiable appetite for slave women and were prepared to pay liberally for their tastes. It was said that the only entrepreneurs in all Cairo who had reason to be disgruntled were the money-lenders. Mansa Musa's caravan spent so prodigiously while in the city that the bottom fell out of the gold market and did not recover for twelve years after his visit.

But it was the African prince himself, as much as the extravagance of his entourage, which startled the city. His physical appearance was a surprise. Cairo had expected a coal-black, half-savage despot from across the desert where the sun's rays were rumoured to bake a man the colour of jet. Instead they found he had a light complexion, variously described as having a red or yellow tinge. Nor did he display those signs of primitive savagery which the Cairoese disparagingly associated with the inhabitants of Negroland. Rather, this exotic prince had greater piety for the Prophet and his teachings than the

Mansa Musa, golden lord of Negroland, on his throne. Facing him a Tuareg on his camel. Detail from a fourteenth century Catalan atlas

Egyptians themselves. Far from being over-awed by their Arab sophistication, there was some difficulty in persuading him that he should deign to pay his compliments to the Mameluke Sultan of the city. The Sultan, it might be added, cared more for Mansa Musa's gold than for any diplomatic slight, and showed himself only too anxious to make his guest comfortable. As the extra-ordinary caravan passed on eastward towards Mecca, similar reports filtered back of its munificent progress; of the profits that could be made from trading with it; of the princely behaviour of Mansa Musa himself who supported Islam with almost childlike generosity; and of the fact that he not only spent his fifteen tons of gold *en route*, but continued to live in such open-handed opulence that he had to borrow ready cash against his by-then impeccable credit.

Reports of Mansa Musa also found their way across the Mediterranean to the ears of European mapmakers who sought to mark this glittering monarch's kingdom in the unfilled spaces of their atlases. In the unknown regions of inner Africa they drew him, the black king in an ornate set of chess pieces, an all-powerful monarch seated on a golden throne or a royal cushion, bearing in one hand a sceptre and in the other a nugget of pure gold. Beside him they wrote the rubric: 'This Negro Lord is called Musa Mali, Lord of the Negroes of Guinea. So abundant is the gold which is found in his country that he is the richest and noblest king in all the land.' One such atlas was drawn for Charles V of France and another was ordered by Queen Mary of England as a gift for her husband Phillip II of Spain. It had not quite been finished when Mary died and the atlas went to her anti-Spanish sister Elizabeth. The offending Spanish coat of arms, originally impaled with those of England, was hastily scratched out, but the picture of Mansa Musa remained, though it was two hundred years since he had gone on his famous Hadj. The golden lord of Negroland had become an immortal symbol of unknown Africa, and his image was still firmly in Europe's mind when her explorers began to look southward towards the mysterious interior of Africa.

But dividing inquisitive European from distant African lay the formidable barrier of the Sahara. No other feature of African geography was to do so much to maintain the continent's mystery. If the outline of Africa is seen as the shape of a giant's skull facing across to India, the entire brainpan of the giant is an enormous desert, the largest in the world, stretching a thousand miles east and west, from the Nile to the Atlantic, an area greater than the continental United States. In Mansa Musa's day only an occasional caravan trail crossed it, like a slender vein through the grey mass of the brain. Only the merest trickle of knowledge passed along each vein from tropical south to temperate north.

If this physical barrier was not enough, popular belief was equally ready to reinforce geographical fact with wild and terrifying theory. Since the time of Pliny the Sahara was thought to be nothing but a single, howling wasteland of sand, fit only for wild beasts and a few strange tribes who, according to Herodotus, could out-run a chariot and spoke a language that sounded like the squeaking of bats. Men of learning, Arab or Christian, knew better, but the public at large had no inkling of the true variety of the desert landscape. Vast areas of the Sahara were not in fact covered with sand at all. There were immense regions of bare rock with a mantle of small, peculiarly shaped stones that seemed designed by nature to cripple man and beast. Nor was one sand zone like another. In places the sand lay flat and monotonous as the ocean on a still day; elsewhere it rose in great ridges that ran ruler-straight across the face of the country for hundreds of miles. It might lie in soft low ripples or hump into the crescent-shaped dunes called *barchans* which inched and groped forward like monstrous beasts as the wind blew across them. Deep in the centre of the desert the bones of ancient mountains poked through the skin of detritus to form stark upland blocks, the home of primitive cave-dwelling tribes; and here and there an intruding water table provided the startling steel-blue of a reed-fringed oasis.

Only the inhabitants of the desert knew the real nature of the Sahara. They had their own, precise word for every feature and every phenomenon, and by such knowledge they survived. Each year the desert men appeared at the settled fringes of the Sahara when the summer heat withered their grazing lands. Very occasionally, too, a town dweller might visit the far oases where the nomads had contemptuously settled bands of slaves to undertake what they considered the menial task of cultivation. But dislike was mutual and constant. City Arab and European alike held the people of the Sahara as little better than fierce predators, battening off the caravans that passed through their territory, quarrelling viciously among themselves, and constituting a special African danger. Christian cartographers, sensing the menace of these alien people, drew on their maps, next to Mansa Musa on his throne, the sinister veiled figure of a Tuareg upon his camel.

So, even before the first European explorers set foot south of the great desert, Africa already had a fearsome reputation. And as time went on, new dimensions were added to this apprehension. The white men found other and equally dangerous guardians of Africa's secrets. Going ashore on her treacherous, reef-ringed coasts they were faced with steep escarpments over which the rivers from the interior tumbled in spectacular but frustrating cataracts. The falls and rapids of the Congo were so daunting that three hundred years after the discovery of its enormous mouth at the end of the fifteenth century, white men had charted no more than one hundred and thirty miles of its lower course. Not until the American, H. M. Stanley, made a small army of porters carry a forty-foot barge, the *Lady Alice*, in five sections overland did a European boat float on the Congo's broad middle reaches. Unlike the North American rivers, which offered an open highway for the enterprising *voyageur* in his canoe, most African waterways were not only impassable but actually dangerous. Time and again the explorers met disaster among whirlpools and rapids. One of the greatest travellers, Mungo Park, was swept to his death over the Bussa Falls when he was faced with the choice between murderous natives and the Niger's cataracts.

Equally hazardous for the river-borne explorer was the wild life in the days when Africa teemed with animals not yet intimidated by rifle and bullet. The bluff Victorian sportsman and crackshot, Sir Samuel Baker, who liked nothing better than to combine exploration with a taste for big game hunting, was nearly sent to the crocodiles by indignant hippos surfacing beneath his canoe. Nor was the explorer on dry land any less exposed to the dangerous fauna of Africa. David Livingstone's career almost ended prematurely when he was severely

Left 'Francis John Pocock. Drowned June 3, 1877'. Pocock, Stanley's last remaining white companion, perished in the Congo cataracts during Stanley's first Congo expedition, and this memorial, edged in black, appeared in his employer's account of the trip. *Opposite* The fate of poor Soudi of Ituru, another of Stanley's followers

mauled by a lion, and throughout his life he lived in terror of snakes. In a letter home he wrote how he trod on a snake in his darkened hut, felt the coils grip his ankle, and leapt out of range with the sweat pouring from him and his limbs quivering with fright. He was luckier than one of his converts who, he reported, was killed 'when a rhinocerous rushed upon him unprovoked, and ripp'd him up'.

Nor was Africa a place for the weakling or sickly. In the high bush the combination of heat and evaporation could shiver the wood in a gunstock or split the felloes of wagon wheels. The traveller by wagon had to carry wedges to drive between the wooden wheel and its iron rim which expanded and rattled in the blazing heat. Among the low steamy jungles a man was a likely victim of fever. With only a rudimentary knowledge of tropical medicine, the explorer might be weakened by dysentery, reduced by malaria, and finished off by any one of a host of African diseases for which he had neither antidote nor acquired resistance. The sea shanties of visiting sailors to the notoriously unhealthy coast of West Africa spoke bitterly of the 'Bight of Benin, where one comes out of nine that go in', and although the wild beasts of Africa were more spectacular executioners, in the last analysis it was disease which threatened the explorer's life. With very few exceptions, the African explorers either returned home permanently broken in health or, even worse, died in the places they went to discover.

So why, then, did the African explorers risk their lives in the dangerous continent? The question has a dozen or more answers. Explorers' motives were

as varied as their personalities. Some went for self-glory. Others, like Baker, assumed an off-hand and sporting manner which fails to cloak their professionalism in the field. A few visited Africa *en passant*, fell in love with the place, and stayed. Many more began their infatuation at long-range – from books and romances read in the security of classroom and library, and these, in the manner of René Caillié, the great French explorer who reached Timbuctoo, sailed for Africa to satisfy a wide-eyed and very personal fascination – in Caillié's case after reading *Robinson Crusoe*. There were missionary figures like Livingstone; dedicated scientists like the German-born Heinrich Barth struggling through the Saharan sands to take meticulously detailed notes on anthropology and linguistics. Soldiers turned explorers because they were ordered to do so; civilian

15

misfits went to Africa to escape a homeland they neither liked nor understood. Indeed the unexpected thing is not so much that the explorers were so diverse, seeing that there were so many of them, but that it took them so long to explore Africa. For it was an irritating fact among the learned societies of mid-eighteenth-century Europe that they knew more about the frozen wastes of Arctic Canada than about places a hundred miles inland from the slaving forts on the Gold Coast. The Amazon river, whose mouth was discovered in 1500 AD, had been fairly accurately known for three hundred years before any white man stood at the most southerly source of the Nile, whose delta had been renowned since antiquity. To a people who prided themselves on their positive approach to geography, such ignorance was tantamount to an intellectual disgrace.

Typically, therefore, the savants began their attack on the African problem by looking up what the geographers of ancient Greece and Rome had written about the continent. Thus a millennium after Herodotus had compiled his series of second-hand reports about Africa, Major James Rennell, among the foremost African experts of his time and a man who personally supervised the survey of India in areas which Herodotus had never heard of, was putting more trust in the Greek historian than in the reports of Englishmen who had actually visited Africa.

It was argued that the Greeks and Romans should have been well-informed about Africa. Greek merchants had long traded down the Red Sea, and in the days of her empire, Rome's African provinces had been a good deal more important and generally closer to the imperial city than far-flung provinces like Britain. Roman troops had marched and counter-marched throughout North Africa. Roman settlers had founded more than a hundred new cities between the Pillars of Hercules and Carthage. And an entire Roman legion, the Legio III Augustan, was customarily recruited from Africa. Yet as so often happened, the intruder only scratched the fringe of the country. Roman rule extended along a strip of the coast. A few days' journey southward saw the limit of her power. The names of Roman towns reflected a frontier atmosphere, places like Castra Nova and Cohors Breucorum. Beyond their garrisons lay the unexplored mountains of Atlas or untameable desert tribes like the Garamantes, whom the Roman circus procurers paid to hunt and trap the wild beasts which swarmed in those days in the Sahara. Their prey – lions, leopards, and the occasional unlucky native – were shipped off to the huge bloodbaths of Rome and her provincial imitators. Trajan, to take a single instance, grandly decreed the destruction of 2,246 animals in a single day's games, and inevitably many of the victims must have come from North Africa. Carnage like this, repeated over six centuries, made Rome and her satellites the graveyard for North African wildlife. By the time Rome fell, animals which had once roamed the Sahara in profusion, were well on their way to extinction.

The ruins of Lepcis Magna

In return for this slaughter, Rome learned surprisingly little about Africa. One energetic army commander took a flying column across the desert and apparently reached the Sudan, for he reported coming to a land swarming with rhinoceros. Another military patrol probed south along the Nile until stopped by the great floating weed beds of the *sudd*. But such trips were rarities, expeditions at a venture. They belonged to no over-all pattern of exploration; they were not followed up; and their results were smothered beneath the voluminous records of the official chroniclers.

A similar fate had already overtaken the results of an even more daring enterprise by Rome's predecessors in North Africa, the Carthaginians. Some time about 500 BC (the date is uncertain) the city fathers of Carthage sent a fleet of sixty ships to sail out through the Straits of Gibraltar and follow the coast where-

Captive 'man-ape' brought back to Europe from Africa, in fact a chimpanzee

ever it led. The expedition was commanded by one of the two chief magistrates of the state, and he pressed his mission with great determination, turning back only when the food supplies ran out. At their farthest south the Carthaginians reported passing a flaming mountain, very likely a volcano in eruption, and hearing signal drums echoing from forest-clad hills along the coast. They also brought back with them the flayed skins of three man-like creatures which they had killed during a shore-landing, and which their interpreters called 'gorillas'. The skins were duly presented to the temple of Tanit in Carthage as a thanks offering, and a grateful inscription was chiselled into the stone of the Chronos temple. But the skins soon crumbled into dust, and the Romans razed the temples when they sacked the city. Only a mutilated transcript of the inscription survived for later scholars to ponder over, and the story of the gorilla became a unique symbol of the enormous gap in the progress of African exploration. Although the name of the gorilla had been learned well before the time of Christ, it was not until 1847 that an American missionary in the Cameroons positively identified the living animal.

It was the Arabs who snuffed out classical knowledge of Africa. As they over-ran the Byzantine rump of the old Roman empire in the latter half of the seventh century, their invasion altered the whole face which Africa turned towards Europe. Roman aqueducts were allowed to run dry; fields and towns abandoned. The large set-pieces of Roman architecture fell into disuse or became little more than quarries for Arab building material, as happened to the sixty Roman columns hauled off to the new mosque at Kairwan. Seldom was decay and change so complete. Obsolete statuary and marble was left to erode where it fell, like the broken-faced busts and sand-scarred vertebrae of the toppled columns lying in jumbled magnificence at Lepcis Magna, a few paces from the waters of the Mediterranean across which Roman galleys had once linked Europe with Africa.

Yet the Arabs also brought a more constructive revolution, for they were the first to undertake continent-wide journeys with the camel. Capable of travelling across two hundred miles of waterless desert where the Roman bullock cart had been hard put to manage a quarter the distance, the camel was as great an improvement in the Sahara as the development of the sailing vessel over the oared galley at sea. And the effects were much the same. Travel across the desert became more reliable; trade increased; new routes were opened; and perhaps most important of all, the people most skilled in the new mode of transport took control of the desert passages. But although the Sahara was less formidable as a physical barrier, the European explorer could only cross it with the connivance of the suspicious, and often fanatical, camel people.

Elsewhere in Africa, too, the newly-arriving European found himself em-barrassingly dependent upon the Arab. All down the coast of East Africa, from the Red Sea to Mozambique, Arab dhow captains had traded and settled for hundreds of years. They called it the land of Az Zanj – from which came the word Zanzibar – and when Vasco da Gama brought his squadron of ships there, searching for a sea route to India, he was piloted past the treacherous coral-bound coast not so much by guesswork and a Portuguese leadsman in the bows, but by an Arab dhow master who knew the waters intimately. Three centuries later, when Stanley's much publicized expedition 'rescued' David Livingstone from the blackest interior, he found the Scots missionary being cared for by a prosperous community of Arab traders who used Ujiji on Lake Tanganyika as their trading base.

Indeed in some ways it seemed that the Europeans were the slowest starters

Sixteenth century map
of Africa. Detail from
Pierre Descelier's
mappemonde

Explorers on the march. 'A South prospect of the River Praa and the Forest of Assin'

in the story of African exploration. When they began their journeys south of the
Sahara at the turn of the fifteenth century, they scarcely knew as much about
the continent as the far-off Chinese – who had at least seen a giraffe, sent to the
Emperor as tribute and admirably painted at the imperial zoo by a Chinese
artist. Another Chinese draughtsman knew enough about Africa to draw an
exquisite profile of its east coast where, between the clumps of palms, he sketched in the flat-roofed houses of the Arab traders. Nevertheless it was still true,
when the age of European exploration in Africa began, that almost no one had
gone into the heart of Africa and returned with any worthwhile account of its
peoples and places. From the north the Arabs, after crossing the Sahara, had
halted on the forest fringes. In the east they preferred to stay close to the coasts.
The outside world had only touched the hem of the dangerous continent. It was
here, in the heart of Africa, that the European explorers were to contribute the
most, as they walked, paddled, were carried in litters, or rode through an extraordinary landscape. They uncovered natural extravaganzas like the Victoria
Falls on the Zambesi, the great gash of the East African Rift Valley, and a lake
(Chad) with fresh water on one shore and salt crystals on the other. They found
too, the incredible diversity of Africa's peoples. With more than eight hundred
languages between them – a source of considerable frustration for the travellers
– native societies ranged from the sophisticated kingships of the Niger to the
Stone Age cultures of the Kalahari bushmen; and their religions from simple
fetishism to a fossil form of Jewry. Several tribes almost surpassed belief –
Masai plastering their hair in dung and sucking fresh blood from their cattle;

22

Sudanese warriors dressed in chain mail like refugees from the Crusades; and the Gulliver world of Ruanda where the elongated Tutsi, some of them as much as six and a half feet tall, lorded it over a race of 5-foot Twa servants.

Europe was to be fascinated by her explorers' tales of strange sights and bizarre adventures. Pliny's oft-quoted remark that there was always something new out of Africa was never more apt than in the eighteenth and nineteenth centuries when every fresh journey only added to the popular appeal of Africa. Public interest was insatiable, swelling into a frenzied crescendo as explorer after explorer dashed off to make his own African discovery before it was too late. It was the great adventure of the day, and even national governments were caught up in the craze, pouring money into grandiose schemes for the exploration and acquisition of some of the most inaccessible, and worthless, territory. It was a stark contrast to the days, three centuries earlier, when African exploration was just beginning and the continent was regarded as little better than a nuisance, an irksome detour in the sea route to the Orient.

In those days, like the sun in eclipse, only the rim of Africa was seen. Portuguese ships had navigated her coasts; a handful of shore bases had been established; and any competent cartographer could have drawn an accurate outline of Africa. The empty interior, however, was reserved for the imaginative mapmaker to draw his griffons and cameleopards, his Negro kings and the wondrous Phoenix on a nest of cinnamon sticks. Under the circumstances it was not surprising that the first large-scale landings of Europeans in Africa below the Sahara should have been inspired by two semi-legendary figures – Prester John, the fabled priest-king of the eastern Christians, and Mansa Musa, Lord of Guinea.

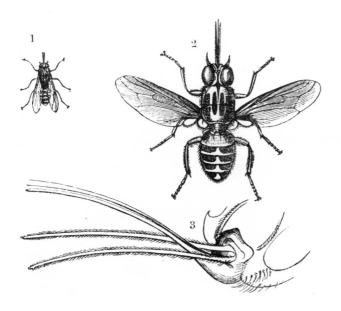

1. The Tsetse; 2. the same magnified; 3. the proboscis. Engraving in David Livingstone's *Travels* to illustrate an insect scourge 'with the ravages of which I have unfortunately been too familiar'

Knights of Prester John

CHAPTER TWO

Prester John was a potentate to rival Mansa Musa. Half monk, half monarch, he ruled, it was said, over forty-two lesser kings and a strange tangle of creatures that included centaurs and Amazons and a race of shrinking giants, formerly sixty cubits tall but now dwindled to twenty. Throughout his realm there was neither lechery, nor poverty, nor robbery. His palace had walls of translucent crystal and a roof of gems, and no traveller or pilgrim was ever turned away, for every day thirty thousand guests sat down there at a miraculous table fashioned from solid emerald and held up by two pillars of amethyst. It was a table which had the marvellous quality that it prevented drunkenness, and sobriety was particularly necessary because the Prester's guests of honour were always clerics, a dozen archbishops at his right hand, and a score of bishops at his left. Indeed so saintly was the Prester that even his domestics were luminaries of the church. His steward was a patriarch, his marshal an abbot, and his cook a prior. Through his kingdom flowed a river that spewed forth gems from a sea of sand; his clothes were made of precious salamander skin washed clean in fire; and the neighbouring kingdoms sent tributes by the camel-load. Yet amid all this magnificence the Prester himself remained a humble man. He used no grand titles but was content with the simple name of Prester, the 'priest', and though he had a flock of adoring wives, he allowed them to approach only four times a year. Each day he sang in person before the altar of the blessed St Thomas who had brought the true religion to his land, and his sole ambition was to crush the snake of Islam. At war he mustered a mighty host – including a division of cannibals who conveniently disposed of corpses after the battle – but in peace he travelled his dominions with only a plain wooden cross and a bowl of earth signifying that from dust he had come and to dust he would return. His death, however, was of no immediate concern, for in his kingdom sprang the Fountain of Life and anyone who bathed in it was restored to the full vigour of a man of thirty-two. The Prester himself, it was confidentially said, had taken the cure eight times and his real age was 562 years.

This extraordinary fantasy-figure had dazzled the minds of imaginative Europeans for at least four centuries before Portugal's caravels rounded the

Prester John on his throne. Detail from a sixteenth century atlas

25

southern horn of Africa in 1497. Quite where his fabulous realm was to be found, no one was sure. Out of Ethiopia came tantalizing snippets of information to clothe the image, reports of a Christian king who was a sworn enemy of Islam and whose court seethed with priests. Naturally it was a disappointment that his realm seemed so small, for even on the crude maps of the day Ethiopia looked a mortal-sized kingdom caught between the upper Nile and the Red Sea. But Europe's theorists quickly found an excuse: they claimed that the Prester had been driven there by the same all-conquering Mongols who had so nearly swamped Europe. Ethiopia, therefore, was the true relic of the Prester's famous empire, and would surely contain the quintessence of everything he had saved.

The Portuguese who first went to look for this Prester John in the 1500's were scarcely suitable emissaries for so Christian a king. Many of them were *degredados*, convicted criminals given a remote chance of redeeming their sins. They sailed with ships coasting around Africa and were dumped ashore at various points along the coast with instructions to search inland for the Prester's kingdom. If they had found it, they would have won full pardon. But the question never arose, for they never came back successful. Only by the northern and eastern approaches to Ethiopia was there any success. By disguising themselves as Muslims, at least two Arabic-speaking Portuguese travellers got through the Islamic cordon. But unfortunately for both of them, the ruler of Ethiopia was so delighted that he refused to let them return home, and the wretched men spent the rest of their lives at his court in gilded captivity.

There was just enough truth in the Prester John legend when applied to Ethiopia, to sustain the hopes of the men who sought the mysterious realm of the Christians. The medieval kingdom of Ethiopia lay sprawled across the high plateau which later generations would call the Roof of Africa. It was a severe and forbidding region, corrugated with wild mountains and ravines and obscured for several months of the year by thick drenching mists which hung over the uplands. In summer there were torrential downpours which made travel almost impossible along the narrow footpaths, and even in fine weather the rough terrain reduced all traffic to single files of porters and pack animals creeping laboriously through the spectacular defiles and over barren mountain passes. Settlement was confined to a handful of towns along the routeways, and to innumerable small hamlets huddling cautiously against the mountains on whose peaks the inhabitants took refuge in time of war. In more settled days their cattle grazed the valleys or their farmers tilled the thin soils of tiny fields scraped out of the hillsides. To the eye of the traveller the country had a striking and bleak grandeur – ridge after ridge of mountain folds extending to the horizon, and all their peaks rising to much the same height like the waves in an endless seascape of grey rock.

The Ethiopians had to scratch a living from the thin soils of valleys lost among the high mountains and treacherous passes

Ethiopia was unique in that she was a long-established Christian kingdom in Africa. In the fourth century AD Graeco-Roman traders had brought the religion to the port towns of the Red Sea, and from there the religion had spread up into the highlands, taking root and flourishing in a spectacular style. The Ethiopian ruler, the Negus, claimed direct descent from King Solomon and the Queen of Sheba; and many of his people held themselves to be heirs to an emigrant race of Jews. Their Christianity was fierce and belligerent. When fortune favoured her, Ethiopia lapped down from her mountain peaks and spread out over the lowlands, reaching north-east as far as the Red Sea coast. In the height of her pride, just before the Europeans found her, it was said that the Negus would beat the ground with his whip and called upon the earth to bring forth more enemies, for he had defeated all his country's foes. When conditions changed and Ethiopia came under attack, she merely contracted back to her mountain fastnesses and the secure protection of the seven-thousand-foot rampart of the great rift valley which formed her eastern frontier.

27

Here on the plateau her Christianity took on strange mutations and splendid emphasis. An astonishing proportion of her population went into the church in one role or another, as monks or priests, as travelling mendicants, or as lay brothers. Women joined as nuns, and children could be baptized as deacons while still babes in arms. Fanatics performed strange acts of penance, wearing iron girdles studded with nails or sitting for days in tubs of freezing water up to their necks. Religious buildings were everywhere, in the villages and towns, as isolated monasteries on the mountain tops, or like the churches of Lalibela, carved from the living rock. The church was a great landowner and in government the clerics rose to positions of immense power. The entire edifice was founded on a peculiar and almost literal interpretation of the Testaments. Drawing upon the Gospels and finding inspiration in the episodes of Christ's life, Ethiopian Christianity had flourished and put forth exotic blossoms in art and architecture, ceremonial and creed. There were the magnificent sad-eyed wall paintings illustrating the Gospel stories with a fascination for the role of Mary; enormous open-air consecrations at which the Abuna or archbishop of the country ordained hundreds of priests in a single ceremony; wild monks with matted hair and leather gowns who fought as berserkers in the imperial army; and mystic baptisms at which everyone, from the Negus downward, reconfirmed their faith by passing through tanks of water.

Beneath this religious fervour were the problems of ruling a warlike and scattered people, divided into clans and factions. At the centre lay the royal court clustered around the person of the Negus himself. His power was absolute, but in such a turbulent country his dynasty lasted only as long as his authority over the powerful war chiefs. So his court never rested in one place for long. A great tented encampment, it moved around the country like the royal pieces in a huge chess game, ready to checkmate the Negus's rivals with the threat of an imperial army. The royal brothers, as potential claimants to the throne, were incarcerated for life in a mountain-top fortress and anyone who contacted them was put to death. Any provincial governor who grew too strong was dismissed; and the Negus himself built up a personal mystique, surrounded by his imperial messengers and the royal lions – the symbols of his authority.

Yet Ethiopia was not entirely isolated. Traditionally the Abuna was a foreigner, appointed by the Coptic church in Alexandria and sent from Egypt. In Jerusalem, too, there was a house for Ethiopian pilgrims to the Holy Land, and one or two religious embassies had carried on to Rome itself. There was, in fact, just enough contact for Europe to nurse hopes of finding Prester John in Ethiopia, a symbol as brilliant in his own way as the lure of Mansa Musa and his gold. The result, when the Europeans explored in earnest, was a feat of Portuguese knight errantry which was to come near to eclipsing the efforts of the conquistadors in the New World.

Alvarez compared the scenes at the Negus's court to the Ethiopian religious paintings. Ethiopic manuscript illustration of the Saint Tekla Haymanot in the company of angels and archangels

Left The Negus and his subjects taking part in a mass baptism to reconfirm their faith. *Right* St Mary in heaven with Jesus. Eighteenth century Ethiopic manuscripts

The first sizeable Portuguese embassy to get through to Prester John made a bad start. They landed on the Red Sea coast of Ethiopia in April 1520 and the local provincial governor, the Bahrnagast, came down to the beach to greet them with an escort of native tribesmen. In his honour, and incidentally as a useful demonstration of their technical prowess, the Portuguese squadron which had brought the embassy, fired off a broadside. Unfortunately one of their guns was still shotted, so that to everyone's consternation a large cannon ball went whizzing through the group of dignitaries surrounding the Barhnagast. Luckily no one was injured, though the ball ricochetted three times on its way past. Full of apologies the Portuguese sent to make amends, only to be greeted with the Bahrnagast's cool reassurance that no one was safe unless God pleased, and that the ball had done no one any harm. The Portuguese were happily ignorant that the Bahrnagast's calm philosophy was based on the extraordinarily low value which he and his countrymen placed on human life. Far from standing on the edge of Prester John's tranquil and prosperous kingdom, the Portuguese embassy was about to step into a turbulent African society which would surprise and shock them with its strange mixture of piety and violence.

The fourteen members of the Portuguese embassy were themselves an ill-assorted group to be representing their country. In command was Rodrigo da Lima. He had only recently been appointed because King Manoel's original ambassador, a seventy-year-old diplomat, had died the previous month and his corpse lay buried in the sand of one of the off-shore islands. Da Lima was arrogant, young, and tactless, and he was already quarrelling with his second-in-command, Jorge d'Abreu, who fancied himself better fitted to lead the embassy. Trying to hold the balance between the two bantams was Father Francisco Alvarez, once a chaplain to King Manoel and now the priest with the task of investigating the religion of Prester John. His diary was to be the first account of Ethiopia published in Europe. Lesser figures in the embassy included a clerk; a painter who was supposed to put on canvas the sights which the party encountered and also to draw and paint for the amusement of Prester John in his palace; a musician in charge of a portable organ (also for the Prester's entertainment); a barber-surgeon; and a number of Portuguese servants, mostly selected for their ability at singing mass melodiously. As a gift they had originally intended bringing a huge four-poster bed complete with blue and yellow taffeta curtains, blankets embroidered with the Portuguese coat-of-arms, and a canopy which showed an emperor crowning a queen while four men sounded trumpets. Unfortunately the bed had not survived the journey, and from a scratch collection among the fleet Da Lima found himself equipped with four lengths of tapestry, the organ, a gold sword with a rich hilt, two obsolete swivel guns together with some powder and shot, some pieces of armour, and a map of the world. It was a shabby offering for so magnificent a potentate as the Prester John they expected to find.

From Massawa on the Red Sea coast where the embassy landed, it was about 450 miles in a direct line to Shoa in the interior highlands where the Negus usually mustered his court. The difficulties of the road can be judged from the fact that the Portuguese took six months to cover the distance. From the decks of their squadron they had seen the forbidding outline of the barren hills rising up beyond the bleached whiteness of the shore. The fortress-like blocks of monasteries on the higher peaks and the miraculous apparition of a cross shining in the night sky over the hills had induced some of the common sailors to desert, swimming ashore for glory and worldly gain. But most of them were soon back, defeated by the wilderness. There were no real roads leading inland, only a few

31

Pass of Rah Eesa

rough tracks which meandered from one monastery or hamlet to the next. From sea level there was a heart-breaking climb to the plateau of Shoa, a laborious journey past baking limestone cliffs, dried up watercourses, and meagre rock-strewn countryside. It was, in fact, depressingly like the worst parts of Portugal. Only the names were different. The familiar table-topped 'mesas' of Iberia were called 'ambas' in Ethiopia; and if – as the embassy later found – Prester John used the most inaccessible crest as a prison for his rivals, it was not much different from the Portuguese habit of incarcerating dynastic enemies in the dungeons of Aljubarrota.

Indeed the similarity between the two cultures, Portuguese and Ethiopian, was one of the more surprising facets to the quest for Prester John. For one, rare moment European and African looked at one another eye to eye. The white men came expecting to find a superior civilization and found instead a society that mirrored many of their own idiosyncrasies. Both nations were devoutly Christian to the point of fanaticism; both ruled by absolute monarchs striving to bring a proud and fickle nobility to heel; and each looked to the other as a possible ally against Islam. It was remarkable, therefore, that Da Lima's embassy failed so utterly to understand Ethiopia.

Bad luck had much to do with it. Everything went wrong from the start. The hot-tempered Da Lima characteristically offended the Bahrnagast by declining his hospitality; an epidemic carried off two of the embassy including their interpreter; and the embassy got bogged down. The root of the trouble was the matter of presents. Da Lima failed to understand that all diplomatic business in Ethiopia depended on the constant supply of flattering gifts, either as bribes or as tribute. Even the door-keepers of the Bahrnagast's chambers had to be bribed with packets of pepper; and when the Bahrnagast asked for Da Lima's best sword, he was deeply offended when the Portuguese commander turned to a companion and borrowed a second-rate weapon for the gift. That night the hut where the Portuguese kept their stores was broken into and two swords and a helmet were stolen. For his part, Da Lima was singularly unimpressed with the Bahrnagast. Instead of some grand potentate of oriental luxury, he found that the Prester's lieutenant was an ugly-looking rogue obviously suffering from eye disease and seated on an ill-made string bed covered with unclean rugs. His audience chamber was a great barn of a place, packed with rank upon rank of natives squatting half-naked on the beaten-earth floor. To one side attendants held four of the Bahrnagast's favourite warhorses, while on a wall near him hung a few poorly fashioned swords and at the head of his bed crouched his wife. Messengers and supplicants who entered the chamber were first obliged to strip from the waist upward, and then bob down and touch the ground with one hand as a sign of respect before handing over the obligatory gifts of spice or cloth. Only the great chiefs could ignore this ceremony. They

Above Ras Gedam from Massawa where the first Portuguese embassy landed on the
coast of Ethiopia. *Below* The pass of Rah Eesa, typical of Ethiopia's severe terrain.
Watercolours by R. Kirk, one of the Shoa Mission, a Victorian embassy to Ethiopia

33

appeared at the entrance on horseback, arrogantly thrusting through the throng behind a squad of heralds who beat back the crowd with their spears and cudgels.

Only Father Alvarez was content. Here indeed, he confided optimistically in his diary, was the land of Prester John. Every hill and crossroads sprouted a church or monastery. In the market place the chief customers were monastic bursars; and on the march every second passer-by seemed to be in holy orders. There were monks in their yellow robes which reminded Alvarez of the Dominicans, half-naked mendicant priests, and nuns with heads shaved and bound up with a leather thong. Alvarez went into the churches to admire the wall paintings and the rich drapes of red velvet and brocade which hid the altars. Only the church furniture seemed inadequate. There were skeins of thin stones instead of bells, which knocked together and made a cracked, tinkling sound, and the clumsy, ill-wrought church plate did little justice to the alleged wealth of Prester John.

Conversely the Ethiopians were taking stock of their Portuguese guests and not necessarily liking what they found. They admired their fine weapons and armour and begged them as gifts. But when the priests invited the visitors to share mass with them, they were shocked by their uncouth behaviour. They talked in loud voices in church and spat openly on the floor, and they seemed always to be quarrelling with one another. Even their holy man was something of a menace, for Alvarez committed the sin of riding up on a female donkey to a monastery where no female creatures of any sort were allowed. Only a hurried deputation sallying forth to make him stop and dismount before he came too close prevented the entire monastery from being defiled. Later there was an even more serious violation of church sanctuary when the hungry Portuguese casually trapped and killed some pigeons they found in a church. The local population was so shocked by this bloodshed that the Portuguese were forbidden to enter the church ever again.

So the embassy blundered on, alternately appalled and delighted by what they found. Da Lima forced the Bahrnagast to provide a few pack animals by threatening to burn the presents for the Negus on the beach if he received no help, and the embassy proceeded by fits and starts on their long journey inland.

Loyally Alvarez enumerated everything worthy of the realm of Prester John. There were communities of nuns who piously insisted on washing the travellers' feet as travellers from the Holy Land; royal guesthouses for people on state business; and an occasional chieftain who was courteous to the passing embassy. But for the most part, the people of Prester John were neither as hospitable nor as decorous as legend would have it. Some of the men strutted about with nothing but a leather strap around their testicles; and women scarcely covered their nakedness with a sheepskin casually dangling from one

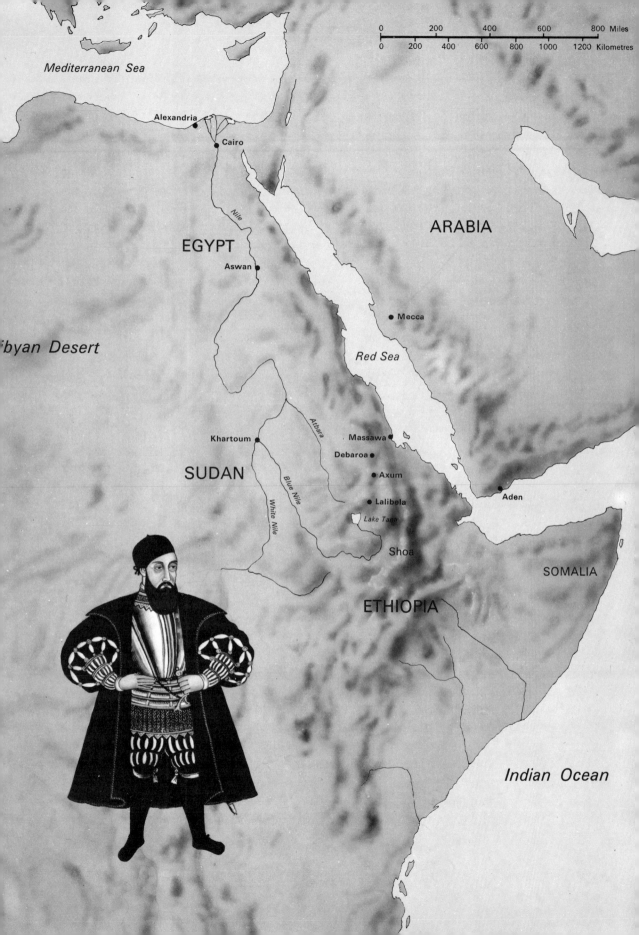

Mediterranean Sea

Alexandria

Cairo

EGYPT

Nile

Aswan

ARABIA

Mecca

Red Sea

ibyan Desert

Khartoum

Albara

Massawa

SUDAN

Blue Nile

Debaroa

Axum

White Nile

Lalibela

Aden

Lake Tana

Shoa

SOMALIA

ETHIOPIA

Indian Ocean

0   200   400   600   800 Miles

0   200   400   600   800   1000   1200 Kilometres

View of the mountain or amba of Devra Damo, on which one of Ethiopia's numerous fortress-like monasteries was built

shoulder. 'In Portugal or Spain', Alvarez commented drily, 'people marry for love, and because they see beautiful faces, and the things inside are hidden from them. In this country they can well marry because they see everything for certain.'

But it was the violence of the country which really shocked the visitors. In several villages the natives turned out to do the embassy the honour of stoning them as they rode through; and Alvarez uncharitably had to send a slave with his mule on ahead to draw any ambushed fire. At night the guides built barricades of thorn bushes against brigands, and in one place the travellers rode through a wood under the rotting heads of eight hundred executed rebels dangling like grotesque apples from the branches. The realm of Prester John, it was becoming increasingly clear, was a place where tempers ran high and blood was easily spilt. Several times the embassy was left stranded when their porters mutinied and marched off after flinging their loads to the ground. In the middle of one dispute, a high-ranking priest suddenly appeared and without a word of warning sprang like a tiger on the captain of the guard, beating him viciously about the head and opening deep gashes. Then he calmly introduced himself as a messenger from the Negus and told the startled Da Lima that the

Emperor was dissatisfied with the progress of the expedition, and proceeded to hurry off as abruptly as he had arrived.

Scrambling on hands and knees over high passes, harried by packs of hyenas so bold they had to be jabbed away with lances, nearly drowned in a flash flood, the Portuguese were heartily glad when in mid-October their guides finally announced that the Prester's camp lay just ahead. The embassy had long since given up any hope of seeing the crystal palace of legend, and so the sight of the massed tents of the Ethiopian court cheered them considerably. It lay like a huge military cantonment, row upon row of tents radiating out from the great, red, central pavilion of the Negus. Several thousand Ethiopians, dressed in their finest clothing, had assembled to watch the embassy arrive. They stood silent and curious, as a company of a hundred heralds dressed in silk shirts cleared a path for the white men, waving and cracking their whips in the air with great gusto. On each side the crowd fell back to form an aisle, flanked by the nobles and by the Negus's horses, drawn up as if on parade with brocade saddle cloths and plumes nodding from their bridles. Next, a double column of imperial messengers ran forward, each man wearing a lion skin thrown over one shoulder and with a gold collar studded with semi-precious stones clasped around his throat. Taking up position on each of Da Lima and his men, they ushered them onward, moving at a curiously formal pace which was a shambling half-run, half-lope. Close to the pavilion the visitors were made to pass between four captive lions, traditional emblems of the Negus and securely held, Alvarez noted with some relief, by massive chains. Finally, at a bow-shot from the mysterious red pavilion, the procession came to a halt, and the Portuguese began a garbled second-hand dialogue with the man they had come so far to see.

The go-between was a court functionary whom Alvarez called the Cabeata. Dressed in a white cotton gown and a high pointed hat, he acted as chamberlain to the Negus who remained hidden in his tent throughout the interview. The Cabeata opened the audience by demanding in solemn tones of Da Lima what he wanted and where he came from. The ambassador replied that he had brought an embassy to Prester John from the King of Portugal and messages from the Viceroy of India. At this the Cabeata turned around and sedately marched back into the red tent. A few moment later he came out and repeated his first question. Again Da Lima stated his business. Back went the Cabeata, only to re-emerge to ask his question a third time. According to Alvarez who was watching closely, the Cabeata performed a curious little minuet each time he came out of the red tent, stepping back and forth with the three Ethiopian noblemen who stood in a line blocking the Portuguese path. At the third time of asking, Da Lima was so nonplussed by the repeated question that he replied that he did not know how to reply. As he thought best, was the Cabeata's unhelpful answer. This retort piqued Da Lima into commenting tartly that he would not deliver his embassy to anyone except the Prester in person. The answer produced an immediate reaction, for on his next appearance from the red tent the Cabeata raised the essential question of gifts. His lord, he announced, demanded to see all the presents that the embassy had brought him. For a moment Da Lima was rude enough to hesitate, but the other Portuguese urged him to comply, and one by one the meagre collection of gifts was produced. Without more ado they were picked up and carried back into the tent for the Negus to inspect. In a few minutes they were brought back. The Portuguese brocades were hung up on the wooden arcade for display, and the other articles were arrayed on the ground for maximum effect. Then one of the Ethiopian nobles harangued the crowd on the great value of the presents and the honour the Portuguese had done their lord by coming to see him. When he had finished the crowd gave a great shout and began to disperse. Da Lima and his companions were left where they stood, utterly mystified by the rigmarole of Ethiopian court etiquette and uncomfortably aware that their first audience with the Negus had come to an end without giving them a chance to pass on their messages from Portugal.

The Portuguese never did get to grips with the eccentricities of Ethiopian court life. Essentially, the entire system was devoted to maintaining the mystique of the Negus as a hidden, all-powerful, despot. In camp he remained shut up in his tent. On the march he was shielded from public gaze by cloths held up on poles by his bearers, while lion-handlers cleared his path of stray onlookers. His power was projected as being absolute and omnipresent. A monk had his eyes put out for disobeying an order; another lost half his tongue because he talked too much. No one, from the highest to the lowest rank, was immune from the Negus's whims. Swift reversals of fortune were commonplace. The Minister of Justice was himself hauled off to be whipped, and great Ethiopian lords might be ruined in a twinkling of an eye, stripped of rank and privileges by the Negus and reduced to serfs. Even the most senile and feeble tribal chieftains were made to stagger around court with great blocks of stone in their arms as tokens of submission. On Sundays and festivals the shrivelled head of a Muslim chief would be brought out and publicly displayed round the camp. But the brutality was softened with unexpected streaks of humanity. A man condemned to be whipped would be seized and marched off by the guards with every appearance of ferocity. He was thrown to the ground, and a great show made of flogging him half to death, but on closer inspection it turned out that most of the blows were not aimed at the prisoner but hit the ground as a token punishment. When it was over the victim got to his feet and calmly returned to the court circle as if nothing had happened. To Alvarez's mind, the most intelligent part of Ethiopian justice was that false accusations were discouraged by the simple device of making the accuser pay all the accused's expenses while the latter was awaiting trial.

To their surprise, the Portuguese found that there were other Europeans already at the Negus's court. Mostly they were artisans and men who had escaped from Moorish captivity and taken refuge in Christian Ethiopia. They lived well and were valued for their skills. The most illustrious of them was a Portuguese, Pedro da Covilham, one of the few messengers who had got through the Islamic cordon by disguising himself as an Arab. In Ethiopia he had risen so high – receiving lands and a high-born Ethiopian wife, by whom he had several children – that he had achieved an almost native identity. He annoyed Da Lima considerably by disappearing off to his estates just when he was most needed as an interpreter.

Indeed considering the number of Europeans the Negus must already have seen, it was surprising how much interest he showed in Da Lima's inept little embassy. He was for ever sending runners to the Portuguese tents to pass on strange requests: the Negus had heard that the Portuguese were great horsemen – would they oblige him with a riding display in front of his tent? and he lent them eight horses to do so. They were asked to send over a musket, or a Catholic cross, or a pair of breeches to inspect. Some of the requests – for example, whether anyone in the embassy knew how to manufacture gunpowder – seemed very sensible; others were more frivolous. The Portuguese were obliged to put on exhibitions of dancing, of fencing, and even of swimming, this last being performed in an artificial tank dug for mass baptisms, and the Negus was delighted to see that they could swim underwater. Probably the oddest request was that the visitors should hold a banquet, and sing and carouse in their own style while observers ran back and forth to tell the Negus how the white men behaved when drunk. The Portuguese carried off their tasks with varying degrees of skill and good grace, and only balked when called upon to fight with the Negus's champion wrestler. An enormous bull of a man, he broke the leg of the first Portuguese sent against him (it was the painter-artist) and the arm of the next. Very wisely the third and last Portuguese challenger withdrew from the contest.

But it was Father Alvarez who attracted the most attention. He had come to examine Prester John's faith, but found instead that he was cast as a performing representative of the Church of Rome. A small tent was set up as a chapel next to the Negus's pavilion, and there Alvarez was asked to demonstrate every ritual in the Church calendar. Fortunately he proved quite a showman. He decorated his chapel with all the trappings he could devise, recruited a choir to accompany the organist from the embassy, performed mass, and even borrowed a baby to demonstrate a baptism in slow time so that the Ethiopians could ask questions at intervals. To everything the Negus paid the closest attention. Messengers came bursting in to ask explanations of such minor details as a change in the hymn tune, and at night they lit the interior of the chapel with candles and raised the tent flap so that the Negus could watch the Catholic priest in action, a situation which Father Alvarez milked shamelessly by flicking holy water from his hyssop across the gap so that it fell on the skirts of the royal tent.

It was significant how much of Ethiopian court life took place in the depths of the night, probably as a device to cloak the activities of the Negus still further. Time and again the Portuguese were roused from their sleep to answer questions sent by the Negus, and Alvarez had to spend one entire night observing the annual mass baptism of the court. A large tank had been dug and lined with planks and canvas to make it watertight, and then a stream diverted to fill it. A marquee was erected over the pool and early in the night – it was bitterly cold on the wind-swept plateau – the Negus entered alone to be immersed and baptized privately at the hands of his personal chaplain standing chest deep in the water. After the Negus had climbed out of the pool and dressed, he took up his position in a small kiosk from which he could watch the rest of the ceremony through a peephole. Only the immediate members of the imperial family were permitted to wear any clothing while being ducked. All the rest entered stark naked, much to Alvarez's embarrassment as he was asked to watch the ceremony from another vantage point, though he and the rest of the Portuguese declined to be re-baptized as well.

The climactic meeting when the Portuguese saw the Negus face to face also took place after dark. It was a splendid *coup de théatre*. Without warning the Portuguese were woken up and told to dress, and then taken to the entrance of the royal pavilion. There they found a thousand of the imperial guard, glittering in coats of mail and armed with shields, swords and assegais. Escorted into the tent, the Portuguese were taken forward past several sets of curtains, each more gorgeous than the last, until the final set drew back to reveal the Negus himself, about twelve feet away and seated on a platform covered with rich carpets. He was a young man, round faced and with large eyes. On his head was a tall crown of gold and silver, a brocade mantle covered his shoulders and across his knees lay a bishop's apron of cloth of gold. Four attendants stood motionless with candles in their hands to form a spectacular backdrop, while on each side of the Negus were men with drawn swords, and at his right hand a page holding a flat silver cross with engravings on it. The general effect, Alvarez thought, was very like the pictures of God the Father which the Ethiopians painted on the walls of their churches.

The meeting with the Negus was the high point of Da Lima's embassy. It turned out that the ruler of Ethiopia wanted the Portuguese army to sweep the Muslims from the Red Sea. With Da Covilham's help, Alvarez was asked to draft the details of a formal treaty, though he had to weed out the bizarre notion that the two Kings should land sufficient Portuguese and Ethiopians in Arabia to form a long line so that they could pass the stones of Mecca from hand to hand and throw them all into the sea. Unaccustomed to such treaty-making, the Negus's advisers spent much time consulting their copies of the New Testament for suitable grammar and vocabulary. Once or twice Alvarez was called to the imperial tent to explain difficult points to the Negus. On one occasion he found the Negus puzzling over his new map of the world given to him by Da Lima, and was asked to show exactly where Portugal was located in relation to Ethiopia. Alvarez temporized by claiming that the whole of Portugal was Lisbon, and all of Spain was Madrid. Shrewdly, the half-deceived Negus immediately retorted that it looked from the map as if France would make him a larger and more powerful ally.

The Ethiopians must have gained an equally strange idea of Portugal from the behaviour of Da Lima's embassy. Everything which Alvarez had found so astonishing in the Ethiopians – their violence, the strange ceremonies, their pride and greed – was reflected in the Portuguese themselves. A tiny band of foreigners isolated in the heart of a strange country, the Portuguese behaved like spoilt children. They quarrelled incessantly among themselves, with Da Lima and D'Abreu in particular arguing over matters of precedence and causing great embarrassment to the Ethiopians by taking their complaints to the Emperor's chamberlain for adjudication. Da Lima complained that D'Abreu was wearing clothes that were too grand for his station; that he was disrespectful; that he did not stay kneeling, as he should, a moment longer than the ambassador after an audience with the Negus, but rose to his feet at the same time. Da Lima even claimed that his lieutenant was trying to poison him. Matters finally reached such a pitch that the Portuguese split into two factions, and one day Alvarez had to rush into the Portuguese tent, swinging his crozier to break up a sword fight between Da Lima and D'Abreu, though not before the latter was slightly wounded.

In the end this quarrel proved to be the Portuguese undoing. The Negus sent them back to the coast to be picked up at Massawa by a Portuguese squadron, but on the journey tempers flared so high that D'Abreu's faction tried to ambush and capture their rivals. One of the Portuguese was shot in the leg, there was an unseemly brawl in a village where the party was billeted, and the horrified Ethiopian escort promptly marched them all back to court for the Negus's judgement. There the entire embassy was obliged to spend another five years, moping like unwanted guests on the fringes of the Negus's camp, awaiting guides and mules to take them to the coast.

Only Alvarez used his long delay wisely. He turned tourist and travelled about the countryside to see its wonders. He visited the astonishing churches of Lalibela; measured the towering stone columns of Axum which he believed were left there by King Solomon; and went hunting for the treasure of the Queen of Sheba. For a while he thought seriously about staying on in the country and joining an Ethiopian monastery. By the spring of 1526 when the embassy finally got away, he had enough material to fill five lengthy parts of his description of the slightly tarnished kingdom of Prester John. His book came out in Europe just when Portugal, having found the long-sought king of the Eastern Christians, learned that they would have to go to his rescue.

Two years after Da Lima's embassy left the country Ethiopia suffered the most calamitous invasion in her history. Striking from the north, Ahmad ibn Ibrahim El Ghazi, commonly called El Gran, 'the left handed', virtually over-ran the country. Gran was one of Islam's most brilliant generals. He had risen from obscurity as a common Somali warrior to command an army whose Turkish musketeers and janissaries completely over-matched the Negus. He had sworn to convert Ethiopia to Islam and he wished to avenge his murdered father-in-law whose head Alvarez had seen as a war-trophy in the Negus's camp. For once Ethiopia's highland fastnesses did not save her. Gran allowed his troops to ravage the country from end to end in a protracted campaign of destruction. Villages were burned and their inhabitants carried off into slavery. The splendid church decorations that Alvarez had so admired, were hacked to shreds. One of the Negus's sons was killed and a second taken prisoner and sent to be a pasha's slave in Arabia. The royal treasure was looted. A thousand years of Ethiopian culture collapsed beneath the onslaught. The Negus's allies fell away; his mother, Sabla Vengel, took refuge on the flat and impregnable crest of the amba near Debaroa; and the Negus himself died like a hunted jackal on the shores of Lake Tana, leaving the crown to his seventeen-year-old heir, Galawedos. Desperate appeals for help were smuggled out to the Portuguese in India, but it seemed that the rising tide of Islam, drawn by the crescent moon of Turkey, was about to engulf the last outpost of Christian Africa.

Suitably, Portugal's champion for Prester John could have ridden from the pages of an Arthurian romance. Dom Christoval da Gama was the quintessential knight errant. Young, gifted, and chivalrous, he was a well-connected and well-endowed darling of the Portuguese. His father, the illustrious Vasco da Gama, had led the first Portuguese fleet to reach India and been created a count. His brother, Estevam, was the reigning Viceroy of India and arranged the relief fleet to sail to Ethiopia's aid. Young Christoval was not yet twenty-six years old, but had already distinguished himself in sea battles against the Turks in the Gulf of Oman. He was adored by his men and had clearly inherited his father's grim tenacity of purpose. He was a story-book figure, the ideal captain to send to the help of Christian Ethiopia and attack the paynim with a

The tribulations of Ethiopia. *Left* Soldiers pillaging a house; *right* a woman being beaten with rods. Ethiopic manuscripts

handful of troops, which was all his brother could spare him. Dom Christoval's task was simply to put fresh heart into the Negus's defence while Portugal raised a proper army to come to his assistance. In the summer sailing season of 1541 he and a small Portuguese expeditionary force were hastily put ashore at Massawa by a Portuguese battle squadron. Where a few years earlier Da Lima had been met by the Bahrnagast, the Europeans now found the beach almost deserted. Gran had swept the coast clean with his ships and cavalry, and there was scarcely a Christian Ethiopian to be found.

The campaign began badly. A hundred fire-eating Portuguese disobeyed orders, deserted the squadron, and marched boldly inland. They bribed the sentries and went off on their own account, confident of winning glory. In less than twenty-four hours, befuddled by heat and betrayed by their guide, they blundered into an ambush set by Gran hovering like a bird of prey in the hills behind Massawa. The Portuguese were taken to his camp, stripped and shut in a cattle pen. Then they were released one by one, like hares from a trap, and ridden down by the Muslim lancers. Only two survived, by shamming dead, to bring back news of the disaster to Massawa. Da Gama told them that their headstrong companions had deserved their fate, and they watched the delinquent sentries hanged.

Christoval da Gama did not need the lesson of the massacre to know that he was facing wretched odds. Unlike the Spanish conquistadors under Pizarro, who were busy toppling the Inca empire half a world away, the Portuguese on the shore of Africa had little advantage in technology, mystique or surprise.

They had come to save, not destroy, a native throne, and they were opposed by troops whose musketry and armour were as good as, if not better than, their own. Moreover in this instance it was the enemy, not the Europeans, who possessed the cavalry. Against Gran's crack Turkish lancers, Christoval da Gama did not bring a single horseman. By tradition the Portuguese relied on the famous shock charge of their pikemen, preceded by salvoes from musketeers. As a military tactic it was scarcely more sophisticated than the wild rush of the Negus's already defeated tribesmen or the fanatical charge of Ethiopia's fighting monks.

Only four hundred volunteers were picked to go inland with their dashing young Portuguese commander. It was a token force to bolster the Negus until more help could be sent the following year, but it was given the finest equipment available. A few crude cannon and a hundred matchlock muskets were landed from the fleet, and every man was issued with a double quantity of personal arms. For maximum effect the volunteers assembled with all the dash and glitter of the parade ground. Every officer was a nobleman, brilliantly dressed from his private wardrobe. Each company formed under its own blue and white banner and above the centre waved a huge battle standard of white damask with a crimson satin cross stitched on it. In the van marched a crisp little band of flutes, drums, trumpets and bagpipes. It was the smartest, most gallant little company that Portugal could muster at short notice, and like the Crusaders whom they so consciously emulated, Da Gama and his men were illogically hopeful that they could defeat the Moor and shore up a tottering pillar of the true Faith.

Da Gama's first objective was to make contact with the imperial family, and since Galawedos was several hundred miles in the interior, he marched straight for the amba where the Queen Mother had taken refuge. It was a remarkable fortress, a flat-topped hill rearing upwards so steeply that any direct assault was impossible. The Portuguese compared it to the fighting top of a man-o'-war, and one soldier described it as 'square and scarped for a height double that of the highest tower in Portugal. It gets more and more precipitous near the top, until it hangs out like an umbrella all round, as if it were artificial, spreading out so that no one at the foot can hide himself from those above.' The only access was a single narrow path along which Da Gama's two messengers had to scramble until they reached a platform. From there, in a wicker basket, they were winched up to the crest to pay their compliments to Sabla Vengel and beg her to come down and join the expedition.

The meeting of the Queen Mother and the young Portuguese commander underscored the unreal air of the expedition. It was like a scene from a tapestry devoted to the allegories of knighthood. On one side was the rescued lady, released from her tower and escorted by thirty serving women, and romantically mysterious behind a veil of black silk embroidered with flowers. To meet her was her saviour, the gallant young knight resplendent in a pleated hose and a vest of red satin and gold brocade. A French cape of fine black cloth hung from his shoulders, and in his hand was a black cap with a rare medallion. Behind him stood his Portuguese troops in burnished armour, firing off two salutes in honour of the Queen before they shouted their battle cry and wheeled into a display of drill and a mock fight.

For the entire rainy season Da Gama stayed near the amba using the Queen Mother's influence to raise auxiliaries among the tribes. The troops drilled almost daily, practising the pike charge and the armoured caracol, a complicated manoeuvre in which several ranks of musketeers advanced and retired between one another while keeping up a continuous fire. Raiding parties went out to seize mules and a handful of horses from the surrounding villages, and an artillery train was constructed. The Ethiopian tracks were much too difficult

Lady escorted by spearmen. Ethiopic manuscript

for wheeled vehicles, so the guns were fitted to sledges sliding on runners shod with old musket barrels, and drawn by cows which the Portuguese painstakingly had to break into harness as the Ethiopians had no draught animals. Da Gama, in true conquistador style, made himself very popular by working alongside his men, but their affection was tinged with respect for his discipline. On his orders a Portuguese deserter lost both hands, chopped off at the wrists, and two of Gran's spies who were caught, were first tortured and then pulled apart by the sledges.

On 15 December the little column, now swollen by two hundred native auxiliaries, pushed forward again. They marched in battle order, for Gran was expected to attack them at any day. The Queen Mother stayed at the rear of the column, surrounded by fifty musketeers with loaded weapons and lengths of lighted match in their hands. A light screen of Ethiopians mounted on mules scouted the expedition's path, and Da Gama himself rode up and down the column twice a day checking the equipment and making sure that there were no stragglers. It was a gruelling march. The sledges were stuck time and again, and had to be lifted bodily over obstacles. The Portuguese, fidalgos as well as footsoldiers, had to do all the work because the Ethiopians did not see the point of wasting effort on cannon which they felt sure would never get across the higher mountain passes. But get through they did, with the Portuguese dismantling them and literally carrying them over on their backs. 'Such was our labour', wrote one Portuguese soldier, 'that as much could have been written of it as the labour of Hannibal in crossing the Alps.'

In February the expedition met with its first check. A small garrison of Muslims were standing their ground on an amba which Da Gama had either to capture or leave dangerously in his rear. Against the advice of the Ethiopians who pleaded the strength of the place, Da Gama decided to take the amba with a frontal attack. Only three paths led to the summit, all of them exposed to a hail of spears and stones from the defenders above. The rocks were so slippery that the Portuguese had to storm the hill in their bare feet, and in some places they were obliged to jam the butts of their pikes into crevices in the rockface to make an improvised ladder. After the defences had been tested with a prolonged bombardment, Da Gama personally led the wild charge up the most difficult approach, while two of his captains simultaneously attacked on the other two sides. Twice the Portuguese assault swept up the hill, and twice they were hurled back in a shower of stones and rocks. Several men died, and many more were badly knocked about by the missiles. But with the third attempt they surged to the top. There were a few moments of desperate fighting on the lip of the amba, and then it became a death trap for its defenders. The Muslim captain died bravely, transfixing one Portuguese clean through his armour with a terrific javelin thrust and knocking another senseless with a sword blow that

Warfare in mountainous Ethiopia — six hundred knights falling over a cliff. An illustration from a seventeenth century history of Ethiopia

dented the man's helmet. But the Muslim leader was overpowered and killed by three Portuguese attackers, and then the Ethiopians came rushing in with the sword, belatedly but enthusiastically, to butcher those defenders who did not hurl themselves over the cliffs. It was a slaughter, as one Portuguese remarked 'which the Abyssinians delighted in doing'.

The victory of the amba cost Da Gama 8 dead and 40 wounded, and though it immensely heartened his troops and allies by proving the vulnerability of the Muslims, it was a tactical blunder. The fight gave Gran time to call in his troops hunting for Galawedos in the mountains and hurry north at the head of 17,000 men, including 1,500 cavalry and 200 Turkish matchlockmen. With this massive force he placed himself directly across Da Gama's path, and the young Portuguese knight had no choice but to try to burst through his cordon.

The battlefield Da Gama picked was a magnificent arena but his second tactical error. He intended, so it seemed, to make war with the elegance and formality of the medieval tourney. Low hills on every side turned the place into a natural amphitheatre, and in the centre Da Gama drew up his men on a small prominence in front of which there was enough room for Gran to deploy his cavalry effectively. At the middle of his position Da Gama placed the Queen Mother, an oriflamme for his paladins to defend. At dawn the rising sun picked out the ominous silhouettes of five Muslim horsemen on the skyline, gravely looking down to inspect the Portuguese position. When they wheeled about and vanished, Da Gama sent two scouts to the same vantage point, and they reported Gran's vast host was on the march. Thereafter everything unfolded with ponderous decorum. Gran himself appeared on the ridge, easily recognized by his three famous war banners, red and white with heraldic moons and arabic mottoes, fluttering behind him. For a time he sat motionless, watching the Portuguese; and then his army rolled over the hill like a living carpet – wild tribal levies from Harar with shields and spears, squadrons of auxiliary light cavalry, and disciplined clumps of Turkish musketeers. The Portuguese could hear the call of their trumpets, the ruffles of their drums, and see the front ranks engaging in mock duels as they advanced towards them.

Nothing was hurried or omitted. The great army slowly lapped around the Portuguese position, and calmly encamped just out of musket shot. Throughout the next night the Portuguese nervously stood to arms, keeping up morale by firing off their cannon from time to time, for they were terrified that the Muslim cavalry would launch a surprise attack. But the etiquette of war was not yet done. At daybreak an Arab rider rode up under a flag of truce with a message for Da Gama. His lord, he said grandly, commiserated with the leader of the Portuguese that he was so young and foolish as to be duped by the Queen Mother of Ethiopia. The Negus's cause was lost, and the Portuguese would be sensible if they surrendered. As a token the messenger brought a friar's cowl and a rosary for Da Gama, a broad hint that he should have been a priest and not a soldier. Replying, Da Gama sent word that he came at the command of the Great Lion of the Sea, the King of Portugal, to restore Prester John to his throne; and in exchange for the Muslim gift, he offered to Gran a small pair of tweezers for plucking eyebrows and a very large mirror, making him out to be a woman.

With these insults dutifully exchanged the battle began. Gran invested the Portuguese position and tightened the noose by sending in his musketeers so close that the Portuguese had to make repeated sallies from their hastily constructed breastwork of stones to drive them away. Whenever this happened, Gran unleashed his cavalry against the exposed Portuguese infantry and cut them up badly. All day the siege went on, and by nightfall it was clear that the Portuguese would either have to break out or be whittled away entirely. Quietly they loaded their baggage on mules, mounted the cannon on their runners, and took up a flying wedge with the Queen Mother at the centre. Then, at first light, they marched forward as a single unit, drums beating and banners flying, straight into the heart of Gran's army. It was a suicidal gesture, and the Muslim army raised a great shout of triumph. Indeed the entire Portuguese expedition would have been wiped out if a lucky musket shot had not brought down Gran's horse, wounding the Muslim general in the thigh. Immediately his three red and white banners dipped as a signal for the Muslims to retire. Gran was caught up by his attendants and carried from the field, and the entire Muslim force streamed away, harried by Da Gama's tribal irregulars who put in their usual tardy appearance to hack up the stragglers. The Portuguese themselves were too exhausted to join in the pursuit. Their losses had been brutal. A quarter of them were wounded, including Da Gama with a musket wound in the knee, and they lacked the cavalry to press home the victory. They were more firmly convinced than ever before that the hand of God was on their

Above The burning of Churches by Muslims and the death of Christoval de Gama; *below* the fall and death of Ahmed Gran, shot by a Portuguese musketeer. Wooden panel painted at the beginning of this century by Kegneketa Jemlieri Hailu of Gondar

49

side, but militarily, the encounter had been wasted. Gran was left to regroup his forces, summon more assistance from his allies, and one day annihilate the slow-moving and unsupported Portuguese expedition.

For almost a year Da Gama and his adventurous army crept forward. They fought and survived another pitched battle, raided desperately for horses, and struggled to link up with Galawedos. But they were groping in the dark. The young Negus was still wary of Muslim raiding parties and refused to be drawn out of his most inaccessible camps; and while the Portuguese were enmeshed deeper and deeper into hostile territory, their fleet failed to arrive in the Red Sea with essential reinforcements. Meanwhile Gran steadily built up his troops, recruiting not only from Africa but from across the Red Sea, until he could come against Da Gama with his full strength: 800 Turkish musketeers, 600 Arab and Persian bowmen, a tribal army, and, most stunning of all, an artillery train of 10 field guns. In his van cantered 30 Turkish troopers, a personal gift from the Pasha of Zebid and so sumptuously equipped that they rode in golden stirrups.

The battle followed its previous pattern, but this time the Portuguese were completely overmatched. Once again their footsoldiers were beleaguered by the Turkish muskets and cavalry. Galled by Gran's cannon and ringed in by his cavalry, there was no question of a general Portuguese advance. Rather, Da Gama and his men sallied out repeatedly from their barricade, using the smashing blow of the Portuguese infantry charge to break the ring closing around them. But each time they returned to their position sadly depleted. Not a single man returned unwounded from the first charge, and one after another the company commanders were killed. Two brothers, both senior captains, fell within yards of one another and their corpses lay side by side. Da Gama's right arm was smashed by a musket shot. Twice the Turkish cavalry got within the palisade and had to be driven out. Finally after a hurried consultation with his remaining officers, Da Gama ordered a general retreat. Covered by a desperate charge from the last company, the remaining Portuguese scattered and fled taking the Queen Mother with them. Soon afterwards the powder store ignited with a tremendous explosion, blowing out the centre of the camp and killing about forty wounded Portuguese as they lay helpless on the ground. Da Gama himself fell into enemy hands. He was betrayed, so it was said, by the Devil disguised as an old crone who led the Turkish troopers to the bushes where he was hiding. The young Portuguese commander was taken before Gran sitting triumphant by a mound of 160 Portuguese heads. Already in great pain, Da Gama was ordered to be stripped and flogged. His beard was waxed and twisted into wicks which were then set alight, and his eyelashes and eyebrows were pulled out with tweezers. Then he was decapitated.

Ironically, his squalid death was also Galawedos's salvation. Gran, confident that he had crushed the main threat, allowed his Turkish troops to disperse and he himself retired to the area of Lake Tana to recuperate. There on 21 February 1543 he was surprised by a large army under Galawedos suddenly appearing out of the hills. With him came the surviving Portuguese, some with muskets, and some mounted at last on horses. Out of respect to Christoval da Gama they had voted to fight without a new leader, and felt amply revenged when a Portuguese musketeer shot and killed Gran himself. His head was brought back at a full gallop by a young Ethiopian, dangling by its hair from his teeth, and his death made the highwater mark of the Muslim invasion. It was also the beginning of a new relationship between Portugal and Ethiopia. The victorious remnant of Da Gama's tiny army was handsomely treated. The Negus offered them lands, high-born Ethiopian wives, and titles; and many of them decided to stay. In their wake came Portuguese priests to argue Coptic theology, and Portuguese architects to design castles and palaces at the Negus's command.

Portuguese art and technology were to influence Ethiopian thought and literature for the next hundred years, and for a while the Negus himself acknowledged the authority of the Pope, until a nationalist revolt expelled the foreigners and their doctrines. Portugal's adventure in Ethiopia died, as it had begun, in an aura of bloodshed and martyrdom that finally quenched the dream of Prester John.

The nationalist revival in Ethiopia and the expulsion of the Portuguese. 'Three Capuchins beheaded in the yeare 1648 by the Comand of Basilides King of the Habessines'

Sidy Hassan, late Bey of Tripoli

Barbary and Guinea

CHAPTER THREE

If the romance of Africa's place names still held any magic after the disappointment of Prester John, the West African coast was the most tempting. Around the western bulge of the continent ran a line of names that signalled profit, luxury and advantage to the European. Each segment of the coast was labelled for the product to be found there. From Cape Blanco to the native kingdom of Biafra marched the Gum Coast, the Pepper Coast, the Ivory Coast, the Gold Coast, and the Slave Coast. Here the Europeans came from the very first days of discovery, settled the mangrove swamps, caressed native princes, haggled with middlemen, and, if they were lucky, made fortunes for themselves. But very seldom did they show any real determination to explore inland. The Portuguese struck six hundred miles into Ethiopia a few weeks after arriving there; but the Europeans in West Africa three centuries later were still, effectively, on the beach. Like sea turtles, they seemed overcome by the effort of leaving the water for the land and lay sluggish on the shore. According to Thomas Astley, the disappointed editor of a collection of explorers' tales in the mid-eighteenth century, their inertia was the result of greed. The merchants on the coast were too busy making a profit for themselves to look inland to see the source of their wealth.

Astley's criticism was not entirely fair. There were formidable obstacles to any attempt to move inland. The waterways were irregular and broken by cataracts; paths were clogged with jungle; and the mortality from unknown and sudden diseases was swingeing. Yet the most important reason for the European's lack of exploring enthusiasm was that the indigenous peoples of West Africa were hostile. Over the three centuries, as they came to know the white man better, they liked his incursions the less. It was a situation which was to be repeated again and again in the record of African exploration. As Da Lima had found in Ethiopia, the best moment for exploration was often the very first contact with the native people. Then a sense of curiosity, a feeling of genuine hospitality, or a flush of optimism in the benefits of new friends, made for good relations. Later, when these feelings were displaced by fear or by disillusionment, the traveller would be hindered, discouraged and sometimes done away with. In West Africa ten generations of European entrepreneurs on the coast were enough to dispel any early euphoria.

A somewhat similar problem was to be found along the north coast of Africa. Here, from the mouth of the Nile to the Straits of Gibraltar and Morocco, the visitor from the north ran afoul of ideology as well as history. The spread of Islam had made a no man's land of the Mediterranean and a front line of the North African coast. A sprinkling of Spanish and Portuguese garrisons remained in North Africa, and merchants from Leghorn or Marseille could be found trading in Tripoli or Algiers. But they were there on sufferance. North Africa lay in the Muslim sphere, and Christian visits, like those in West Africa, were very much coastal exercises. Consuls, ambassadors and traders stayed on the coast where they had their business in the population centres. Inland lay only mountains, deserts, and wild tribes over whom the pashas and deys exercised only sporadic control. Africa's northern shore, like its western one, was a ledge on which the foreigner trod gingerly. Its very name, the Barbary Coast, was an index of the evil reputation it held, and the French traveller Blaquiere summed up a long memory of distrust when he stated at the end of the seventeenth century that 'to look for virtue or principle in a Barbary chief would be an idle task'.

Yet these coasts, Barbary and West African, were also the nearest parts of Africa to Europe. It took less than a month to sail from Bristol or Brittany to the Pepper Coast, and a Spanish officer in the Tetuan garrison had but to step beyond his pickets to find himself in Moorish Morocco. Africa of the tawny Moors, as the north was called, and Africa of the dark or Black-a-Moors, south of the Senegal river, was remarkably close. How the Europeans felt about these areas, therefore, was of great significance. It coloured their expectations of inner Africa for the better part of three centuries.

First contacts in West Africa were notably cautious. A favourite technique with masters of trading vessels was to stand close inshore and hurl samples of bells, cheap bugles, and other trinkets on to the beach. Only if these were picked and accepted by the natives, would serious trading begin. Even then the sailors preferred the natives to come out in their dugouts to the waiting ships, a process which had its own dangers, for the Negroes would take barrels of gunpowder into their canoes and happily sit on them with sparks showering from the bowls of their pipes, until told to stand clear. There was little system to this trade. A working vocabulary from the Pepper Coast brought back by an English captain, summarized the general needs. It began with a native phrase for 'good day', gave translations for 'give me a knife', 'pepper grains enough' and 'have you enough?', and ended brusquely with 'hold your peace', 'you lie!', and 'put forth and row'.

The Portuguese being earliest on the scene, it was one of their captains who

Early trading technique between ships and West African canoes

had the dubious distinction of depressing future contacts still further when he initiated the slave trade. He presented seven horses and their trappings to a friendly chief and received in return a very desirable young Negress for his own use. Professional slave traffickers a couple of generations later would have found this deal outrageously expensive as by then they were buying in bulk, and by 1537 the Lisbon slave market claimed to be handling 10,000 slaves a year, though not all of them were Negroes. The Portuguese were the first to prove that the West Africa trade was lucrative, and 'as soon as these voyages appeared to be attended with gain', wrote Astley, 'the English were ready to put in for a share.' So too were the French, the Dutch, the Brandenburgers and almost any nation able to finance a company for the West Africa trade. In a welter of enthusiasm the French alone managed to run through four disastrously mismanaged West African companies before the fifth survived through to a profit. Each nation sent its ships to the coast, struck up treaties with local chiefs, and promptly built seaside forts to protect these claims, as much from one another as from any aggrieved native. The Portuguese, too thinly spread and too poorly supported from home to resist, consolidated into favoured places like the great fortress of St George of the (Gold) Mine, or withdrew inland where their blood became diffused within the native populace. Years later, white explorers would be coming across light-skinned mulattoes and Portuguese-speaking chiefs in

'A View of the New Settlement on the River at Sierra Leona on the Coast of Guinea'. The slaving ship in the foreground has a protective barricade amidships to prevent rioting slaves from attacking the crew and taking over the vessel. *Inset* Benin bronze plaque showing a Portuguese trader with his staff of office and the symbols for money

Left Episode at a trading fort. 'An elephant came to the town of Elmina and was shot dead'. *Right* Scenes of African life recorded by a late seventeenth century traveller. Native musician, and a baby kidnapped by a monkey

the interior. But Portugal's knowledge of West African geography was either hidden in her archives or died with her pioneers. 'Ginny and Binny', as the English traders called Guinea and Benin, had to be re-explored by the newcomers.

André Brüe, chief factor for the French Senegal Company at the turn of the seventeenth century, was a more than usually talented example of this breed of explorer-merchant. Successively director, head of administration, and commissioner-general of the company, he was the virtual architect of French Senegal. Grossly fat and prone to much sweating, he seemed poor timber for an African traveller. In the opinion of his doctors he was liable to be stricken down at any moment by one of those mortal pestilences which were supposed to result from undue exertion in the tropics. Yet Brüe survived at least half a dozen inland treks and with his elephantine bonhomie won himself an unparalleled reputation among the Negro princes. His initiation to Negro court life was with the Damel of Kayor, a powerful slaver-chief of the middle Senegal. Outside the royal enclosure Brüe found thirty to forty Negro guards clad, Crusader like, in shirts of chain mail. Behind them a royal choir of sycophants

58

bellowed out the praises of the Damel whenever a stranger was in earshot. Entering by a wicket gate, so low that the corpulent Frenchman had to crawl through on hands and knees, Brüe found the Damel seated on a low stool in his audience chamber. Every native suppliant, as he approached, had to strip naked to the waist, grovel on his face, and throw three handfuls of dust on his head as a sign of submission. Brüe's reception proved to be less formal as he brought with him two ten-gallon kegs of brandy which were immediately broached, and the Damel got so resoundingly drunk that it was four days before Brüe could get a sober word out of him. Negotiations then took a typically wandering pattern of guile, bombast, and inebriation. Brüe had to inspect a march-past by the Damel's wild-looking army of black musketeers, accept a condemned Negress as his personal slave, and admire dancing displays by the King's sixteen wives. They were, the Damel boasted, twelve more than the Muslim priests approved, but being a King he felt himself above such ridiculous restrictions. As for the King of France, the Damel enquired about an extraordinary rumour that he possessed only one wife. What does he do, he asked Brüe, when this wife was sick or with child? 'He waits till she is well', replied Brüe loyally. 'Bah!' the Damel snorted, 'Your Grand Monarch, as you call him has more wit than that.'

For eleven years in the Africa trade, Brüe dealt with most of the important coast chiefs, from the 'King' of Biafra who affected a black petticoat, black pumps on his otherwise bare feet, a black cloak and trousers, and a great black hat on his head 'so that he was all over black except his Teeth and the Whites of his eyes', to the Brak of Maka who was comfortably swaddled in a flowing blue and white surplice and an enormous pair of breeches so baggy that they trailed on the ground behind him. A scarlet cummerbund half a foot broad was stuck through with a vast silver-mounted sabre and the whole effect was topped off with a soaring cloth bonnet, arranged so as to cascade down over one ear. This, like the Brak's other clothing, was hung with scores of gaily coloured amulets dangling at strategic points around his body on the theory that their virtue protected the nearest part of his anatomy. Scarcely less gorgeous in his own French court dress, Brüe handled each encounter with a nicely judged blend of respect, flamboyance, and an uncanny ability to select the right bribes. Brandy was always the staunchest ally, but for the Damel he proposed a great French bed and a suit of armour; and for the paramount chief of the Fulis a burning glass, telescopes, pistols, and a scarlet surtout in the latest French vogue with a belt, sword, and beaver hat to match. To the royal Fuli harem, which arrived slung on each side of their master's camels, cooped up in great ozier baskets like so many chickens with only their heads sticking out, Brüe gallantly explained the fashions and feminine society of France, and utterly won them over by demonstrating how to make open-faced tartlets baked in the ashes.

First day of the Yam Ceremony in the Kingdom of Ashanti on the West African coast

Brüe and a handful like him – Compagnon who followed him up the Senegal to look for gold mines, and the Englishmen, Thompson, Jobson, and Stibbs, who opened the Gambia for the Royal African Company – were the front runners of West African exploration. Usually they went by river, a gruelling slog against the current and punctuated with sodden and often futile efforts to dig channels through shallows or drag their longboats through cataracts. Food was obtained by barter with the natives who had to be watched constantly for signs of treachery. Compagnon calmly reported that among the clans around Bambuk the most passionate were for knocking him on the head; others more moderate were for sending him away without giving him time to examine the country. The rivers teemed with crocodile and hippo, and along the banks the travellers saw extraordinary numbers of elephant and lion. Curiously enough, there is no report of anyone actually being bitten by snakes though all the travellers uttered hideous warnings about venomous reptiles whose bites had to be treated instantly by cutting, gouging, or firing gunpowder in the wound, a treatment that was sure to leave a scar.

Against really big game such as elephant, hippo and crocodile, the feeble musketry of the explorers had little effect. It was not unusual to fire at them and afterwards find the spent musket ball on the ground, flattened where it had impacted uselessly against the tough hide. Hippo were the greatest menace. Every explorer had at least one bad scare from the massive beasts, and several lost their boats to irate animals which were said to make a terrible roaring noise and grind their teeth mightily just before they charged. Richard Jobson was in so many collisions with hippo on his way up the Gambia that he was obliged to frighten them off at night by floating stumps of lighted candle downstream on chips of wood. The only sure way to bring down a hippo was to fire bar shot at its legs and then finish it off with an axe. The hunter then took care to remove the animal's tusks as they were in great demand in Europe by manufacturers of false teeth and by apothecaries who ground them up and used the powder as a surgical coagulant. Elephant, on the other hand, showed such massive indifference to the explorers that some bizarre misunderstandings arose. It was commonly supposed that elephants destroyed lions by seizing them with their trunks and thrusting them headfirst into mudwallows to drown, or by catching the lion's head in the fork of a tree and leaving him to starve. The comforting notion that a nimble man could always elude a charging elephant on its left-hand side because it could not turn handily in that particular direction, was matched by the more logical idea among Negro boatmen that they could wade in perfect safety in the rivers when accompanying a European because his white skin drew the first attack from any crocodile.

In the final analysis, however, the dangers of up-country travel were considerably over-rated. Most of the early travellers returned safely to the coast. The up-country factors who manned the trading posts in their wake, established a comfortable enough existence of a colonial sort, with horseback rides in the cool of daybreak, breakfasts of Chinese tea laced with honey, fresh chickens purchased at three gunpowder charges apiece, large and obedient households, and business that seldom took more than three days a week, and then only in the afternoons. It was on the coast, rather, that West Africa was really loathed. Shut up in the little stone boxes of trade forts, it was little wonder that the life gave the coast a bad name. Surrounded by marsh and swamp, the sun glaring off the water, the beaches literally stinking with decaying matter, the fetid heat, and the grim tedium of their own society, the men were prey to drunkeness, brutalizing habit, and cafard. At the English fort of Cape Coast, the garrison actually walked over the underground dungeons beneath the main square where slaves waited in befouled darkness, each branded D.Y. on his right breast for the Duke of York. At James Fort on the Gambia anyone who ventured beyond the walls after dark was liable to be found next morning with his throat cut. Claustrophobia and pettiness rasped away any veneer of decency. Deaths by drunkenness, suicide and melancholia were so common that they bred a callous unconcern among the survivors. The chief factor at James Fort mysteriously split his skull on the threshhold of his chamber 'while correcting his black boy', and the blacksmith there got so drunk that he fired a musket at the ensign's head. He missed narrowly, the musket ball nearly penetrating the dining hall where the governor was entertaining. The culprit was drummed out of company service with a halter around his neck and shipped home, probably much to his delight.

Looming behind all was the spectre of disease, unknown and incurable. Visiting ships, just a few weeks on the coast, could lose so many men that they were burned for want of crews. Inside the forts the mortality was even greater. Holland's base at Mouri was known as The Dutchman's Graveyard, and among the English garrisons dying men were known to beg their comrades for a decent burial because grave-diggers had grown so slipshod that they did not put the corpses deep enough, and wild animals gnawed them in the night. Company surgeons were able to identify the everyday symptoms of fevers, cholera morbus, ulcers, and frequent convulsions, but they could do little to cure them. They applied native medicines, warned their patients against irregular living or sleeping with bare stomachs under a full moon – a sure invitation for fever – and excessive use of palm wine or native women. Then, likely as not, the surgeons themselves went on the brandy bottle. Death was a little dulled, and tropical chores such as extracting guinea worms from the living flesh, were made a little more bearable.

Yet despite their stagnation and immobility the men of factory and fort were, in their own way, seminal to Europe's growing knowledge of Africa. Every one of them was a listening post on the fringe of the unknown continent. Their trade demanded a minutely detailed knowledge of their native customers and they compiled unexpectedly comprehensive inventories of the coastal tribes. It was necessary to know, for instance, that Joloffs took red and green frieze

The north-west prospect of Cape Coast castle, the main British trading fort on the West African coast

cloth, but the Fuli paid highest for trumpery of yellow. The successful merchant took into account the tastes, economy, trading customs and character of every chief and tribe he dealt with. Such knowledge was gradually accumulated, codified, and circulated up and down the coast. The Mandingo were held to be cheerful, light hearted gossips, great smokers, liable to wrangle amongst themselves and almost the only major tribe who spurned wine and brandy. Meeting them one shook hands in the European manner until the joints cracked, but always with the right hand because to use the left was considered a mortal insult. The Quoja had a reputation for lewdness; the Joloffs for being the most drunken, deceitful, hospitable, and handsome of the 'flat nose' Negroes. With the Joloffs a sharp look-out was necessary for they would stare you in the eye with an air of utter innocence, while their incredibly dextrous feet would be sidling out from under their baggy trousers and picking off anything within reach. The Fuli were industrious and reasonable, while the natives of the Ivory Coast were the most frank and civil traders to be found. Unfortunately the latter also filed their teeth, wore perriwigs made of their wives' hair, and loaded themselves with iron rings weighing up to 50 pounds on each leg. Said Astley, 'they much admire the noise these rings make when they walk, and therefore the greater a man's quality is, the more rings he wears. In short, they are a hideous people, and stink exceedingly.'

Stench or sweetness, it was in the Europeans' interest to deal with every tribe they could. Profits on manufactures were at least 170 per cent, and though the supply of gum and ivory (happily known as 'gum and teeth') dwindled, and the malaguetta chilies of the Pepper Coast were ousted by oriental spices, the trade in gold and slaves more than made up the deficit. Enough West African gold dust was brought into England for coins made of it to become known as 'guineas'; and the austerely teetotal Mandingo alone supplied as many as two thousand slaves a year. The slaves were in themselves a source of geographical intelligence. Negro traders travelling the interior brought out men from the farther tribes which no white man had ever seen. Armed raiding columns of warrior tribes struck into virgin country and brought back prisoners so primitive that the black sophisticates of the coast laughed at them for wearing animal-skin clothes with the tails still attached.

Widening ripples, the contacts of the coast merchants spread until they lapped against the great inland kingdoms of West Africa. Dahomey, belligerent, victorious, and expanding with alarming speed towards Whiddah, caused the greatest stir. Bullfinch Lamb, stolidly named servant of the Royal African Company, had the misfortune to be the second white man the Dahomey King had ever laid eyes on, the first being an old Portuguese mulatto bought by the Negro despot for £500. In a pathetic letter to his company written on 27 November 1724, Lamb begged his employers to release him from the clutches of

Torture scene in Barbary

the Dahomey King, a savage and sadistic despot who alternately cuffed and humoured him like some albino curiosity. Lamb was frightened and dispirited, yet his mercantile opportunism still flickered. His company were to send up gifts to please the royal whim. The King had specially asked for an English saddle, a small dog, and a pair of shoe buckles. Lamb also suggested adding some picture books, two quires of paper, and a large ball of twine. The picture books were to replace a dog-eared Latin missal which the King always carried and, though he could not read, pretended to consult before he passed sentence. The paper and string were so that Lamb could make the King a kite, a device which the Dahomeyan had heard about but never seen 'though I told him it was only fit for boys to play with.' But the company's trump card would be a cast-off white prostitute from one of the forts. If she could be placed in the harem, said Lamb, great commercial advantages would follow.

Kites, whores, and shoebuckles would have been laughable if the coast merchants had not learned that such presents brought immense rewards. Bullfinch Lamb, after enduring two years in Dahomey before he could get away for ever to America, was quickly followed by more courageous colleagues. They found in place of some self-inflated village confederation, a powerful and ruthless monarch, backed by a professional Negro army and with his royal enclosure circled by a ring of human skulls. Dahomey embassies were conducted with respect. It was difficult to belittle a ruler who sent palanquins and relays of runners down to the coast to greet his guests, and then met them under the great imperial umbrella, dressed in gold-flowered robes and with a personal escort of four magnificent women musketeers, glistening and naked from the waist up.

Europe's increased respect for the natives, however, was not always reciprocated. The white man, as the Negro saw him, was tarnished. There was too much cheating, profit taking, and double dealing on both sides for awed admiration to last. West African merchants minted counterfeit spread eagle dollars for the native trade. Tricky surgeons sold ship's bilgewater as medicine; and unscrupulous factors held mock investitures with worthless parchments, thin salvos of muskets and heroic speeches in order to appoint some gullible native their sole agent in the area so as to fleece him all the more pitilessly. The natives reacted with violence or theft, taking the white men as greedy fools. Natives of the Gold Coast passed fake nuggets doctored with copper. Factors in charge of lonely storehouses were beaten up and robbed, and it was said of the Joloffs that they could steal the contents of a barrel through the chinks between its staves. Sharp practice was indiscriminate of race or tribe. Negro middlemen drove some of the most brutal slave bargains and were described as 'beggarly, greedy, faithless, and of a turbulent inconstant Disposition'.

Calculated dishonesty, drunkenness, cruelty, and rampant sensuality were traits which both races saw in one another. For every rumour – and there were many – that the whites were prodigious sexual athletes (some of the Senegal rulers actually asked for instruction), there was a tale which gave the Negroes similar appetites or sexual organs enlarged by nature. White visitors to the Gold Coast found it diverting to attend native law courts where adultery trials were pleaded with particular verve and pantomime. Negro husbands gladly prostituted their wives and set up their fourteen-year-old daughters as courtesans in the shadow of factory walls. One splendid mulatto at Cape Corse won the reputation of keeping the most comfortable bawdy house on the entire coast where the visitor would be served with banquets of guinea-fowl stuffed with eggs and spice and washed down with brandy and good palm wine.

The European merchants of West Africa, though on the beach, had not prevented the white man's reputation from running inland ahead of him. Few explorers would profit from the advertisement. Native tribes, who had caught only the faintest echoes of the white man, would have the same pessimistic expectations as the European who saw Africa at its darkest.

Slavery, in its mirror image, was also a recurring motif to European ideas about North Africa. Along the Barbary Coast, however, it was the European who was enslaved, not the slaver. A West African merchant, bound for Benin and cast away on the sand dunes of Morocco, saw another side to the slave business if he finished up as the half-starved chattel of some Berber princeling in the desert. Africa of the tawny Moors, it was generally agreed, was a place best avoided, a country of irrational fanatics who abused the Christian, and whose meagre towns were separated by vast barrens of sand and rock, infested by brigands. Half the population, it was said, lived in abject poverty brought about by the robbery of the other half. Maltreated ambassadors, shipwrecked merchants, and redeemed or escaped slaves – the leading sources of information about Africa north of the Sahara – had scarcely a kind word to say about their experiences there.

It was curious therefore that Europe's chief informant about the area was not a slave of the Moors, but of the Christians. Hassan ibn Mohammed al Wezaz al Fazi had been captured some time around 1520 by Christian corsairs operating near Djerba, Homer's Mediterranean island of the lotus eaters. Son of a wealthy refugee family from Granada who had gone to live in Morocco, he was as well educated as he was well travelled. About the time that Da Lima was seeking Prester John in Ethiopia, Hassan ibn Mohammed had gone across the Sahara with the caravans, visited Timbuctoo and the Niger, and toured many of the oases and cities of North Africa. He was, in effect, a walking gazeteer of Moorish Africa and must have brought a good price from that cultured slave master and discerning patron of learning, Pope Leo X, Giovanni de Medici. Under the Pope's guidance, Hassan converted to Christianity, took the Pope's name as his own, and turned out several scholarly works, including a Spanish-Arabic dictionary and a geography of Africa based on his travels. The geography book won him the title of Leo Africanus, and he was to be regarded for nearly three centuries as the undisputed authority on Africa north of the equator. It was a mark of the slow pace of African exploration during these times that two hundred years after Leo's death, his text was still appearing in translations and European explorers still were setting off into the Sahara confident of finding the same places he had visited so many generations earlier. As late as 1800 most maps of the north were still based on his badly out-of-date itinerary.

Leo's book gave a skeleton of knowledge about North Africa, but the flesh and colour came from reports by Christian slaves. Thomas Pellow, a Cornishman from Penryn, was only eleven years old when in 1715 he was taken by corsairs. He was captured by Moorish raiders from the Moroccan port of Sallee, who promptly sold the boy to their overlord, the Emperor of Morocco. Pellow turned Turk by becoming a Muslim, and for the next twenty-three

Mediterranean Sea

Atlantic Ocean

Strait of Gibraltar •**Tangier**

Madeira

Barbary Coast

Sallee
Rabat • •**Tetuan**

•**Mequinez**

Atlas Mountains

MOROCCO

•**Agadir**

Canary Islands

•**Algiers**

TUNISIA

•**Tunis**

Djerba

•**Tripoli**
Lepcis Magna

ALGERIA

LIBYA

Fezzan

•**In Salah**

Mourzouk •

Sahara Desert

•**Timbuctoo**

Songhai

SENEGAL
Bondou

Senegal

GAMBIA •**Bambuk**
•**Maka**
Medina • •
Kingdom
of Woolli

Gambia

GUINEA

Sansanding •

Niger

White Volta

Black Volta

Volta

DAHOMEY

Sokoto • •**Cashna**

•**Kano**

Lake Chad

Bornou

+ *Bussa Falls*

NIGERIA

Niger

Benue

Pepper Coast

Ivory Coast

Gold Coast

Cape Corse

Whiddah
•

Badagry
• •**Lagos**

Accra •

Slave Coast

•**Benin**

CAMEROONS

Bight of Benin

Fernando Po

Gulf of Guinea

GABON

Oguwe

Congo

200   400   600   800 Miles

200   400   600   800   1000   1200 Kilometres

years led an extraordinarily eventful life as a renegade soldier of fortune. He learned Arabic, served in the harem guard, received a Moorish wife from the Emperor's own hands, and campaigned extensively with the imperial army. In its service he was wounded several times before he finally switched religions once again and slipped away to England where he wrote up his picturesque adventures. He described a seventy-day trek which he had made across the Sahara with a large military column sent to gather tribute from the Emperor's vassals on the far side of the desert. It was the first account by an English eye-witness of the great trans-Saharan trade. The column's guide, Pellow reported, was an aged Arab, stone blind and yet so experienced after thirty crossings of the sand sea that he could lead the caravan entirely from memory, predicting exactly how many days the caravan would have to march between waterholes, and the amount and quality of the water to be found there. Several of these waterholes were no more than scoops in the sand, covered over against the sun with animal skins, and the column had to locate them by watching for the flocks of ostriches which gathered in the vicinity. At other times the guide found his way by sniffing the sand, recognizing each area by its distinctive smell. A soldier, said Pellow, hoping to disprove this faculty, kept back a sample of sand with him for two days before offering it to the guide to smell. He was sharply told that either the caravan had moved in a circle or that an old man's blindness was being mocked.

Sadly, Pellow and humble travellers like him were of little consequence in their day. Like the Portuguese traders in West Africa, many of them vanished without trace. Part of the problem was that North Africa, by virtue of its classical heritage, was held to be the preserve of men of scholarship, most of whom took the line that nothing significant had changed since the time of Hannibal. In their view more was to be gained from a study of the ancients than from any examination of the current Muslim inhabitants. In 1789 a popular

Experiences of Christian slaves in Barbary from a seventeenth century anti-Moor propaganda book. *Far left* 'Selling slaves in Algers'; *left* 'Execution with A batoone' (bastinado); *opposite: left* 'Turks burning of A Frier'; *centre* 'Divers Cruelties'; *right* 'Making the boat & their Escape to Mayork' (*Majorca*)

geography-cum-history, Thomas Salmon's *Present State of All Nations*, pronounced that

> The Moors are said to be covetous, inhospitable people intent upon nothing but heaping up riches, to obtain which they will be guilty of the meanest things, and stick at no manner of fraud. And as they know themselves to be such deceitful, treacherous wretches they are very suspicious of foreigners. The Arabs also have always had the character of a thievish, pilfering generation, and 'tis said will even rob and destroy one another when they have nobody else to prey on.

Such views were not calculated to attract the learned traveller to Barbary any more than the immense popularity of atrocity stories about the Barbary slaves was likely to improve public opinion. Of the first twenty books printed in English about North Africa, half were concerned with the plight of English captives there. To this lament was added the strident propaganda of professional ransom-brokers and redemptionists seeking to interest the public purse in their cause. They all cried up the torments of Barbary and spared no harrowing detail. With bland disregard for similar conditions in the slave forts of the West Coast, they spoke of the underground dungeons of Morocco – the *matamores* – ankle deep in water, where the slaves were herded at night, the frequent beatings and the hard labour of mixing mortar for new palaces or quarrying stone for the great mole at Algiers. Christian charity was invoked for co-religionists who had to empty the latrines of Mequinez, or plough in harness with a mule, or walk behind a horse which had been to Mecca, with cloth and pan to wipe its tail and collect its droppings.

Based on fact but carefully selected for bias, the atrocity stories failed to mention that many of the prisoners turned Turk or elected to stay in Barbary when they were set free. North Africa was drawn at its worst, and hardly anyone tried to set the record straight. Cervantes, who was a prisoner of war of the Algerines, failed to mention how well he was treated though he tried to

escape several times. Sir Jeffrey Hudson, Charles II's court dwarf, went so far as to claim that his own sufferings as a Barbary captive had made him grow from 18 inches tall to 3 feet 6 inches.

Even Dr Thomas Shaw, the first of the genuinely learned scholars to spend much time in Barbary, fell into the hostile mood. A remarkable man who was later principal of St Edmund Hall, Oxford, and professor of Greek at the university until his death in 1751, Shaw was chaplain in Tangier* and travelled widely in Tunisia and Algeria during the 1720's. Protected by a delightful mixture of academic myopia and solid common sense, Shaw moved about with only a tiny escort of two or three armed men, dressed himself as a native, and refused to take tents for fear of attracting robbers. He relied instead on hospitality in the 'hovels of the Kabyles or the encampments of the Arabs'. When that was unavailable, he slept out under bushes or in caves. Inevitably he was more interested in tracking down pilasters and pediments than in geography, but as he went his scholarly way, lamenting here over a Corinthian capital used as an anvil base, there at an old mosaic floor covered by a tattered rug, he built up a picture of Barbary which, as his editor put it, has 'always been esteemed for the solidity of his observations rather than for the brilliancy of the style.'

Shaw's observations, in fact, underlined the shortcomings of taking a historical approach to Africa. The Moors, he noted with donnish disapproval, were sadly fallen from their traditional skills. The chief astronomer in Algiers had not the knowledge to construct a sundial; the famous Islamic science of chemistry was reduced to mere distillation; and 'the whole art of navigation, as practised at Algiers and Tunis, consisted of nothing more than what is termed pricking of a chart and distinguishing the points of the compass.' Shaw's obsession with the past, as with Pellow's escapades, overshadowed the fact that the man himself was an excellent practical explorer. Behind the querulous scholasticism, he gave a first-class description of the countryside and its people, distinguishing carefully between Turk, town Moor, hill Berber, and desert Bedouin. With grave deliberation he ignored the petty details of his own itinerary and re-worked his notes into a systematic account of Barbary. It was an immense step forward, for it removed much of the fear and ignorance, and was widely read by the important men of the day. Moreover it left an inland journey as the next logical step, now that he had surveyed the coastal belt. But Shaw warned the traveller not to expect too much. He wrote:

> When I was at Tozer in December, AD 1727, we had a small drizzly shower that continued for the space of two hours; and so little provision was made against accidents of this kind, that several of the houses which are built only, as usual, with palm branches, mud, and tiles baked in the sun, fell down by imbibing the

* As was Addison's father who wrote a remarkably good account of people of Western Barbary.

Left The Emperor of Morocco, under the sunshade, riding to his castle which was built by English slaves. *Right* Thomas Shaw in his study

moisture of the shower. Nay, provided the drops had been larger, or the showers of longer continuance, or overflowing in the Prophet's expression, the whole city would have undoubtedly dissolved and dropt to pieces.

It was all a sad decline from the more solid architecture of Hasdrubal, Hamilcar, and Scipio.

There was a third element also to the growing awareness of Barbary. Diplomatic exchanges between the courts of North Africa and Europe were on the increase, and the ambassadors had something to add to the reports of slave and savant, in counterpoint to the dry precision of Dr Shaw or the dashing boldness of Pellow. John Windus, chaplain of Commodore Stewart's embassy to Morocco, described very well what it was like to meet the most infamous of the North African potentates, the Emperor Mulai Ismail. Preceded by two sergeants on horseback and an English band playing its music, the ambassador and his livery men rode to the palace through a crowd of curious onlookers. Any spectator who came too close was pointed out by the Moorish escort and thrashed by the Moorish soldiers. At the rear of the column humbly walked the English sea captains whom Stewart hoped to ransom. Inside the palace the ambassador was kept waiting for half an hour, before he and his party were led forward on foot into the Emperor's presence. The moment they appeared, Mulai Ismail fell face down on the ground and made very ostentatious devotions towards Mecca. Then, mounting a horse, he conducted the interview glaring down at the Englishmen, and constantly and rudely interrupting the interpreter so that it was very difficult for Stewart to make himself understood. The dread which Ismail commanded among his subjects was very evident from the trembling attitude of his slaves and courtiers who stood nervously watching his every movement, ready to fawn or prostrate themselves at the slightest whim. Their attendance was made all the more alert by the menace of a squad of Bokharis, Ismail's devoted praetorian guard of Negroes. With these bullies, the

71

âteau de l'Empereur

Le Château neuf
ou de l'Etoile

MER

View of Algiers and its notorious harbour mole built and
maintained by Christian slave labour

Mouillage Dangereux

Le Môle

Château du
Fanal

MEDITERRANÉE

1. Fort de la Marine.
2. Galiotte de Garde.
3. Porte de la Marine.
4. Porte de Babbazira et
   de la Pescaderie.
5. Fort de Babazon.
6. Casseries ou Cazerne.
7. Maison du Roi.
8. Porte neuve ou de Ba-
   baxedit.
9. Porte de Babalouet.
10. Maison d'un Morabou
    fort distingué.
11. Esclaves qui charrie
    des Pierres.
12. Fort de Babalouet.
13. Fours à Chaux.
14. Lieu d'Assemblée des
    Officiers de Marine et
    du Port.
15. Porte de Babazon.

Emperor was said to have developed a simple sign language: a nod of the head
meant that a man was to be beheaded; a quick turn of the wrist that he was to
be garotted.

But at least the slow pace of African exploration in Barbary and on the West
Coast allowed for moments of mutual relaxation. There were a few intervals
of gaiety and compliment to compensate for some of the sourness and mistrust
on the surface. Brüe, though embarrassed, danced a drunken dance with the
Damal of Kayor, and from the benign King of the Fuli happily accepted the
offer of a nubile seventeen-year-old princess whom he had been eyeing appre-
ciatively. Another West African trader, Captain Snelgrave, shared 'a Pye of
minced meat' made at home by his wife with the chief minister of Dahomey;
and the ambassadors to North Africa sometimes held secret drinking bouts
with the Muslim pashas, sending them reeling home under cover of darkness in
contradiction of their pious abstinence. French, English or Dutch, the explorer-
traders on both coasts stamped and swore, wheedled and grimaced, played the
buffoon or handled a bribe if it meant that they won trade concessions from an
African. Perhaps because there was no driving motive for outright exploration
– no pressing hurry to push ahead and explore – the self interest and plain
speaking approach of these early travellers made them, in a sense, more human
and more sympathetic figures than those who came after them.

A European ambassador has an audience with the King of Morocco

Agents from Soho

CHAPTER FOUR

Beginning in 1788, an elegant London townhouse was the unlikely hub of African exploration for the next twenty years. From 32 Soho Square, its slim windows overlooking the green patch of Soho garden, a private club calling itself 'The Association for Promoting the Discovery of the Interior Parts of Africa' prosecuted the intention of its title with an almost military dedication. Indeed the military flavour of the club was inescapable. It operated like an army intelligence department, selecting field agents, training and paying them, and sending them to Africa to gather information. The men who stayed behind in Soho Square were the controllers – powerful, calculating and not a little ruthless. Of the first seven agents they sent to Africa, only one survived the experience. Of the remainder, the most illustrious perished on his second mission, and the other five were never seen again.

The townhouse in Soho Square was the property of Sir Joseph Banks Bt, Commander of the Bath and President of the Royal Society. Officially he was only the Treasurer of the African Association, as the club came to be called, but in reality he acted as its director. Meetings were held at his house and he dominated its councils. Benign, arrogant, and immensely energetic, Joseph Banks sat at the centre of a web of political and academic influence which he had devoted his life to weaving. He had inherited a massive fortune at an early age and had deployed money and family connections to achieve a unique position in society. He was extraordinarily thorough. He had been at school at both Eton and Harrow, had registered at Oxford but lured his tutor to come across from Cambridge, and at the age of twenty-six got himself elected a Fellow of the Royal Society. Three years later he persuaded Cook to take him and his staff, Negro manservant included, aboard *Endeavour* to the South Seas. When the huge success of that voyage reverberated around Europe, it was Joseph Banks rather than the self-effacing Cook who made the thunder. The King received Banks at Windsor long before he ever met Cook; the newspapers were full of the young gentleman's exploits; the Royal Society applauded their Fellow's observations on the Pacific and, at the precocious age of thirty-one, elected him their President, a post he was to hold for the next forty-two years. From this immense puff Banks never faltered. He was the juggernaut of

British science, its acknowledged expert on foreign travel, a leading authority on several aspects of botany and the practical side of estate management (he had a large estate of his own at Revesby in Lincolnshire), and the man to whom His Majesty's Government instinctively turned for advice on every scientific matter, from the design of the breadfruit storage aboard Captain Bligh's *Bounty* to the best way of exploring Africa. It was a nice conceit that Pacific chieftains treasured ceremonial brass clubs sent to them by Sir Joseph and engraved with his coat of arms, and that a note from him was sufficient to obtain safe conduct for an Association agent across France at the height of the Napoleonic wars.

Banks's strength was not his intellect – in fact, he was overshadowed by several contemporaries – but his enormous capacity for work. His far-ranging mind was linked to a pen that pursued his interests to the farthest corners of the earth. He had friends, correspondents and admirers everywhere, and his ability to call upon their help was invaluable to the Association. He also had an ideal second-in-command in Henry Beaufoy, secretary to the African Association. Beaufoy, Quaker son of a London wine merchant, was master of the closely-written analysis to support the crisp, three-line notes which Banks dashed off with such effect. It was Beaufoy who kept the Association for Promoting African Exploration upon its precise course, drawing up the lengthy instructions for its agents, editing and evaluating their reports, and busying himself with the assorted details of minute books and ballot papers.

The other members of this extraordinary club for African exploration were also rather unusual. At the outset it was ruled by a Committee made up, besides Banks and Beaufoy, of an Irish peer who was a friend of the Prince of Wales and had political ambitions, a well-to-do lawyer, and a bishop. The latter, of Llandaff, was notorious for his non-residence and pluralism. Simultaneously Cambridge Professor of Divinity and of Chemistry, it was an index of Llandaff's style that he even failed to attend the very first meeting of the club at which the Committee was elected. There was nothing democratic or plebeian about the Association. It had been thought up by the twelve members of the Saturday Club, a private and fashionable dining circle, and it was ruled that only Saturday members could sit on the Association's committee. Thus at the start the Association was composed almost entirely of friends of Saturday Club members, and later the Club vetoed unsatisfactory applicants for the Association. It was all very simple. Saturday's picked the Committee; the Committee ran the Association; and the Committee were all members of Saturday's. Privilege was further enshrined, and the impecunious excluded, by the stiff fee of five guineas for membership of the Association, pledged for three years in advance. For this money the ordinary subscribing member got very little – copies of the Association's *Proceedings*, an invitation to the annual general meeting, and a chance to hear returned travellers lecture at first-hand of their

The east side of Soho Square, London. Number 32, on the right, was the home of Sir Joseph Banks and the birthplace of the African Association. Painting by T. H. Shepherd

journeys. Yet there was not much difficulty in finding members. Over the years the Association's list included three former Prime Ministers, a clutch of banking Coutts, Hoares, and Childs, and a steady supply of Cabinet Ministers. Gibbon, the historian of Rome, was a member, so too was Hunter, the surgeon; Wedgwood, the potter; and Wilberforce, the abolitionist. They paid their subscriptions and occasionally attended the annual general meeting, but largely left the actual running of the organization to the Committee.

The autocratic nature of the Association did have the immense advantage that it could move with amazing speed. The Association was founded on 9 June 1788. Just four days later the Committee – still without the errant Bishop – met at Banks's house to select their first agent or 'geographical missionary' as they preferred to call him. He was Simon Lucas, the Oriental interpreter at the Court of St James, and his task was to strike southward from Barbary into that 'wide extended blank' of the map of Africa which the Committee announced was 'a reproach upon the present age'.

The selection of Simon Lucas as their first agent was a yardstick of the Committee's inexperience. Frankly, they had little idea of how to set about exploring Africa. They had before them the examples of Captain Cook in the

77

Pacific, James Bruce the Scots explorer returned from Ethiopia, and a certain Mr Forster who had recently made a great stir by walking back from India at the end of his tour there with the East India Company. But Cook had used his ships as floating bases, Forster had his Oriental experience to fall back on, and James Bruce had retired to Scotland to write up his memoirs and met all enquiries with very discouraging, if not curt, answers.

The selection of Simon Lucas was, therefore, a safe and somewhat obvious choice. He was the one man in London who could be expected to have a working command of Arabic. Like Pellow, he was a former Barbary slave who had been sold into Morocco after being captured by Muslim pirates. Ransomed after three years, Lucas had agreed to return to Morocco as British Vice-Consul, so he obviously had no deep-rooted aversion towards his former captors. Indeed he now expressed himself to the Committee as quite willing to go back to Barbary a third time on condition that his court interpreter's salary of £80 a year was maintained. Nothing could have been easier for Banks. A brief word in the ear of Lord Sydney, Secretary of State responsible for the Barbary Consulates, and Lucas was seconded on full pay. The Committee told him to proceed to Tripoli, ingratiate himself with the Pasha, and then join a caravan going southward into the desert.

If Lucas's appointment had been swift, the selection of the Committee's second field agent was positively breakneck. While Banks was still negotiating Lucas's release from the Court, there arrived on his doorstep the ragged figure of the extraordinary American traveller John Ledyard. To the fledgling Association, he must have seemed sent by providence, the very man they were looking for, a professional adventurer looking for work.

But Ledyard was more of a self-publicized explorer than a successful one. Born in Connecticut, he claimed to have lived several years among the Red Indians in order to study their ways and learn survival among primitive peoples. Next he had gone off on Cook's third (and fatal) voyage, signing on as a corporal of marines so as to find a berth on what was a popular and very exclusive expedition. Finally, he had attempted to walk around the world by starting at Ostend and heading for America by way of Siberia. This last scheme had petered out in central Russia, and he had struggled back with some difficulty to London to see Joseph Banks, who at once suggested Africa to him and sent him round with a note to call on the Association's secretary. Henry Beaufoy was hugely impressed by the American's bold manner and sturdy appearance. He wrote:

> Before I had learnt from the note the name and business of my visitor, I was struck by the manliness of his person, the breadth of his chest, the openness of his countenance, and the inquietude of his eye. I spread the map of Africa before him and, tracing a line from Cairo to Sennar, and from thence westward in the

latitude and supposed direction of the Niger, I told him that was the route by which I was anxious that Africa might, if possible be explored. He said, he should think himself singularly fortunate to be entrusted with the adventure. I asked him when he would set out? 'Tomorrow morning', was his answer.

Ledyard's melodramatic reply was typical. For all his bubbling self-confidence and experience, something about him rang hollow. On closer inspection his flamboyant record as an explorer was distinctly flawed. Putting aside his eccentric claim to have been a disciple of the Red Indians, Ledyard's contribution to the Cook expedition was nothing to boast about. He had served in a very minor capacity indeed, and then deserted in order to go home and rush into print with a book that inflated his own importance at the expense of his dead commander. Certainly Ledyard's acquaintances in America wasted little time on him and refused to finance another escapade. So he went off to Siberia and, after one false start when he tried walking on the ice around the end of the Bothnian Sea, got deep into Russia. From there he was deported on the orders of the Empress. A couple of Russian soldiers, according to Beaufoy, 'placed him in a sledge, and conveying him, in the depth of winter, through the deserts of the Northern Tartary, left him at last on the frontiers of the Polish dominions. As they parted they told him that if he returned to Russia he would certainly be hanged, but that if he chose to go back to England they wished him a pleasant journey.' This crisp farewell brought Ledyard semi-destitute to London where he borrowed thirty guineas from Beaufoy to tide him over.

John Ledyard, as the Committee should have realized, was something of a Jonah. Banks had only to consult his own financial ledgers to see that the American had been sponging off him for years: an explorer's outfit for Siberia; a bill for twenty guineas drawn against Banks, and without Banks's knowledge or permission, in St Petersburg; another bill for five guineas drawn in similar circumstances in Königsberg. For years Ledyard had been hurrying off on ill-prepared expeditions and finishing up stranded in some out-of-the-way spot. Yet now when he vowed to the Committee, perhaps a little desperately, that he could explore Africa on a pittance, they dipped into their pockets to send him to Cairo. From there he, too, was to strike out into the great desert. In a typical flurry of haste, Ledyard left London almost as swiftly as he arrived. He sailed on the last day of June 1788, proclaiming that his knowledge of the Red Indians would be invaluable among the Bedouin and that for want of Arabic he would carry a dictionary.

If the Committee had managed somehow to yoke their first two agents into a team, they might have done better. But in practice of course, it was impossible: Ledyard and Lucas would have driven one another mad. Yet their strengths and weaknesses were strangely complementary. Ledyard could have injected some urgency into Lucas's prevarications, and Lucas could have made up for

Ledyard's massive ignorance of North Africa. As it was, the Association's first agents went their separate ways, one to Cairo and the other to Tripoli, with equal lack of success.

Lucas got to Tripoli in a somewhat leisurely fashion in late October. There he won over the Pasha with the gift of a pair of double-barrelled pistols mounted in silver, but failed to press home his advantage. The trouble, as a rival diplomat tartly observed, was that Simon Lucas had spent so much of his life with the Moors that he had become as easy-going as they were. Certainly there was a Moorish touch in the way in which he set about his preparations –

Well-to-do horseman in Barbary with his wife riding concealed in a travelling tent

parleying endlessly with caravan masters; picking himself a sumptuous desert outfit in the latest Turkish style, complete with crimson embroidered waist-coat; buying a couple of good carpets; borrowing the Pasha's tailor to run him up a grand tent; exchanging gifts and compliments with the Tripolines, and generally sinking into the comfortable existence of Barbary's most indulgent capital. The Pasha actually presented him with a fine mule to speed him on his way, but that was as far as Simon Lucas got. A brief excursion out of the city lasted just four days before the first rumour of rebel tribesmen sent him scurrying back. After eleven months' absence Lucas arrived back in London with absolutely no first-hand experience of desert Africa and only some hearsay reports of conditions in the interior. His mission, by any standards, was a disappointment.

In the meantime Ledyard's venture crashed more spectacularly. Before Lucas left England, the American arrived post-haste in Cairo. Promptly he bustled off to call on Rossetti, the Venetian consul who was looking after British interests in the city, and asked him to arrange a meeting with the Egyptian authorities. Rossetti entertained Ledyard to dinner but offended him by not asking him to stay the night, so that Ledyard stalked off in a huff to put up instead at a convent for Christian pilgrims. Rossetti, it seemed, was worried about the abrasive effect the impetuous American might have on the Turkish rulers of the city. As it turned out, he was quite right for Ledyard despised the Turks. Writing to Beaufoy, he poked fun at the geographical ignorance of the minister responsible for passports to the interior:

> He told me I should see in my travels a people who had power to transmute themselves into the forms of different animals. He asked me what I thought of the affair? I did not like to render the ignorance, simplicity, and credulity of the Turk apparent. I told him, that it formed a part of the character of all savages to be great necromancers; but that if I had never before heard of any so great as those which he had done me the honour to describe; that it rendered me more anxious to be on my voyage, and if I passed among them, I would in the letter I promised to write to him, give him a more particular account of them than he had hitherto had.

Ledyard was a first-rate busybody. He was forever going down to the caravan market to interrogate slavers and slaves from the interior or try to arrange passage into the desert. His inquisitive manner usually won him abuse and threats of violence, and Consul Rossetti, whose coolness hid a decent concern for the novice, took to sending an assistant from his office to accompany Ledyard, ostensibly as an interpreter but really as a warden to keep him out of trouble. Ledyard's letters to the Committee also showed him in a poor light. They were impatient, vain and intolerant. The Moors were 'a trading, enterprising, superstitious, warlike set of vagabonds', and he had a depressing knack of culling from them only the most banal items of bazaar gossip which he then used as a vehicle to flaunt his own travel experience. There were constant references to the similarities – mostly imagined – between Arabs and Polynesians, Arabs and Siberians, Arabs and Red Indians and any other people Ledyard boasted of meeting on his former travels. Equally tedious were his strident claims to his selfless pursuit of Africa's geography. 'Money! It is a vile slave', he wrote to Beaufoy. 'I have at present an economy of a more exalted kind to observe. I have the eyes of some of the first men of the first kingdom on earth turned on me . . . fame from them bestowed is altogether different, and is closely allied to a well-done from God.'

Ledyard's sycophantic despatches ended with appalling suddenness. The Committee received a note from a genuinely regretful Rossetti to say that their agent was dead, by his own hand and by accident. It appeared that just as

Ledyard was at last on the verge of leaving the city with a caravan, he had suffered a bilious attack brought on, the Committee generously felt, by the frustrations of his Egyptian stay. To counteract his distress Ledyard had taken too large a dose of vitriol, and then sought to allay the burning sensation with a strong draught of tartar emetic. The interaction of the two medicines brought on a fatal haemorrhage. Ledyard collapsed, and though Rossetti sent for local doctors it was too late. Ledyard, impatient to the last, had died in Cairo and had been buried in the British graveyard.

The news of Ledyard's death reached a Committee already embarrassed by a more light-hearted failure closer to home. While their two field agents were abroad, the Committee had enquired if there were any Moors living in London who could give information about Africa. Through the recommendation of a London doctor they got hold of a glib Moroccan called Ben Ali, who claimed to have been to the far side of the Sahara. He told the Committee that for a weekly fee of three guineas, he would give them the benefit of his experience. Furthermore, if they wanted to check his knowledge, he would gladly conduct two explorers of their choice to the far side of the Sahara, paying for the venture with the profit on £300 worth of trade goods which they were to provide. Ben Ali's suggestion was all too smooth, yet Banks and his colleagues were duped into paying Ben Ali his fees, voting the £300, hiring an interpreter, and even casting around for a suitable explorer to go with him. But they were soon disillusioned. After a couple of months' useless chatter, Ben Ali suddenly disappeared. The interpreter called at his lodgings to find him, but he was not there. Ben Ali had vanished, leaving all his belongings behind. Luckily it was not easy for a Moor to conceal himself in London for very long and Ben Ali was tracked down to a house in Hampstead. There he was found to be under siege from various women who were claiming him as the father of their children. It cost Ben Ali's original sponsor £100 in bail money to call off the constables and hush up the embarrassing affair.

With a trio of failures to its record, the Association might have been expected to be on the verge of disintegration, or at least of changing its Committee. But the Committee's brisk self-confidence and their invulnerability to criticism from the rank and file made them impregnable. Moreover, they claimed that the Lucas and Ledyard affairs had produced valuable results, and they were, in a sense, practice runs for later missions. Certainly there was no lack of volunteers for more exploration. The Committee was receiving a steady stream of letters from all sorts of men who wanted to go off on expeditions to Africa provided the Association would pay their expenses. From these hopeful offers – some optimistically vague, others mildly fraudulent, including one suggestion that the cash be paid in Paris, whence the writer would presumably never have been seen again – the Committee picked themselves the likeliest sounding candidate.

He was Major Daniel Houghton, an Irish soldier who had spent three years as Fort Major at Goree on the West African coast and had picked up some Mandingo language. His offer was obviously serious, because seven years earlier he had volunteered on his own initiative to explore up the Gambia river on behalf of the British Government. What Houghton did not say in his letter to the Committee, but was clear from its tone, was that he was desperate for work. He was middle-aged and without a military posting, he had no money of his own, a wife and large family to support, and an application for a half-pay pension bogged down in the machinery of an unsympathetic government. In fine, Daniel Houghton was driven to exploration by poverty and the Committee had a very good bargain of him.

He wanted, he said, only enough to meet his basic needs. Much more important would be an undertaking that the Association would take care of his wife and children while he was away in their service. It was a humble, almost pathetic offer, and the Committee met at Soho Square to accept it with alacrity. Houghton was to use the technique suggested by Ben Ali. He would have £260 given him, part of it to be invested in trade goods, and travel inland from the West Coast as an itinerant merchant. The profits of his trading would help to pay for his expedition. His wife was to receive a gratuity of £10, and if this miserable sum was not sufficient proof of their parsimony, the Committee primly added that 'she be at the same time informed that this assistance is the utmost which the Committee conceive themselves at liberty to afford.' By way of counterpoint they simultaneously turned down an offer from a Captain Mason, seconded by one of the Whitbreads, that he go off to Africa for them on condition that he could draw at least £1,200.

So, in October 1790, the Irish major set out. He was underpaid and equipped at second-hand. Beaufoy had given him Simon Lucas's old wardrobe, including the crimson waistcoat and a matching skull cap, and also a long list of questions to which Houghton was to find the answers. Most of the questions were about the Niger and the site of Timbuctoo, and if Houghton had managed to answer half of them, the Association would have solved the two great mysteries of North African geography for a pittance. As it was, Houghton nearly confounded his penny-pinching sponsors by coming remarkably close to success.

In fairness to Banks and his friends there was a feeling of grand, truly continent-sized, logic to this latest venture by the men of Soho Square. They had tried penetrating the interior in three ways – from Tripoli, from Cairo, and by interrogation in London. All had failed. So now they were putting in an agent from the West, the hitherto untried approach. Houghton was to proceed to the Gambia river in West Africa and contact an 'Old Coaster' by the name of Dr Laidley. The doctor would equip Houghton, find him a guide, and act as his African letterbox. Whenever Houghton had anything to report from the interior, he was to write out a dispatch, and on the back of it draw up a bill for £5, payable to the bearer from Banks's account. The African messenger had only to present the letter to Laidley or any British consul and he would receive the money. It was a superb expression of confidence in the power of the pound sterling to penetrate where no explorer had set foot.

Houghton's letters, as it turned out, came erratically out of Africa. From them the Committee learned that he had set off from Laidley's with an interpreter, a horse, five asses, and some trade goods. Almost immediately there had

Above Cane bridge over the Wallia Creek on Houghton's route inland. *Opposite* Medina, Capital of Woolli, where Houghton lost most of his equipment in a fire

been a narrow escape when Houghton overheard a Mandingo woman gossiping about a plan among the Negro traders to attack and stop him. But Houghton had evaded his enemies by swimming his beasts across the river at low water and keeping to the minor trails. There then followed a long silence as Houghton moved inland, his next report being a letter to his wife, which he wrote from the little native kingdom of Woolli at the head of the Gambia. He had been greeted enthusiastically by its King, who was anxious that the British establish a trading fort at his capital Medina. Houghton wrote glowingly of the place. 'You may live here almost for nothing', he told his poverty-stricken wife. 'Ten pounds a year would support a whole family with plenty of fowls, sheep, milk, eggs, butter, honey, bullocks, fish, and all sorts of game.' But there was also bad news to report.

While writing my letter to Mr. Beaufoy, the city of Medina took fire nigh my hut, which was also in flames in five minutes. It happened at noon-day, or I should have lost all my things. As it was, I lost all my bedding, except my counterpane and pillow; all my arms, my saddle and holsters, three jackass saddles; my shot and ball melted. I saved a little shot and all my powder, but not a gun. I am trying to get two sent up the river to me from the merchants. I lost my broad beaver hat I bought at Beavan's to keep off the sun, my razors, scissors, and shaving case, and my silver-mounted hanger.

The fire proved to be only the first of a series of misfortunes for Houghton. A cheap trade gun which he obtained as a replacement burst in his hands,

wounding him in the face and arms. His faithless interpreter ran away with the horse and three of the pack asses. And the ruler of the next petty state, the King of Bondou, robbed him of several valuable items including the blue coat in which Houghton had fondly hoped to appear before the Sultan of Timbuctoo. But the Major was getting canny in the ways of Africa. Before going to see the Bondou King, he had hidden his more essential belongings in his hut.

A low-keyed optimism still gave a cheerful cast to Houghton's letters. Although he was suffering from regular bouts of fever and had been abandoned by his guides, he was still confident of getting through. He was now so sun-burned, he informed the Committee, that he was often mistaken for a Moor, and could therefore travel more easily. His misfortunes, he felt, had toughened him. Moreover, he had one vital piece of information to report: reliable witnesses told him that the Niger flowed *eastward* towards the centre of Africa, and not westward as many geographers supposed. There were said to be large trading vessels on the river and he proposed to sail aboard one of them

'Gregree men' – witch doctors of West Africa

to Timbuctoo. In London it seemed to the Committee that their third agent was on the verge of success. Delightedly they circulated the Association's membership telling them to expect great news, when they heard unexpectedly from Dr Laidley.

He reported he had received a smuggled and crumpled note from Houghton, dated 1 September 1791. It read: 'Major Houghton's compliments to Dr Laidley, is in good health on his way to Timbuctoo, robbed of all his goods by Fenda Bucar's son.' It was the last that anyone heard from the Irishman. Soon afterwards rumours trickled back of his death. Some said that he had been killed by the King of Bambuk; others that he had died of dysentery, or been killed for his possessions. Laidley offered a reward for positive information or the recovery of notebooks and papers, but there was no response. He was reluctantly obliged to write to Beaufoy to tell him that Houghton was most probably dead. Not for another five years did the Committee learn the true facts: poor Houghton had been robbed by his Moorish travelling companions and marooned on the fringe of the desert. Somehow he had managed to stagger to a waterhole and called for help but the people there refused to assist him. Worn out by his trials, Houghton had died of fever and maltreatment, and his body left to rot in the bush.

The Committee reacted to this death of a second agent with a curious mixture of callousness and decency. Very churlishly they announced that Houghton had brought about his own death because: 'Contrary to all the suggestions of prudence, and the remonstrances of his friends in England, the Major had encumbered himself with an assortment of bale goods, consisting of linens, scarlet cloth, cutlery, beads, amber and other merchandise, which presented to the ignorant Negroes such temptations as savage virtue could not resist.' This was hardly fair, for the Committee had originally agreed that Houghton was to travel as a merchant, and although they had stressed that he was to avoid carrying too many tempting trade goods, they had not laid down any precise limits. Yet for all their mealy-mouthed criticism in public, the Committee's private behaviour was better. Despite their earlier warnings, they had been paying Houghton's widow a decent stipend ever since her husband's departure and they continued to do so for three and a half years. And in 1794, when Mrs Houghton so mismanaged her affairs that she landed herself and her family in Kings Bench Prison for debt, the Committee agreed not only to give her another £300 for her relief, but also applied for a government pension for her. Banks's influence had its usual result, and she was awarded £30 a year, while the Association itself put her children through school. It was a revealing glimpse of the two sides, outwardly stern and inwardly gentle, of Joseph Banks that even as he was complaining to the Association about the 'Canker worm of over-anxious humanity' which threatened to sap the Association's funds, he was also giving handsome charity towards the widow of the persevering Irish major.

Houghton's glowing account of the upper Gambia had found an interested audience among English business and government concerns. With the advice of the Committee, the government cooked up a scheme to establish a consulate-cum-trading post in the area, and capture the inland trade. A good deal of money was lavished on the preparations. A consul was selected and put on salary; volunteers recruited for a garrison; trade goods assembled; and two ships engaged to take the whole conglomeration out to West Africa. The project proved an expensive fiasco, as war with France and the blockading of the Gambia by French privateers put an end to it. The only man to profit, as the Committee found in its subsequent enquiries, was the putative consul. Not only had he been drawing his full salary while waiting in England, but the two schooners hired for transport turned out to be his own property and he had been paying himself a fat rental for them while they lay at anchor. Almost by accident, though, one brilliant success did sprout from the rubble of the consular debacle. To accompany the consul on behalf of the Association, the Committee hired their fourth field agent, a young Scots surgeon, lately returned from a voyage to the East Indies. He was to be the most famous of their choices – Mungo Park.

Mungo Park was closer than any previous Association agent to the type of ideal African explorer recommended by Thomas Astley. As a surgeon he had a useful practical skill, and as a keen botanist he possessed some scientific qualification. He also knew how to handle a Hadley's quadrant, and his Indian voyage gave him tropical experience. Only in his total ignorance of Arabic or West African language and customs was he entirely lacking, and these the Committee proposed to remedy by having Dr Laidley provide him with an interpreter and some reliable Negro travelling companions. Yet neither the Committee nor Astley guessed the main reason for Park's phenomenal success: his ambition.

Seventh child of a well-to-do farmer on the Duke of Buccleugh's estates on the Yarrow, Park had been brought up to a very Scots creed of self-betterment through application and hard bargaining. In a typically middle class pattern he had been apprenticed to a Selkirk surgeon, done his medical studies at

Edinburgh, and then set off for London to make his fortune with diploma in pocket and an introduction to a well-connected relative. This relative was his brother-in-law, William Dickson, an important seedsman based in Covent Garden and, through botany, an acquaintance of Sir Joseph Banks. Inevitably, therefore, Mungo Park was yet another Banks protégé. Banks arranged his voyage to the East Indies; Banks must have seen the descriptions he brought back of eight hitherto unknown tropical fish; and almost certainly Banks recommended Mungo Park to the Committee as their next geographical missionary. It was the sort of opportunity which Park would not let slip. He appreciated, as his memorialist put it, 'the distinction which was likely to result from any great discovery', and he saw the African adventure as a chance for fame and fortune. The Committee would learn that Mungo Park reckoned African success, when it came, as much in terms of hard cash as in the advancement of human knowledge.

Two romantic views of Park from popular books of his day. *Opposite* Mungo Park resting in a tent. He found he had a way with native women who always treated him with great kindness. *Right* Park on his travels, drying himself after a bathe

But Park had something more in his favour than mere driving ambition. His qualifications, mental as well as physical, marked him out as a suitable traveller. Tall and erect of bearing, he was good looking in a well-chiselled way, and women found him attractive. This was to be important as more than once their kindness saved him on his journeys. He also possessed to a quite remarkable degree the stamina and strength to perform great feats of physical endurance and to survive illnesses which would have killed lesser men. Such qualities enabled him to pursue his ambition with a single mind and a certain coldbloodedness. He did not travel, like later Scots explorers, out of missionary zeal, nor did he use his medical skill as anything more than a convenient grace. He explored because it was his shortest route to eminence, and he never forgot this fact. It was not altogether surprising, therefore, that when he eventually vanished into Africa, he left a long trail of broken men who failed to keep pace with his drive and determination.

His first dash for the Niger was an epic that became so well known in his own day that there were readers of his *Travels into the Interior Districts of Africa* who could recite every village he visited. Park told his tale with great verve and a nice eye for the romantic. The great journey began when he left Laidley's house on the Gambia. He was dressed in the normal European clothes of the day, carried an umbrella, and on his head wore a tall hat in whose crown he later carried his notes. For his Arabic he relied on a copy of Richardson's Arabic grammar, and for protection on a brace of shotguns and a couple of pistols. Fortunately he was much better served in his travelling companions than poor Houghton. Laidley had provided him with an ex-slave named Johnson who had been in the West Indies and spoke English as well as Mandingo, and also a cheerful young Negro called Demba who was promised his freedom if the mission succeeded.

To begin with, Park followed Houghton's track and so fell straightaway into the rapacious hands of the King of Bondou. By a stroke of genius Park managed to divert the King's greed by presenting the black despot with his umbrella. It was a sensation. The old King repeatedly furled and unfurled it 'to the great admiration of himself and his two attendants, who would not for some time comprehend the use of this wonderful machine.' Park was about to take his leave 'when the king, desiring me to stop a while, began a long preamble in favour of the whites, extolling their immense wealth and good dispositions. He next proceeded to an eulogium on my blue coat, of which the yellow buttons seemed particularly to catch his fancy; and he concluded by entreating me to present him with it.' Observing that 'the request of an African prince, in his own dominions, particularly when made to a stranger, comes little short of a command', Park very quietly took off his coat, the only good one he possessed, and laid it at his feet, thankful that he like Houghton had taken the precaution

A view of the bridge over the Ba Fing or Black River. From Park's *Travels* – the figure in the bottom right-hand corner is supposed to be Mungo Park himself

of hiding the smaller and more valuable items of his equipment in the thatch of his hut.

The young Scotsman also discovered that he had a way with the local women. He made a great hit with the royal seraglio, ten or twelve handsome young girls who clustered around him quite unabashed and teasing him about his appearance. They claimed his skin was so white because his mother had dipped him in milk as a child, and she must have pinched his nose ceaselessly to make it so high and boney. Park's suave replies earned him the name of 'honeymouth', though they were not displeased because gifts of food were later sent over to his hut from the women's quarters. Later Park was to write of Africa that he never met 'a single instance of hardheartedness to me in the women. In all my wanderings and wretchedness, I found them uniformly kind and compassionate.'

The most dangerous moment of Park's advance was his first encounter with fanatical Muslims. He was staying quietly in a village when a party of black Moors burst into his hut and ordered him out. He was hustled away to see the

Moorish chieftain who, no sooner than Park had appeared, thrust a broken musket into his hands and told him to mend it. Park explained that he did not have the necessary skill, and was promptly told to hand over the knives and scissors of his trade stock. When Park's interpreter intervened to say that Park did not have such articles, the enraged Moor snatched up a musket, cocked it, and put the muzzle to the interpreter's ear. He would have blown out his brains if his companions had not stopped him.

The Moors who kept Park prisoner for four months, were not deliberately cruel. They were more curious than vicious. After the initial baiting when pork was offered to him as a Christian to eat, and a pig was tied up and tormented in front of him, his captors turned inquisitive. He was made to dress and undress several times as no one had seen buttons in use before. His skin was poked and scraped to see if it would change colour; and his belongings pilfered. But it was not enough to dishearten Park, who consoled himself with small victories. The tormented pig ran for refuge under the chair of the Muslim chief and caused an uproar, and when the camp women came *en masse* to inspect if the Christian was circumcised, he put them to flight by suggesting that only the prettiest could have a personal demonstration. When the Moorish chief took a fancy to his pocket compass, Park told him that the needle was bewitched, pointing always towards his own mother who lived beyond the great desert. Even if she died, he said, the needle would lead him to her grave. Shaken, the Moor gingerly handed the powerful fetish back to its owner. The hardest blow

came when the young slave, Demba, was taken away to be sold, despite the fact that Park promised to send several times his value in trade goods once he regained the coast. Demba was never seen again, though the other slave, Johnson, was spared, the Moors saying he was too old and addled to be of any value.

The Moors lived a hard, semi-nomadic life with little to spare for useless mouths so once their curiosity had been satisfied, Park became a useless pet. Like an unwanted cur, he was tied up in a hovel, sometimes kicked and abused, but more usually ignored. In consequence his opportunity to escape came surprisingly easily. One night when the camp guard was more lax than usual, Park simply gathered up his few remaining clothes in a bundle, waited for Johnson to give the all clear, and at daybreak rode out of the camp while the Moors were still asleep. Johnson refused to go with him, pleading that the risk was too great, and so Park committed himself to the bush alone. Without trade goods, money, or an interpreter, and in constant risk of re-capture, it was greatly to his credit that he chose to push ahead for the Niger rather than return to the Gambia.

For three weeks he had a very hard time of it. He wandered through the bush, hiding from Muslims and begging food at native huts. As usual the womenfolk helped him out. He paid them with thanks or the gift of a button from his coat. Once he left behind several hanks of his hair to an old man who considered it a great fetish. Finally, on 20 July, he was trudging along in the

Opposite The Moors' camp where Park was kept prisoner for four months.
Right A young West African Negress

wake of a small caravan when he heard the scouts raise the cry that there was water up ahead. Running to the front of the column, Park saw before him 'the great object of my mission, the long sought-for majestic Niger, glittering in the morning sun, as broad as the Thames at Westminster, and flowing slowly to the *eastward*.'

Park's eyewitness account of the Niger was the great coup of his career. Wracked by fever, he struggled back to Laidley's and sailed to England to carry his report to the Association which had given him up for dead. He arrived, unheralded, in London on Christmas morning. Not wishing to disturb his friends, the Dickson family, he loitered in the public gardens behind the British Museum. There, quite by chance, Dickson found him as the seedsman was on his way to inspect some plants in his care. It was a moment of great feeling, the Association's annals reported – 'What must have been his [Dickson's] emotions on beholding at that extraordinary time and place, the vision, as it must have appeared, of his long-lost friend whom he had long numbered among the dead?'

Park's dramatic reappearance provided the Association with almost as many problems as Houghton's calamitous loss. At the outset all was effervescence. Congratulations poured in from every side. Park was feted. The Committee voted him an extension of salary while he wrote up his book; the Secretary (a new one, as Beaufoy had died during Park's absence) agreed to act as editor; Major Rennell, the leading geographer of his day prepared a learned commen-

Costumes of Sangara

tary. Publication was a huge success. The first edition sold out within a few months, and the enlarged edition was embellished with a 'native song' by the Duchess of Devonshire to celebrate Park's rescue by a kindly African woman. At a stroke, Park's name was a household word and he had £1,000 in royalties.

But this success, the fame and fortune which he had always sought, had another side. Park was canny enough to realize that he was now a valued commodity, and that as the successful explorer he could set a high price on himself. He had always held a good opinion of his abilities, and now acted very independently. Rather brusquely, he severed his connection with the Association and went off to the Borders with his royalty money. There he looked around for a farm to invest in, and married Alice Anderson, daughter of the Selkirk doctor whom he had once served as an apprentice. Banks wrote asking him to go off on an exploring trip to Australia, but Park received the offer very coldly. He made such extravagant demands for pay and privileges that Banks grew petulant. Exploration, Banks suggested, was not a matter of cash but of the pursuit of knowledge. 'Pecuniary considerations', Park sharply wrote back, 'however contemptible in themselves, serve as a good interest by which to judge the importance of any office or any pursuit.' It was a crushing retort, for which even the President of the Royal Society could not find a suitable reply.

But in the end it was Banks, aided by Park's own restlessness, who won. Park began to find the Border dull. Land was so expensive that instead of farming he had set up as a surgeon. But he thought the life of a country doctor very dreary. Visitors who expected him to regale them with tales of his adventures, found him distant and silent. The notion of going back to Africa became increasingly attractive, both as an escape from boredom and as an opportunity to improve his lot still further. Almost contritely, he wrote to Banks to tell him that 'I will gladly hang up lancet and plaister ladle whenever I can obtain a more eligible situation.'

Banks of course already had another trip planned for him. This time Park was to try to trace the course of the Niger downstream of his previous visit, but in an altogether more grand fashion than his first expedition. He would be the leader of an officially sponsored government venture with the rank and pay of a captain and the privileges of a representative of His Majesty's government. He could choose his own officers and take an escort of thirty soldiers from the Royal Africa Corps garrison at Goree. Four artificers from the Portsmouth dockyard were to accompany him to Africa to build a forty-foot boat, in which he would float down the river, mapping its course, showing the flag, and making commercial treaties with the tribes.

It was a supremely generous offer and Park leapt at the chance. As second-in-command he selected his brother-in-law, Alexander Anderson, and a friend, George Scott, was to be expedition draughtsman. A long list of requirements was drawn up: the army was to provide leather gaiters, mosquito nets, and double issue of firearms for the escort. The soldiers were to be encouraged with extra pay and the promise of discharge on return. The army mules were to be numbered in red paint on their hides so as to make sure everyone knew his own beast. It all seemed eminently well organized and sensible, but everyone overlooked the fact that Park's earlier success had been due to his single-handed determination and endurance as a sole traveller. His new entourage in their heavy uniforms and thick hats would be more a hindrance than a help. Few of them would be able to stand the gruelling pace which Park set.

So began Park's second, and fatal, journey. It was a hideous failure relieved only by his fantastic record for stamina. Against all advice and logic, he led his column out into the bush during the West African rainy season. Soldiers and mules slipped and slithered. Baggage grew sodden. Ten days out from the coast, Park recorded the first case of dysentery; thereafter the expedition simply leaked away. When the soldiers felt sick, they begged to be allowed to drop out of the column and recuperate in wayside villages. Often they failed to reappear. One man died of an epileptic fit; Lieutenant Martyn, their officer, began drinking heavily, finding, in his own words, that native beer was as good as Whitbreads. Yet, all the while, Park kept up a blind optimism. 'Everything looks favourable', he wrote confidently to his wife as he set out. 'We have been successful far beyond my highest expectations . . . In five weeks from the date of this letter [26 April] the worst part of the journey will be over.'

After those five weeks had passed, he refused to revise his estimate. 'I am happy to inform you that we are half way through our journey without the smallest accident or unpleasant circumstance . . . I see no reason to think that our stay in the Interior will be longer than I first mentioned.' Very probably he was trying to keep up his wife's spirits, for he did not tell of the death of the epileptic, that seven asses were missing and that a disastrous fire had destroyed nearly all the expedition's baggage. On 4 July Isaaco, the guide, was nearly carried off by a crocodile, and only saved himself by thrusting his thumbs into the creature's eyes. By the middle of the month the column was a shambles, every man either sick or in a state of great debility. Park worked like a demon to hold it together. He seemed indestructible. At one ford he carried virtually the entire expedition, man by man, across the water on his back, dumping them on the other bank and then returning for the next person. Effectively, he was turning his second expedition into another one-man effort. If he could not persuade a soldier to continue forward or carry him personally, then he simply abandoned him to his fate. It may have seemed callous and cruel, but Park did not spare himself. He too was suffering from fever and was not prepared to let other men off more lightly. By the time his column reached Sansanding on the Niger, only eleven of the original forty Europeans on the

Miniature of Mungo Park.
After an engraving by H. Eldridge

expedition were still alive and all three officers, Anderson, Scott, and Martyn, were very weak.

For the best part of two months the expedition recuperated at Sansanding, while Park tried to open formal relations with the chiefs. But the hand of death was on his tiny force and it was dwindling fast. On 19 November he wrote to his wife of the deaths of Scott and her brother. 'It grieves me to the heart to write anything that may give you uneasiness, but such is the will of Him who doeth all things well! Your brother Alexander, my dear friend, is no more! He died of fever at Sansanding on the morning of 28 October.'

It would have been difficult for Park not to be aware that his decision to set out during the rains had caused the deaths of his men. To the Earl of Camden, one of the Principal Secretaries of State, he confessed, 'Your Lordship will recollect that I always spoke of the rainy season with horror, as being extremely fatal to Europeans; and our journey from the Gambia to the Niger will furnish a melancholy proof of it.' Only five Europeans were now alive: Lieutenant Martyn, three soldiers, of whom one was deranged in his mind, and Park. Either he was no longer able to face the thought of going back to confess his faulty leadership, or he truly thought he had a chance of getting through. Whatever the reason, he decided to press on and, if the worst came, to shoot his way downriver. With the help of one of the soldiers, he converted a native canoe into a leaky schooner which he dubbed H.M.S. *Joliba*, the native name for the river, and in a grimly jaunty mood hoisted the British flag in her. With this crank vessel, he told Camden, he proposed to 'set sail to the east with the fixed resolution to discover the termination of the Niger or perish in the attempt . . . '

Sending Isaaco back with final dispatches, Park and his dying companions floated off down river. Each man had fifteen muskets beside him, and all the supplies they could salvage. Soon the news began to be whispered on the coast that they had perished. Isaaco was hired to return inland to learn the truth and collect what evidence he could. He reported that H.M.S. *Joliba* had come under running fire from hostile natives and, seeking to escape, had been swept over the Bussa Rapids. Park and all his companions were dead. The only clue Isaaco had been able to find was a belt which had belonged to Park.

The precise details of the explorer's death were never cleared up satisfactorily. For years there were men in England who believed that Park was too skilled in African ways to have made such a mistake on the river. He would re-emerge, they claimed, from the bush. His detractors said that Park had caused his own death by antagonizing the natives with rough treatment and arrogant demands. Others feared that the *Joliba* had been ambushed by a marauding band of Tuareg, or her crew had failed to pay tribute to the river chiefs and been executed. Years later Park's own son visited the river in disguise to try to solve

Opposite One version of the death of Mungo Park, published soon after he had been given up for lost

Sandwind in the desert by G. F. Lyon

the mystery but without success. A favourite explanation, allegedly by an eyewitness, said that Park had died a hero's death. As the *Joliba* was swept towards the rapids and hostile natives swarmed on the bank, Park and Lieutenant Martyn had each taken a white man, presumably a non-swimmer, in their arms and leapt into the water, only to be dashed to their deaths over the falls. It was a glamorous conclusion to Park's flamboyant career and the one which the African Association, and most of their public, preferred to believe.

The Committee of the Association, however, already had other agents to worry about. The responsibility for the Niger debacle, as far as they were concerned, belonged to the Government which had sponsored it. Their own prestige was so great that there was talk in Spain, France, and Germany of setting up similar clubs for exploration and the Committee was getting hopeful enquiries from young men all over Europe who wanted to go exploring in Africa. Out of all these applications, they picked a young man who was to be one of the most talented African explorers.

Professor Blumenbach of Göttingen University had recommended the applicant and Blumenbach's word carried considerable weight for he was something of a Banksian figure in his own right. Professor of Medicine at Göttingen University by the age of twenty-six, he was an authority on the geography and ethnology of Africa. Naturally he was also one of Banks's correspondents, exchanging treatises and learned journals with Soho Square, and in May 1796, while Park was on his first trip, he wrote to Banks about a young student who was an African enthusiast clamouring to go exploring there. His name was Frederick Hornemann and, wrote Blumenbach:

> There will hardly be a man better qualified for the purpose in question than he is. He is universally known by all his acquaintances as a man of excellent character, and besides other good qualities, as a very good Economist who, tho' in very moderate circumstances (having lost his father, a clergyman, who left a widow with several children) yet always managed his Economical arrangements in such a way, that he lived decently without ever incurring the least Debts etc.

The one thing the Committee could seldom resist was the offer of an inexpensive explorer. They wrote back immediately to Blumenbach, agreeing to pay Hornemann's expenses while he studied Arabic and prepared himself for a venture into the interior of Africa using the Cairo route which Ledyard had attempted. It was typical of Hornemann that, by the time he heard from the Association, he had read up so much about Africa that he knew as much about the place as anyone in the Association. Indeed the Secretary of the Association was unable to answer several of Hornemann's questions about former field agents. Quiet, unassuming, and diligent, Hornemann was, above all, efficient. Whether studying Arabic or learning to use a sextant, Hornemann showed a streak of calculated discipline that all his predecessors had lacked. In a letter to

Banks he explained how he had always wanted since childhood to travel in Africa, and that this desire had only increased as he grew up. He was so ingenuously grateful to Banks and Blumenbach and threw himself so whole-heartedly into the venture, that there was never any doubt that he was the African explorer *par excellence*, both by dedication and inclination. He was also the first of the great German travellers in Africa.

In the Autumn of 1797, Hornemann crossed war-time France with a safe-conduct that Banks's influence had obtained for him. At once the young German made for Cairo and there enrolled as the pupil of a Greek priest who was willing to improve his Arabic. He stayed with Rossetti, the Venetian consul who had helped Ledyard, and every day he went to his lessons. He was about to leave with a caravan when plague broke out and he had to postpone his trip. Scarcely had the plague abated than Napoleon landed in Egypt with an army and the Egyptian authorities interned all foreign citizens. Hornemann kept his patience. He was eventually released by the occupying forces and Napoleon personally promised to forward his letters to London, provided only that they were written in French. Then, ignoring warnings that Europeans were now so unpopular that it required a small army to make a desert passage, Hornemann joined up with a caravan for Fezzan. Of all the Association's agents he was so well prepared that he was the first to disguise himself successfully as an Arab.

It was, as he wrote to Banks, a considerable risk. If his disguise were pene-trated there was little doubt that he would be done away with. But his Arabic was now quite good and he hoped it would improve with use. He proposed to pass himself off as a simple trader, merging quietly into the lower echelons of a caravan. If anyone asked about his telescope or quadrant, he would say that they were merely articles for sale; and he would take care to use them only when he was sure that he was unobserved. Neither the Association nor any of the European consuls were to make any inquiry after him, in case the word spread that there was a Christian with the caravans. Hornemann intended to rely utterly on his own resources and accept the risk involved. He would strike for Bornou on the far side of the desert, and even if nothing was heard from him for three years, no one was to worry. He would report back by secret means, using 'some bale of goods with an ordinary letter of advice in Arabic, making my real despatch the package or covering of some article of trade.'

A year later Hornemann surfaced. From Tripoli, he wrote jubilantly to Banks that his disguise had been a complete success. He had been into the Fezzan, lived successfully as a native, and though challenged once or twice as a spy he had talked his way out of trouble. His command of Arabic and his knowledge of Islamic law now exceeded all but the most learned Muslims. 'Pray Sir,' he wrote, 'do not look upon me as a European but as a real African . . . I look upon my Travels done as upon the work of an apprentice; – Now I think I have the experience of at least a young Master.' A couple of months later the Committee heard again from him at Mourzouk on the fringe of the desert. He was headed, he told them, for Bornou and after that for Timbuctoo. He hoped that his next letter would be sent from the further coast of Africa.

That letter never arrived. Hornemann, the most professional of the desert travellers, was swallowed up by the Sahara. He was so well disguised, so much the chameleon, that for years the Association continued to hope for his safety. Unlike Park or Houghton there were no rumours of a white man dying in the interior. Not until 1819, did a British explorer come across definite news of Hornemann's death. The German had got an immense distance, passing through Bornou and Cashna, and penetrating two-thirds of the way to the far coast of Africa. He succumbed, not from maltreatment or attack like his predecessors, but from the effects of dysentery brought on by his exacting way of life. According to the British explorer, the local population mourned him as a learned 'Marabout', a wandering holy man. It was a considerable compliment for the son of a Lutheran pastor.

Hornemann's journey was the pinnacle of the Association's efforts in the North African desert. Their next explorer, a Swiss by the name of Johan Ludwig Burckhardt, travelled successfully in the Levant and Mesopotamia, where he was the first to describe Petra. But Banks himself retired from the Treasurership in 1804, crippled by increasing gout, and with his death in

1820, there came a slump in the activity of the club. Conceived and raised by the original enthusiasts, their departure meant decline. The Association sponsored a few more expeditions but they could not compete with the lavish efforts of national governments, particularly the French and British, who were beginning to take an interest in the routes which Banks and Beaufoy had once sketched. In 1830, when the Royal Geographical Society was founded, there were only fourteen members of the African Association left, and they considered whether or not to merge it with the new group. They had not sponsored an expedition for a decade, and the new Society had wider aims and membership. In one last touch of decorum the fourteen survivors sent themselves a resolution that, from the £700 in the Association's funds, any member who wished could have his life subscription paid to the Royal Geographical Society. Those who did not want to join would have £20 returned direct. The remainder of the joint fund would be made over to the new Society.

So, forty-two years after its foundation by the *bon viveurs* of the Saturday Club, the African Association slipped quietly out of existence. It had broken through the crust of unknown Africa and uncovered the broad outline of North African geography. All this had been achieved by parsimony, shrewd direction of its agents, and a total outlay of some £9,000. By later costs, it was the greatest bargain of African exploration.

Opposite The Castle of Mourzouk, one of the main caravan centres on the north side of the Sahara. Drawn by G. F. Lyon. *Above* Sir Joseph Banks 'the Juggernaut of British Science' as President of the Royal Society. Painting by Thomas Phillips

The
Social Spectrum

CHAPTER FIVE

By 1830 it was increasingly clear that the African adventure was open to all comers. The Association's agents had not been the only people in the field. Entirely independent of Banks and his friends, a selection of other travellers had been in Africa at the same time, tramping about the continent with equal gusto and at least as much success. Some were sponsored; others freelance. A few adopted native disguise, but most of them decided to stay firmly, and often passionately, European in dress and manner. More important, they came from almost every social class that European society had to offer. Beginning with a Scottish aristocrat and ending with a Cornish manservant, they ranged in steady progression from one social extreme to the other. The lesson to be drawn was that performance in Africa depended more on a man's reactions to his exotic surroundings than on his background or training.

James Bruce, laird of Kinnaird, was the leading example, both in time and standing. His journey preceded the foundation of the African Association by some twenty years and had a double effect on its creation. Bruce demonstrated not only what could be done in Africa by the determined individual, but also that it helped enormously to have the money – and for most people, therefore, the sponsorship – to do it. James Bruce, however, was the exception. Of all the African explorers of his day, he was the only one who was genuinely wealthy. He alone could afford the great escapade as a private whim and indulge himself as the gifted amateur. Able to pay his own way, he was delightfully free of interference from sponsors or governments, and this independence set his style as an explorer – colourful, erratic and domineering.

Bruce's physique had a great deal to do with it. He was a great hulk of a man, more than six-foot tall, barrel-bodied and red-haired, and despite a sickly childhood when he was too tall for his strength, he had become an excellent shot and horseman. He was also a hypochondriac, a person easily offended, and had such a violent temper that when he became angry his nose would burst out bleeding quite spontaneously. With some slight justification he claimed he was related to the family of Robert the Bruce, and therefore prided himself as superior to what he called 'the lower orders'. Very much a creature of his times, he was admirably equipped in purse and boldness to be an African traveller of note, and it was not surprising that he should also prove a highly controversial one. In the end, however, there emerged from within this mountain of a man a gnawing dread that he was not being taken seriously, and this fear was to destroy him.

There was, to begin with, a touch of deliberate extravagance to his notion of going off to Africa. People of his background normally confined their travels to Europe, usually a tour of Mediterranean antiquities such as Dr Johnson prescribed so heartily. Bruce, however, proposed to extend his scope in a grandiose manner. His intention was the same, namely to study traces of the ancients, but the hunting ground would be much more spectacular. He announced he would go to Egypt and Nubia to look for Greek and Roman relics, and in Ethiopia solve that hoary question so loved by Roman geographers as to the source of the Nile. A trained Italian draughtsman was to accompany him to illustrate the finds he was sure to make, and his merchant bankers would arrange credit with Julien & Rosa, their correspondents in Cairo, so that he could draw money on his wanderings in the interior. As it happened, Bruce had no financial worries because the newly formed Carron Iron Company* had recently contracted to buy coal from his estate, and an agent was left in charge of day-to-day affairs. Nor did Bruce have any family cares. His parents were dead; his first wife had died childless; and although he felt certain he had found her successor in Margaret Murray, daughter of a neighbouring laird, he was so confident of her attachment to him that he expected her to wait until he returned from Africa. His immediate concern, as he saw it, was to do something elevating by enlarging knowledge of classical times, bring fame to himself, and increase his country's prestige.

Mr Bruce contemplating the source of the Nile, from a popular chap book

For James Bruce was a patriot at heart, and his African saga was closely intertwined with his wish to serve his country. He boasted a belligerent patriotism, and had once proposed to lead a British military invasion of the Spanish port of Ferrol. During a short spell as Consul at Algiers he was such a fire-eater – recommending a naval demonstration against the city to teach it respect for the British flag – that he was obliged to resign. This prickly chauvinism was to be one of his hallmarks throughout his travels and partly explained why, although he wore local dress, he did not try to pass himself off as a native. He was, as he saw it, a grandee of Britain travelling abroad, and so the correct way of establishing his status was to behave like an African of equivalent rank. To this end he wore rich clothing, dispensed valuable gifts, and ostentatiously carried rare and expensive scientific equipment and weapons. His quadrant, for example, was so large that it took eight men to carry it over rough ground; his rifle was particularly well made and accurate;

---

* Later famous for giving its name to a short-range cannon known as the carronade.

and for emergencies he kept an exquisite Brescian-made folding blunderbuss under his cloak. The latter he used at least once, threatening a recalcitrant Fung chieftain with it. He was never averse, when disturbed at camp, to loosing off a charge of small shot into the darkness to clear off any intruders. In short, James Bruce was a formidable person who expected, and usually received, the deference due to a traveller of position.

Thus it was lucky that he should have picked an area of Africa where this attitude was particularly effective. Ethiopia, which had scarcely seen a white man since the days of the Portuguese, was in the throes of a bloody civil war. Bruce rode boldly into the middle of the fray and, if he is to be believed, soon established a fearsome reputation. His horsemanship impressed the Ethiopian gentry, and the range and hitting power of his rifle, which he showed could shoot a candle through several shields stacked together, won him all contests for marksmanship. With Luigi Balugani, his Italian artist, he crossed the country in the wake of the warbands, sketching plants and animals, collecting fossils and Ethiopic manuscripts, and keeping up a diary on long scrolls of paper which he covered with his hasty, firm handwriting. With Balugani too he made a highly emotional pilgrimage to the prime object of his trip, the source of the Blue Nile near Lake Tana, though he intentionally omitted any mention of his Italian assistant or of the Portuguese travellers who had identified the place before him. The natives, Bruce proudly claimed, were immensely appreciative of his feats. The Negus created him an Ethiopian noble and awarded him a provincial governorship; and once, when he stood up to a bullying official, he swore that an onlooker burst out in admiration, 'A brave man! *Wallah Englese*! True English, by G-d!'

It was all the more galling, therefore, that he should find himself ridiculed when he came home. This mockery was totally unexpected. He had travelled slowly back across Europe, stopping at spas to shake off his malaria and cure the guinea worm which riddled his left leg. It was true that there had been an unhappy moment in Italy where he found his imagined fiancée, Margaret Murray, had apparently forgotten him and was married to an Italian Marchese, whom Bruce impetuously and foolishly challenged to a duel. But in general he was applauded by the learned academies of Florence and Paris. Buffon, the French biologist, spoke very highly of his achievements and when Bruce returned to England, the King graciously accepted his collection of drawings of antiquities, and the Royal Society voted him a Fellow. But that was as far as the honours went. 'The Abyssinian traveller', as he was called, soon became London's laughing stock instead of its hero.

It was a cruel fate for which Bruce was partly to blame. He was altogether too cantankerous and dramatic. Boswell called him 'a tiger that growled whenever you approached him'. Moreover, the returned traveller made the

Opposite James Bruce, *top left*, as a confident young man, painted by Pompeo Batoni; *below* brooding and ravaged, Bruce shortly before his death. Painting by Weichert

Above Departure of an Ethiopian army for the field.
Below Banquet in the hall of the Negus's palace

dreadful mistake of choosing the drawing-room over the printing press for his sounding board. Instead of publishing a serious account of his journey, he talked at dinner parties and soirées, and the London wits cut him to ribbons – though never to his face because they were frightened of his reputation for violence. In a sense Bruce's social eminence was a curse, for his contemporaries would probably have been less vindictive towards a man with less social pretension. Dr Johnson, who thought he knew something about Ethiopia and had written *Rasselas* about it, declared that Bruce might never have been to the country at all. The satyrist, Peter Pindar, wrote a mocking and very funny ode about him and an edition of Baron Munchausen's escapades was maliciously dedicated to Bruce. The educated public, the very people whose opinion Bruce had set out to pamper, showed that it did not want to hear about a blood-stained Ethiopia and certainly not from an arrogant Scot.

It was not entirely a matter of Bruce's clumsiness. The trouble was that the whole tide of geographical opinion was running against him. A contemporary navigator, James Cook, was bringing back tales of sun-drenched South Sea islands and causing a sensation with Omai, a Polynesian chief whose gravity, good sense and cultured bearing made a profound impression. By comparison, a swashbuckling African traveller with yarns of derring-do and drawings of Roman ruins seemed mildly embarrassing. Learned societies demanded more scientific observation and the public preferred its savages happy.

The disappointment preyed on Bruce terribly. The swagger and dash went out of him. He was a man who nursed his grudges and now, retiring to Scotland, he allowed his chagrin to rankle. He eventually wrote his book, a ponderous, rambling account that was part narrative, part fantasy, and marred by personal grudges. He plunged into a long and complicated lawsuit against the Carron Company. Visitors found him gruff and unresponsive, and when Banks wrote civilly asking for advice on African travel, he got curt, negative replies. The truth of the matter was that Bruce was a little unhinged about Ethiopia. He wandered about his estates wearing a turban, and rigged up a room as a museum of himself and his travels. Before he died in 1794, after falling down a flight of stairs and striking his head, his portrait showed him as a ravaged, brooding man. Tragically, of all the explorers in Africa he had been one of the most enterprising and yet, in the end, the most ill-used. Neither success nor failure had ruined him, but only his own erratic brilliance. The same colourful performance which had carried him so splendidly through Ethiopia, marked him out for destruction in the more sophisticated atmosphere of London.

Few critics, it was noticeable, mocked Bruce for his high patriotism. Rather, he heralded a growing national pride in exploration. In 1820 a British naval captain, G. F. Lyon, returning from the desert, walked into Tripoli singing 'God Save the King' and 'Rule Britannia' at the top of his voice; and his

Sketching ruins in Tripoli, by the patriotic G. F. Lyon who sang 'Rule Britannia' as he returned from his explorations outside the city

successor, Major Dixon Denham of the 64th Foot, firmly stated that his party 'were the first English travellers in Africa who had resisted the persuasion that a disguise was necessary, and who had determined to travel in our real character as Britons and Christians, and to wear, on all occasions, our English dresses; nor had we, at any future period, occasion to regret that we had done so.' Denham was forgetting that Mungo Park had also travelled in European dress, but then the Major's chauvinism did have the excuse that he led an official, government-sponsored expedition. It went in 1821 under the aegis of the Colonial Office, whose Minister, Lord Bathurst, was keen on establishing contact with the supposedly wealthy Sultanate of Bornou on the southern edge of the Sahara. Taking a leaf from the African Association's book, Bathurst was prepared to sponsor the necessary exploration. Unfortunately he then partnered Major Denham with a companion of the same social class but totally opposing temperament, Lieutenant Hugh Clapperton of the Royal Navy. The result was calamitous.

There was a perverse logic to the spectacle of a navy man being sent to interior Africa at this time. The supreme questions of African geography were all concerned with its drainage: where did the great rivers rise? where did they flow? did they join? and were they navigable by commercial craft? The Niger and the Nile, in particular, were held to be the keys to the economic penetration of Africa, and it seemed sensible to dispatch naval officers to sail down them and map their courses. This was precisely the sort of plan which appealed to Hugh Clapperton. He was a dashing and ambitious officer, fretting in Edinburgh on half pay after distinguished service in the Napoleonic war. Only thirty-three, widely travelled, and in excellent health, he was a good friend and neighbour to Walter Oudney, a naval surgeon who had been corresponding with the government about the projected Bornou trip and was already selected as its doctor-scientist. Oudney suffered from consumption and, though eager for the venture, there was reason to doubt his stamina. So nothing seemed more natural than for him to take along the strapping Clapperton as his assistant. Permission had been asked of the Colonial Office when Major Dixon Denham abruptly shouldered his way on to the scene.

Although not as boastful of his breeding as James Bruce, there was no doubt that Dixon Denham was uncommonly well connected. When many other officers were on half-pay, he had a post at the Military College at Sandhurst, and there were hints that the Duke of Wellington himself took an interest in his career. Certainly Denham set about getting himself on to an African expedition with remarkable assurance. Somehow he arranged a personal interview with Bathurst and within a few days followed it up with a very cool memorandum outlining his ideas. He proposed to go south from Tripoli, taking a party of slaves as attendants. Going first to Bornou, he would then proceed to investigate if the Niger was in any way connected with the Nile. 'I do not stipulate any reward', he added in a matter-of-fact manner, 'but promotion in my profession of a soldier . . . ' Understandably, Lord Bathurst decided that the best way of dealing with this self-assured and well-recommended applicant was to pack him off with Oudney and Clapperton.

It was the worst of arranged matches. None of the partners was consulted beforehand and all their expectations were rudely crushed. Denham was saddled with two unwanted companions; Oudney was demoted and given a civilian appointment as prospective vice-consul to Bornou; and Clapperton, instead of helping his friend, learned that he would be taking his orders from an army officer whom he had never met, and who showed such little enthusiasm for his company that no meeting was arranged between the three explorers for six weeks after Denham's official appointment. Even more disastrously, the authorities failed to define the boundary of civil and military authority between Oudney and Denham, and the Bornou Mission, as it was officially called, seemed so certain for collapse that it did not even sail to Africa as a unit. The two friends, Oudney and Clapperton, arrived in Tripoli in late October, but Denham stayed behind, grumbling that official procrastination had given him

insufficient time to prepare his effects. Not until the following month did he show up at the British Consulate in Tripoli where the Consul, Hanmer Warrington, had been charged by the Colonial Office with arranging the expedition's supplies and escort from the ruler of Tripoli, the Bashaw.

Consul Hanmer Warrington was one of the more notorious figures of the Barbary coast. He was, in many ways, remarkably like James Bruce who, it will be remembered, had also served as a North African consul. Warrington, too, was wealthy, choleric, and active. He had risen from Cornet to Major in the Dragoon Guards and boasted how he had led the charge to retake the British guns in the Malaga campaign. Being a hundred yards in the van, he was the first to enter the French battery, his horse was killed under him and he took two musket balls through his coat tails. Nimrod, the sporting journalist, called him 'a great ally of mine, being just about my own age, and equally fond of horseflesh', and as Consul in Tripoli Warrington liked to send Arab horses as gifts to his friends in England. Rumour had it that he was a great crony of the Prince Regent and it was later said he lost £40,000 to George IV in a single night's play. More intimately, his wife was alleged to be an illegitimate daughter of the King, and certainly this influence could explain how Warrington

managed to hold on to his post as Consul-General in Tripoli despite his rollicking behaviour.

He was a great drinker and hard swearer who lived in considerable style in a mansion he had built himself on a hill overlooking the city. The house was almost a state within a state. Escaped criminals used it as sanctuary if they could get over the garden wall, and whenever Warrington, in one of his moods, ordered the Union Jack to be struck from the flagpole, the Bashaw regarded it as tantamount to a declaration of war. Throughout his consular career, Warrington was obsessed by the fear that the French consulate was plotting mischief against him. The Tripolines played on this mania so skilfully that on one occasion Warrington rushed fuming down to the Bashaw's courtyard, shouting that he was a rascal, and threatening to horsewhip him. It was typical of Warrington's ebullient manner that he was next seen entertaining the Bashaw to dinner, clapping him on the shoulder and sharing a glass of wine with him. The intervention of this flamboyant and opinionated plunger was all that was needed to ensure that the Bornou Mission floundered deeper into trouble.

The chief culprit was Denham. Shortly after reaching Tripoli he handed his two colleagues an extraordinary manifesto which set out his ideas on the expedition's conduct. It began:

> As the Mission is about to depart for Mourzouk Captain Denham submits to his companions the propriety of establishing that regularity during the March of the Caravan which cannot but contribute to both the comfort and safety of the party. Duty when chearfully (sic) performed, is ever a source of pleasure and satisfaction, rather than of pain; and as all have been accustomed to serve, all must be aware of the necessity of subordination and system . . .

While laying down rules for mounting guard, issuing stores, punishment of offenders, this priggish directive made it clear that Denham regarded the mission as his personal command, and that the others were to do as he said.

Not unnaturally, Oudney, as a civilian appointee, immediately refused to accept this high-handed approach, and told Denham so. Clapperton, for his part, merely turned insubordinate, and whenever he disagreed with Denham's orders, appealed to the Vice-Consul to adjudicate in his favour. Denham flew into a rage and accused them of a Scottish plot, and by the time the caravan had reached the staging point at Mourzouk was writing to his brother: 'My lieutenant's conduct has been such, both here on the road and at Tripoli that had I reported it, he must have been broke or at least sent home, so vulgar, conceited & quarrelsome a person scarcely ever met with.' To Lord Bathurst he complained formally that Oudney had made a total mess of the travel arrangements, and that:

Never was any man so ill qualified for such a duty. Neither had his professional or pleasurable pursuits ever placed him three times on a horse in his Life and except by Water, I think, he had never travelled thirty miles from Edinbro'. Still every thing would he arrange and on we went, blundering in misery, altho' at a considerable expense. Not one word of any language could he speak but his own, Yet did he undauntedly harangue those around him who bowed, walked off and of course cheated him – My opinion which I absolutely forced on him sometimes was always received with 'Thank ye Sir, but I dare say we shall do very well', and generally the contrary system adopted . . .

Denham had also been behaving very badly. When the mission reached Mourzouk, it was delayed for want of the escort promised by the Bashaw and Denham, frightened of the approaching plague season, decided to abandon his companions. Incredibly, he was convinced that his efforts had already earned him a promotion, and so he headed back for London to claim a Lieutenant Colonelcy. He only got as far as Marseille before he learned that the expedition was about to move again, and turned back. He reached Mourzouk a second time to find Clapperton and Oudney debilitated by hemma, the local fever, and the Colonial Office furious with him. They sent a sharp reminder that his job was to get on with the expedition, and also wrote sourly to Warrington asking why the Mission's finances were so chaotic. The Colonial Office had paid the Bashaw £4,000 for his assistance and wanted to know why no Tripoline help was forthcoming. Denham and Oudney, acting as independent leaders, had both been drawing large sums against the expedition's account, and costs were soaring far beyond Warrington's original estimate.

This unceasing flood of letters, memoranda, and written instructions was something new to African exploration. It characterized the official expedition, and was the price of government finance and government help. Thus from Oudney the purse-conscious functionaries of the Colonial Office wanted signed receipts for all expenses, utterly disregarding the fact that most of his money went to Arabs who were illiterate or, if they could write, used a script which would have meant nothing to a London ledger clerk. Neither Bruce nor the Association's agents had been exposed to quite the same bombardment of mail carried at great cost and some danger into the wake of an expedition. That most of the correspondence was out of date and irrelevant by the time it arrived, only added to the burden. Warrington, Oudney and Denham were all expected to justify their actions regardless of circumstance, and the whole process became more and more complicated as they each continued to advocate their own lines of policy.

Everything – and particularly the suppurating feud between Denham and Clapperton – was committed to paper, usually in triplicate. As the caravan proceeded into the desert, the quarrel intensified. Denham ordered the naval officer to provide him with observations of the latitude of various places along

Consul Hanmer Warrington's country house near Tripoli, possibly painted by Warrington himself

the march so that they could be entered into the official diary. Clapperton refused, saying that the observations were his own work and he was not going to allow Denham the credit for them. Denham persisted, and again Clapperton refused. The two men were barely on speaking terms and began to conduct their quarrel by letter, each sitting down to write a formal complaint to the other and have it carried between the tents by messenger. 'Tents, Jan 1st, 1823' Clapperton dated the following:

> Sir,
>
> I thought my previous refusal would have prevented a repetition of your orders.
>
> You take upon yourself a great deal to issue orders which could not be more imperative were they from the Horse Guards or the Admiralty. You must not introduce Martial system into what is civil and scientific; neither must you expect from me what it is your duty to execute – Call on me and I will assist you; but any other labours are my government's and shall be forwarded in the proper manner.
>
> > I have the honour to be
> > Sir,
> > Your most Obt. humble Servant
> > Hugh Clapperton
>
> To Major Denham

Two weeks later Denham wrote to Warrington that Clapperton had 'thrown off all Control and refused to act under my orders.' More to the point, it appeared that Denham either would not, or could not, use a sextant to make the necessary observations himself.

To be fair, Denham was not entirely to blame. Clapperton had a very excitable temperament and often let his emotions get the better of him. He threatened to knock down an Arab who dared argue with him; and one of the servants asked to be sent home because, he said, Clapperton had beaten him up, drawn a pistol on him, and threatened to shoot him. Denham himself had heard Clapperton shouting at the servant 'You B - - - r! I'll pick your teeth for you', and, as was Denham's unpleasant habit, carefully made a note of the abuse in his list of grievances for Bathurst. In his own defence, Clapperton wrote that he had not beaten the servant, but certainly should have done so as 'the breakfast he brought was not fit for a dog; what was intended for the breakfast having been laid aside – for the Major's breakfast.'

Denham's trick of storing up hints and details to use against Clapperton reached its peak in mid-April, when he brought forth his most damaging charge: the Arabs of the caravan were saying that Clapperton was having homosexual relations with one of the native servants.

The enormity of this accusation tore the Bornou Mission into shreds. Frenzied letters passed between London, the Tripoli Consulate, and the protagonists in the desert. From Warrington:

> Great God!!! . . . A more Infamous, Vile, diabolical Insinuation to blast the reputation of Man was never before resorted to, and I have not the smallest hesitation in the Presence of my God to say that it is false, malicious, and conspiring against the future happiness of an Individual. Lieutenant Clapperton I know little of, but in that little, I would with my life answer for Him that he would never disgrace Human nature by such foul and damnable Conduct . . .

Denham, in all probability foreseeing the explosion that would follow, had gone off on a side-excursion from the caravan, leaving Oudney to launch an immediate enquiry into the charge. The story was tracked down to one of Clapperton's former servants, a man named Abdullady 'apparently above forty and very ugly', who was being teased by his Arab companions. Somehow Denham had picked up the story and seen his chance for a major scandal. He was careful not to subscribe to the charge himself, but merely brought the rumour into the open. Thus when Bathurst himself pronounced that 'no suspicion whatever attaches to Lieut't Clapperton's character', Denham was able to write blandly to Warrington asserting that he himself had never believed the charge and of course knew it to be completely false. But to Clapperton himself, Denham never apologized personally. The rift between the two men was absolute.

These spectacular ructions within the Mission nearly overshadowed its considerable achievement. The most important discovery on the far side of the desert was Lake Chad, which Denham – perhaps with a sponsor in mind – wanted to call Lake Waterloo, and which provided a neat piece of evidence for the fashionable theory that the Niger lost itself in the 'Great Sink of Africa'. Near Chad the expedition split up, Denham to try to make the circuit of the lake, and the others to strike westward for Kano and Sokoto. Denham failed in his attempt, and Oudney died before making any distance. The surgeon had been weakening steadily under his consumption and on his last morning had to be dressed by Clapperton. He was trying bravely to climb on his camel, when he collapsed. Taken back to his tent he died soon afterwards, a courageous little man, according to his biographer, 'with a pale, grave face, pleasing manners, and possessed of much enterprise and perseverance'.

Clapperton's health also broke. By the time he got back to Chad from Sokoto,

Denham scarcely recognized the gaunt, fever-stricken skeleton he found curled up in a blue shirt on the floor of a native hut. He was just about to turn and walk out, when the man moved and called his name.

It took this condition of extreme distress to patch up the quarrel between the two men, and even then the truce only held until Tripoli on their way home. Scarcely had they reached civilization than the letters of complaint started up again. Clapperton demanded a full investigation of all charges held against him; Denham accused everyone, including Warrington, of conspiracy; and the Colonial Office muddied the waters still further with demands for the official records of the expedition which had disappeared with Oudney. Neither Clapperton nor Denham ever made any real attempt to solve their differences. Clapperton went off to West Africa to trace the course of the Niger from the opposite approach, but he perished at Sokoto, being the first white man, in effect, to have crossed the western bulge of the continent. He died of dysentery, calling out to his Cornish manservant that he could hear the tolling of an English funeral bell. Denham, vindictive to the end, wrote up an official *Narrative* with so much rancour that by the time a wary editor had trimmed it to size, the book left the impression that Denham, and Denham alone, had master-minded the Bornou Mission. Denham eventually also went back to Africa, and was at Fernando Po when he heard of his naval rival's death. Appointed Governor of Sierra Leone he too was dead within a year. He let himself grow soft and flabby and took to doctoring himself with odd medicines. Five years later his simple grave of brick and lime was covered with weeds and half-forgotten.

Lord Bathurst did not, as might have been expected, give up African exploration in disgust, but instead mended its style. Even while the Bornou Mission was on its way home, Hanmer Warrington learned that another explorer was due to arrive. This time his target was the mysterious city of Timbuctoo, reputedly centre of the gold trade, and the Colonial Office expected the Consul-General to render all assistance necessary. Quite how far this assistance was to go, Warrington could not have guessed: within nine weeks of his arrival the new explorer, Major Gordon Laing, was his son-in-law, having married Warrington's second daughter, Emma, against the vehement objections of her father.

Undoubtedly one of the disadvantages, from Warrington's point of view, was the social disparity of the couple. Gordon Laing did not have anything like the pedigree of the Warringtons; and, if anything, came a shade farther along the social spectrum than his predecessor Denham. His regiment, the 2nd West Indian, was unfashionable, and his background was worthy academic rather than gallant military. His father ran a private school in Edinburgh, and Gordon Laing himself had done a spell as a schoolmaster before going into

Saharan scene: camel conveying a bride
to her husband by G. F. Lyon

the army. As might have been guessed, he tended to make up his lack of army influence with an abrasive intellectualism, a habit which sometimes led him to poke fun at senior officers. It was felt in some conservative military circles that Major Gordon Laing was a clever but somewhat conceited officer, and probably there was a feeling of mild relief when he applied to lead a new expedition into the Sahara. At least his credentials as an explorer were impeccable. Already, when serving with the Royal African Colonial Corps, he had made a foray into Mandingo country to calculate the height of the Niger's course at Mount Soma. From his observations he had shown that the gradient from Mount Soma was insufficient to carry the Niger as far eastward as the Nile; and his conclusions, published in the *Quarterly Journal of Science*, placed Laing in the growing ranks of Africa experts.

Once again Warrington was having trouble in making the traveller's arrangements with the Bashaw. As usual Tripoline performance fell short of its promise; and it was this delay while Warrington made repeated visits to see the Bashaw to ask for an escort for Laing, that allowed the friendship between Gordon Laing and Emma Warrington to ripen into love. Warrington had been so badly scalded over the finances of the Bornou party that he was too preoccupied to see what was going on in his own home. While Laing was writing privately to friends in London asking them to send out a 'handsome little cabinet of mineralogical specimens, such a one as will suit a Lady of taste & refinement . . . which I should like to have addressed to Miss Emma Warrington', the Consul-General was bemoaning the obstinacy and wiliness of the Bashaw. Major Laing, wrote Warrington to his master in London, was a great consolation in this time of frustration. He was displaying 'Enthusiastic Spirit and Indefatigable Exertion', and 'extreme Gentlemanly manners, Honorable Conduct, & sound moral principle', which made Warrington view him 'in the Character of an Old Friend'. Then on 14 July, without a word of warning, came a shocked note to tell Lord Bathurst that the 'Old Friend' had married the Consul's daughter that same morning.

Warrington's dispatch had an uncharacteristically abject tone, the defeated note of an overruled father. He pleaded that he had tried everything in his power to stop the marriage pointing out that it was rash and ill advised, especially as Laing was about to go off into the desert and might never be seen again. But, he said, 'I found my wishes, exertions, Entreaties, and displeasure, quite futile & of no avail; & under all circumstances, both for the Public good, as well as their Mutual happiness, I was obliged to consent to perform the Ceremony . . .' At least, he had imposed one face-saving condition: the couple were on no account to cohabit until the marriage, which Warrington had performed in his role as Consul, had been confirmed by a clergyman of the Church of England. Until then either Warrington or his wife stood guard over the couple, so that when Major Laing rode off for Timbuctoo he was a husband of a few days and his marriage was still unconsummated.

On this frustrated note began one of the more agonized trips into Africa. To avoid a repetition of the Bornou squabble Bathurst had sent a single explorer, but the events leading up to Laing's departure and the character of the man himself meant that the journey brimmed over with emotion and self-inflicted distress. Once again a long trail of letters told the story. Laing was obsessed by three thoughts: his love for Emma; his conviction that he deserved promotion; and his constant fear that someone else – in particular Clapperton,

Alexander Gordon Laing. Engraving by S. Freeman. 'It was felt in some conservative military circles that Major Gordon Laing was a clever but somewhat conceited officer, and probably there was feeling of mild relief when he applied to lead a new expedition into the Sahara'

who was known to have started for West Africa – would solve the Niger problem before him. Over and over Laing referred to these worries, nagging at Warrington to do something on his behalf. The loneliness of the caravan journey reinforced his wild imagining. In his isolation he conceived that there were plots against him in the War Office to block his promotion; that Warrington was bungling the finances; that the Arabs of the caravan were deliberately mistreating him; that Emma was sick. He sent back long lists of petty grievances: his barometers were shaken to bits; hygrometers were useless because the sun had evaporated the ether in them; thermometers broken by warping of their ivory holders; a camel had trodden on his rifle and snapped the stock.

:heer him up, the Consul forwarded a locket with Emma's picture done by rador, the Spanish Consul, and at once a hysterical letter came back ng:

Good God, where is the colour of her lovely cheek, where the vermillion of her lear lip – tell me, has Mr. Herrador, or has he not, made a faithful likeness? – if ie has, My Emma is ill, is melancholy, is unhappy – her sunken eye, her pale cheek, and colourless lip haunt my imagination, and adieu to resolution – Was I within a day's march of Tombuctoo, & to hear my Emma was ill – I wou'd turn about and retrace my steps to Tripoli – What is Tombuctoo? What is Niger? What the world to me? without my Emma – Shou'd anything befall my Emma, which God forbid, I no more wish to see the face of man; my course will be run – a few short days of misery and I shou'd follow her to heaven . . .

These extraordinary letters, punctuated with dashes, jerking from one thought to the next, sprinkled with half-digested quotations in foreign languages, were quite beyond Warrington's grasp. Clumsy in his kindness, he only made matters worse by writing to reassure Laing that Clapperton would probably meet up with him and was a sterling explorer who would be pleased to help. Cut to the quick, Laing cast scorn on Clapperton, accusing him of ignorance and condescension. If the fever of Benin did not kill him, Laing insinuated, Clapperton's indolence would keep him on the coast.

A more cynical reader than Consul Warrington might have doubted the exaggerated tone of these letters. Laing's over-blown emotionalism and his constant appeals to love and honour seemed sham, and his behaviour no more than play-acting in the role of the tormented explorer. But any such suspicion was wiped out early in February 1826. At three o'clock one morning, about a hundred and fifty miles south of the oasis of In Salah, Laing's caravan was viciously attacked by a band of Ahaggar Tuareg. The raiders concentrated their fire on the tents and baggage of the white man. A musket ball struck Laing in the side as he lay asleep, passing through his body and grazing his spine. As he staggered to his feet, the Tuareg rushed his tent and before he could arm himself, he was dropped by a sabre slash on the thigh. Jumping up again, Laing received one cut on the cheek and ear, and another on the right arm above the wrist which broke the arm. He then fell to the ground where he took seven more cuts, the last in the back of the neck. One of his servants was hacked to death; a second ran away into the sand dunes; and the third managed to crawl to safety dragging a broken leg behind him. The rest of the caravan was scarcely molested.

Despite his terrible wounds, Laing somehow managed to survive, though it was not until mid-May that he was able to send his next dispatch. He wrote with his left hand, because the right hand been sliced three-fourths across, and his letter was barely recognizable either for the handwriting which now sloped

Tuaregs

back where once it had sloped forward, or for its tone of resolution. Without carping Laing confessed that he was badly mangled and it was obvious he was permanently disfigured. In addition to his other wounds, he had a broken jaw, one ear cleft into two parts, and he was suffering blinding headaches from five sabre scars on his scalp where the bone had chipped away. But Warrington was not to alarm Emma. The worst was now over and in a short time he would be in Timbuctoo. It seemed that the savage violence which every explorer had feared had been a catharsis for Gordon Laing. It had exorcised the actor in him, and he went forward to Timbuctoo confident that he had passed his greatest test.

Emma Laing never did see her mutilated husband again, which was perhaps fortunate, though she learned of his suffering through chance remarks in his letters. The Tuareg attack was symptomatic of a mounting militancy among the desert Muslims against interlopers, and after getting through to Timbuctoo and spending several weeks there, Laing had scarcely started home when he was murdered on the orders of a fanatical Sheik of the Berabich Tuareg. The precise circumstances of his death, like Park's, were obscure. One account said that he died in a second night attack; another that he was cornered by the Tuareg and asked to renounce his faith. When he refused, he was stabbed through the chest with a spear and decapitated. Both accounts agreed that the superstitious Arabs then tore up or burned all Laing's papers for fear of their magical properties. The Warrington family was left with the single letter that Laing had managed to send out of Timbuctoo. It ended:

> My dear Emma must excuse my writing, I have begun a hundred letters to her, but have been unable to get thro' one; she is ever uppermost in my thoughts, & I look forward with delight to the hour of our meeting, which please God is now at no great distance.

Not for another two years was her husband's death confirmed, and the long-drawn-out suspense undermined Emma Laing's health. In April 1829 she married again, to the British Vice Consul at Benghazi, who took her at once to Italy for a cure. But within six months 'my dear, dear Emma', as Laing had called her was dead, the victim, according to her anguished father, of 'Watchful Days and Sleepless Nights' waiting for Laing's return.

Towards his son-in-law's death Warrington reacted with both sorrow and pride, and – typically – suspicion of French intrigue. On Laing's last letter he attached a note in his own hand which read

> From Major Laing to Consul Warrington dated 21st September at Timbuctoo, being the first letter ever written from that place to a Christian.
> H. Warrington.

Then, stirred up by his loathing of the French, he turned on their Tripoli consul, Baron Rousseau, accusing him of poisoning the Bashaw against Laing, stealing his journal and possibly inciting his murder. These crude charges had slim foundation beyond the fact that Rousseau was on excellent terms with the Bashaw's chief minister and had employed several of Laing's couriers as spies. But Warrington pressed home his accusation so vehemently that Rousseau was forced to leave Tripoli altogether. A Committee of Enquiry, set up by the French Government, cleared their Consul of blame, but this did not stop Warrington from sending a final vituperative letter – a copy of which was lodged with the United Service Club – in which he threatened to hound Rousseau to the ends of the earth. To the finish, Warrington blamed the French for the deaths of his daughter and son-in-law.

To sharpen the edge of this ill-will there was a new sense of national rivalry to African exploration. The Geographical Society of Paris, in 1824, had offered a prize of ten thousand francs, genteely calling it a 'premium', to the first man to enter Timbuctoo and bring back a worthwhile account of his journey. If Laing's diary had been found, a British explorer would carry off the glory, but while Warrington was still fulminating against Rousseau, another contender – a young Frenchman named René Caillié – arrived from Africa claiming to have made the journey single-handed and without sponsorship.

Son of an alcoholic baker who had been convicted of theft, René Caillié took the shine off the more grand officer style of exploration, particularly as his method of travel was at least as successful. Orphaned at the age of eleven and inspired by nothing more lofty than the tales of Robinson Crusoe, Caillié had left his native town of Mauzé in western France to become a professional drifter-adventurer. After knocking around the world for some time and raising money by a variety of means, including collecting and stuffing wild birds in West Africa, he had joined a trade caravan for Timbuctoo as a common traveller. His entire luggage was a single bundle of goods, the usual umbrella and compass, a basic medical kit, and a calfskin portfolio for his notes. He claimed that he was a Muslim and to explain his sketchy Arabic and slipshod knowledge of the Koran he added the implausible story that he was an Egyptian, taken as a boy to France by Napoleon's army and raised there. Now starting from Sierra Leone, he was trying to get home, and the obvious route lay diagonally across the desert, via Timbuctoo, to Cairo.

Whether or not this unlikely yarn was believed, it had the merit that it threw him on the traditional hospitality of the Muslims. This, and Caillié's small purse and unassuming manner, took the Frenchman across the continent with remarkable ease. His closest escape was when he hid from the Tuareg under a pile of mats, and his worst mishap was a heavy fall from a camel. Apart from these, and occasional bullying and a bad case of mouth sores, his journey was very straightforward. In Timbuctoo he was a guest in a house on the next street from where Laing had stayed, and in the mosque he was given alms by a benevolent passer-by. In a continent notorious for its dangerous animals, he only saw a few snakes in the desert, and on the Sahara crossing he was the only man in the entire caravan allowed to stay mounted because he was so ill with dysentery. Indeed his worst troubles began when he reached the comparatively well-known territory of Morocco. Penniless and in rags, he was turned away by the French consul in Rabat and had to sleep in the streets where he was attacked by dogs and obliged to take refuge in a nearby cemetery. And in Tangier he had to be smuggled into the consulate after dark and publicly spurned by day. Finally, disguised as a sailor, he was taken secretly out of the country on a French sloop.

René Caillié's caravan at the well of Telic. The disguised Caillié is probably the figure
standing with a staff

Caillié's journey earned him a government pension and a place in the Legion d'Honneur, as well as the geographical prize, but it had one serious flaw. By travelling in his disguise, his scientific work had been severely restricted. His compass bearings had all been taken while hiding in the bushes pretending to gather herbal samples for his medicine chest, and his notes were written up under cover of studying the Koran. He had not even been able to inquire closely into Laing's fate for fear of arousing suspicion, though he had seen a copper compass which he presumed to belong to the Major, and heard rumours that other belongings were in the possession of the Bedouin. The French proudly called him 'the Marco Polo of Africa', but his book, which the Prize Committee praised for its 'tone of simplicity and sincerity', was really a flat, dull affair. Caillié had, in fact, run a solo marathon. He never went back to Africa but returned to Mauzé where he served briefly as mayor. At the age of thirty-eight he died in comparative obscurity from an unspecified illness which it was popularly supposed he had contracted in Africa. Jomard, the doyen of French geographers, came out to read the funeral oration, and a statue was erected in his memory. But by then the Timbuctoo affair was fast becoming a dead letter. The heat of the Laing-Caillié rivalry began to cool when the Geographical Society in Paris awarded Emma Laing its gold medal in honour of her dead husband's achievement, and Caillié's account of Timbuctoo had stripped most of the glitter from a perennial African myth.

Caillié's success left only the question of the Niger's lower course among the traditional major problems of West African geography. It was solved by a pair of Cornish brothers who landed through the surf at Badagry on the coast on 22 March 1830. They came ashore from His Majesty's brig *Clinker* dressed in baggy Turkish trousers, bright red loose-fitting gowns, and sporting a pair of enormous straw sun hats, each as large as an umbrella. The local girls found the sight so extraordinary that they turned aside to conceal their giggles; yet the elder of the two brothers, Richard Lander, was already one of the most experienced African travellers and considered his rig-out ideal for the venture in hand.

Now twenty-six years old, and son of a Cornish innkeeper, he had been Clapperton's personal servant on the latter's second expedition, and when his master died at Sokoto, had buried him wrapped in a British flag. The only white member of the expedition left alive, he then made his own way back to the coast, carrying his master's papers and survived an ordeal by poison, imposed by a suspicious native chief, by swallowing a massive quantity of emetic immediately afterwards. Returning to England so bronzed that he was mistaken for a Jew, he took a post in the Customs service at Truro, and was working there as a weighing porter on £50 a year when he offered his services to the British government as an explorer in his own right.

There was something chillingly callous about the way in which the government took advantage of Lander's modest offer and dumped him again in Africa. 'Would not Lander, who has been pressing to go again, be the fittest person to send?' wrote one civil servant. 'No-one in my opinion would make their way so well and with a bundle of beads and bafts and other trinkets, we would land him somewhere about Bonny and let him find his way.' Laing or Clapperton would have expected a few thousand pounds worth of expenses, but Richard Lander asked only £100 for his wife during his absence, the same amount for himself on his return, and permission to take along his brother John, unpaid. For equipment the government meanly gave him less than £400, most of it in presents for the natives including fifty yards of Staff Sergeant's scarlet cloth, a vast quantity of needles, a number of inferior mirrors, and two large silver medals bearing the royal portrait. The medals had originally been struck as gifts for loyal Indian chiefs in the North American war but now, clearly, were surplus to requirement. For armament the Landers had just two fowling pieces and four pistols, and they were not even provided with a flag. Their Union Jack was borrowed from a fort commander on the coast.

Though they looked alike, the two brothers in fact had very different temperaments. Richard, the experienced traveller and with the chubbier face, had a cheerful smiling personality. He was a great hand at winning over the natives by teaching chiefs' sons to play penny whistles or entertaining audiences with tunes from a brass bugle that he always carried with him. Setting out with Clapperton, he had enlivened the occasion by standing up in the canoe and playing 'Over the hills and far away' to the cheers of the sailors. In the depths of Sokoto he had kept up his master's spirits by reciting long passages from Scottish ballads. John Lander, on the other hand, was altogether more brooding and introspective. Three years younger, he had been an apprentice

The Lander brothers, after landing at Badagry. 'They came ashore from His Majesty's brig *Clinker* dressed in baggy Turkish trousers, bright loose-fitting gowns, and sporting a pair of enormous straw hats, each as large as an umbrella. The local girls found the sight so extraordinary that they turned aside to conceal their giggles'

compositor with the *Royal Cornwall Gazette* and was much influenced by the vogue for romantic sensibility. Frankly, he never liked Africa, finding it too raw and dirty for his taste which ran to flowery descriptions and extracts from Gray's elegies. Yet his genuine affection for his footloose brother led him to give staunch support throughout their trip and the partnership was one of the very few among African explorers which survived without a tremor. In practical matters it worked very well indeed. Richard's energetic drive was complemented by John's thoughtful caution, and for some reason, they were seldom ill at the same time. When one went down with fever, the other was healthy enough to nurse him.

The Government's stinginess soon began to make itself felt. Cloth and needles were at a glut on the West African market, and as they worked their way inland the travellers had to distribute their manuals of natural history as gifts. Richard even gave away his brass bugle, which the startled natives had originally thought was a metal snake. When all else was exhausted, the Landers took to making presents by removing and polishing the metal labels from food tins. 'We have been highly diverted', they wrote, 'to see one man in particular walking at large, and strutting about with "Concentrated Gravy" stuck on his head in no less than four different places. He appeared quite vain and proud of these ornaments, and was simpering with pleasure wherever he went.' It was a stark contrast to Denham's Bornou Mission which still had bottles of port to enjoy when it reached its farthest point.

The Landers wanted to search for traces of Mungo Park, and near the Bussa Falls they found a gun which they identified as his, as well as a tailor's bill made out to Alexander Anderson, his brother-in-law. Then, travelling in leaky punt-like canoes, they turned downstream to follow the Niger to its mouth. Teams of paddlers hired from the villages had to be cajoled or made drunk before they would continue. An awning was erected to shelter the explorers, though as often as not they had to take the lead in paddling, and their borrowed flag was run up on an improvised jackstaff. Richard, like G. F. Lyon before him, tried to raise morale by singing 'Rule Britannia'.

This jaunty progress came to an abrupt halt near the coast when the Landers were attacked by large canoes of the Ibo river pirates mounting six-pounder cannon. In the scuffle the brothers were thrown in the water; their souvenirs and papers were lost; and they themselves finished up as articles of trade, lying wretchedly in the bottom of a canoe beneath the legs of a Negro entrepreneur and his wife who took them downriver to ransom with the captain of an English ship. Only by promising to work as sailors could the Landers persuade the English captain to redeem them, and in June 1831, after eighteen months' absence, they brought back definite news to England that the Niger emptied into the Bight of Benin. Characteristically, the newspapers scarcely mentioned their return and the government rewarded them as promised: Richard received his bounty of £100, and John got absolutely nothing.

The ill-treatment from the government was one of the few contrasts between the Landers and René Caillié, whose humble origins they shared. The King did eventually summon the Landers and talked to them for an hour, and the Royal Geographical Society awarded Richard a small prize. But the richest reward came from John Murray, the publisher, who was seeking a corner in Africana, and bought the Landers' story for £1,000. Their book made it abundantly clear that working class Europeans were at least as adept at the African adventure as their more socially august rivals. Laing had suffered greater pain and Bruce had endured longer, but Caillié and the Landers had put up with more humdrum conditions at a level that their predecessors would not have undergone willingly. Accustomed to less, they accepted less, and from their sponsors' point of view they were the least trouble. It was ironic that just when they proved the advantages of the humble traveller in Africa, the African adventure was about to blossom into high complexity with its specialized camp equipment, weapons and paraphernalia. Richard Lander himself saw the new style of exploration come in. Financed by a consortium of Liverpool merchants he went back to the Niger in 1834 with two of the new-fangled paddlesteamers. One – inappropriately named *Alburka*, arabic for 'blessing' – was the first sea-going vessel to be built of iron. The steamers got into trouble, ran aground, and were ambushed by the natives. Richard Lander, jaunty to the last and waving his hat at the enemy, was shot and wounded, and died a few weeks later at Fernando Po.

The Lander brothers were captured and ransomed by Ibo river pirates in war canoes flying battle standards copied from European ships

The Great Trek

CHAPTER SIX

Cape Town, in the 1830's, was the white man's most confident footstep in Africa. The hamlet planted by the Dutch two hundred yards up the beach to raise fresh vegetables for passing fleets, had grown enormously. Now it spilled confidently up the slopes of the encircling hills, towards the sharp edge of Table Mountain and the rearing outline of Lion's Head. The most fashionable residential street, Long Street, was lined with solidly elegant houses that would not have been out of place in Georgian Bloomsbury. The town boasted half a dozen churches and chapels of assorted sects, three hospitals, a magnificent parade ground where the militia regularly exercised and the well-to-do went for their evening promenades, and a small menagerie. It was a prosperous, self-satisfied town which had seen the Colony change hands so that a British governor now sat in the Castle where the Dutch once ruled. But it made little difference to De Kaap, as the Hollanders called it. The town still lived by its trade with the outside world. Sailors referred to it as 'the Tavern of the Seas', and there was more concern in the burghers' homes about sheep prices, which had risen dramatically since Spanish merinos had been brought in, and about the slump in wine production due to a new tax on Cape wines, than about colonial politics. Cape Town stood with her back to the continent and looked outward. She accommodated anyone who dropped anchor in the bay, and Thomas Astley had claimed as long ago as the 1750's that there were so many visitors on passage to the Orient that 'there is scarcely any place in the world more frequently described in books of travel than the Cape of Good Hope.'

But few of the visitors ever bothered to press inland. Out there, beyond the sand barrier of the Karroo, lay a very different world. Across an arc of 500 miles one found only a few small market towns and, in the east, a batch of English settlers trying to establish themselves after being dumped ashore at Delagoa Bay. Otherwise this was Boer country, the land of the cattle and sheep farmers, a vast, empty-looking tract with an occasional homestead, a few Hottentot servants dreamily watching over the white man's flocks and herds under a Mediterranean sun and, very rarely, a pedlar or a farmer travelling the road in a cart or on horseback. A feeling of timelessness hung over the countryside, a pastoral archaism which stretched undisturbed to the vacant horizon.

In truth very little had changed here since the first Boer farmers had journeyed, 'trekked' as they called it, into the backveld to take up land grants, six thousand acres at a time. Foreign influences were spurned. Traditionally a Boer only went into town to pay his land rent, pick up gunpowder and coffee, and register his marriage before a magistrate. He prided himself on self-sufficiency and adherence to the old ways which his forefathers had laid down. To him Cape Town was 'Little Paris', a trifling and inconsequential place where men did not understand the correct life of Africa.

Yet for all its apparent emptiness there was a feeling of claustrophobia among the up-country Boers in the early nineteenth century. Mentally as well as physically they felt hemmed in. A bewildering series of laws from the Governor had upset their lives. New land grants were to be auctioned off instead of given at a nominal rent, formerly as little as £5 a year. The natives were being accorded full protection of the law and, with the missionaries to back them up, had taken their grievances to court. A 'Black Circuit' had already investigated some atrocity stories, and even now an Aborigines Commission was sitting in London to take evidence from anti-Boer witnesses. The Boers did not trust officialdom. Slavery had just been abolished, and though the Boers had not owned many slaves, there had been hitches over the payment of compensation money. Above all, the frontier was closed. In the past when the Boers wanted more lands for their sons or their increased flocks, they

A view of Cape Town and Table mountain at the end of the eighteenth century

simply pushed back the native tribes or moved into unoccupied territory. Now the government forbade them to extend past the demarcation line, built frontier forts, and sent out patrols of the unpopular Cape mounted troops, Hottentot sepoys in green jackets. Prodded, constricted, and nervous, the Boers had been murmuring with discontent for years. Like angry bees in the hive, they met together in discussion, elected leaders, and formed into groups. Then, quite suddenly, they swarmed. Crossing the Orange river and abandoning the colony, they moved north, ten thousand or so land-hungry white men who formed the Great Trek, an entirely new phenomenon in African history and the first large scale advance of white men *en masse* into Africa.

They moved into vaguely defined regions where the names were still being pencilled in by an advance guard of ivory hunters, traders and missionaries – Mashonaland, Basutoland, Zululand, Matabeleland, Griqualand of the half-caste Bastaards and quasi-official Kaffraria. This was, or recently had been, tribal territory, and the Great Trek followed a similar upheaval among the black Africans. Inter-tribal war and Bantu migration had dislocated or dispersed the earlier inhabitants. The Basuto, badly beaten, posed little threat as they were only just beginning to reassemble under their gifted King Mosheshe. But farther north lay the ferocious Matabele, and alongside them the battle-trained Zulu under Chief Dingaan. Blandly the Boers maintained that they would not disturb the tribes. They came, they said, to live in peace, buy land by treaty, and trade amicably. Of course, it was absurd. Six consecutive Kaffir Wars in the colony had shown that native and Boer could not co-exist. The problem was that they were too alike. The Boers were as much cattlefarming pastoralists as the Bantu. Both races counted their wealth in herds, grazed the same pasture, and used the same waterholes. Some of the Boers' best customers were natives who sought bride price, and when Boers raided native villages, they went after native cattle and native 'orphans' who could be apprenticed to white masters now that slavery was ended. Cattle made the bond. In neither society did the menfolk work the soil. Women ran the home, and herding was for serfs.

There were striking parallels, too, between the black and white leaders in the confrontation which was about to take place. Umzilikazi, reigning chief of the Matabele, had himself trekked out of Zululand at the head of nine hundred pure-bred Zulus and carved a kingdom for himself with the assegai, dispossessing the Barotse from their grazing lands. Like the Boers, he had resented centralized authority and wanted land and freedom for himself and his followers. In 1837 Umzilikazi was some forty years old, about six-foot tall, heavily built, and with the air of a natural leader. He had been an adviser-officer, an induna, to Chaka Zulu and his own battle honorific was 'the Path of Blood'. He was also something of a dandy, sporting a head-dress of three

Above A Boer's house set in the peaceful South African countryside shortly before the Great Trek. *Below* Boers returning from hunting

137

tail-feathers from a green parakeet, a necklace of blue beads and belt hung with leopards' tails. His equivalent among the Boer leaders, Gerrit Maritz, was scarcely less gorgeous. Among men who usually wore sober clothing Maritz, who was the same age as Umzilikazi and of much the same temper, was famous for his latest fashions. He wore a sharply waisted frock-coat with flowing tails, pantaloons of recent cut, a tall beaver hat, and a gaily flowered waistcoat carefully displayed.

By contrast his colleague and co-leader of the Boer trekkers, Piet Retief, cut a much less glamorous figure. Then in his mid-fifties Retief had been a government building contractor before taking up cattle farming. He was the most popular of the Boer leaders, an unimposing figure of medium height, grizzled hair, and a dark complexion. He dressed unassumingly in a dark jacket, flapping trousers and a wool hat; and until the day of his bloody death he was rarely seen to carry a gun.

But it was Dingaan, paramount chief of the Zulus, who was perhaps the most interesting of the main protagonists. A good deal was known about him from the reports of the missionaries stationed at his great kraal of Umgungundhlovu – 'the Place of the Elephant' – in Natal. Like Zulu chiefs before and after him, Dingaan had come to power by family murder. He killed his brother Chaka to gain the throne and then proceeded systematically to exterminate rival siblings. Undisputed leader of the Zulu nation, he lived warily. Where Chaka had been

Boer trekkers on the march. Painted by Charles Davidson Bell

a great war leader, Dingaan preferred the politician's arts. He played off opponents against one another, maintained a delicate state of impermanence among his indunas, particularly the two greatest, Umblela and Dambuza; and when he attacked, struck without warning and absolute sureness. In the winter of 1837 one of his impis, the Zulu guild regiments, cut off and virtually annihilated a unit of Umzilikazi's Matabele raiders.

With power of life and death over everyone in his realm, Dingaan took care to foster a personal mystique reminiscent of the Negus in Ethiopia. Visitors were obliged to crawl up to him on hands and knees as he reclined on a mat surrounded by some of his hundred wives, or sat on his favourite throne, an armchair carved for him by his loyal indunas. Sometimes strangers would be interviewed across a wall of stakes with Dingaan peering over, his head half-hidden by a fringe of beads. Towards white men he could be friendly, obtuse, or utterly capricious. He would appear smiling and making jokes, his well-fleshed body draped in green baize, and shaking hands with the newcomer. Then suddenly he might turn aside abruptly to condemn some wretch to death for a trivial breach of etiquette. He loved novelties – he had collected a telescope, a lathe, locks and anything mechanical – and always asked to be shown their uses. He appalled one white visitor by seizing hold of a Zulu attendant and charring a hole in the skin of his arm to test the function of a burning glass. The unfortunate victim squirmed with pain but never uttered a sound. To do

Matabele justice: a prisoner, condemned for witchcraft, is taken away and executed by the traditional Matabele method of having his brains beaten in with a knobkerrie. By Charles Davidson Bell

No. 127. *Machaka (unre: Wanine)* Conducting a train of tributary Bacquains with Supplies for Matzelikatze — 1835

Above Matabele warriors escorting a file of serfs carrying tribute to Umzilikazi. *Below* First reception by Umzilikazi. Paintings by Charles Davidson Bell

No. 104. First reception by Matzelikatze — 1835

so would have meant instant death. The white men, it is clear, both fascinated and disturbed him. He associated their technical capabilities with their religious beliefs, and he was always badgering the missionaries at his kraal to explain the power of their God and to provide him with weapons, gunpowder, and bullet moulds as well as sermons. Once he even made a determined effort to catch their magic by learning to read, but soon lost interest and threw away his reading card. He was, according to observers, volatile, easily distracted, and arrogant. He behaved like a despot, which is precisely what he was, and no one felt quite safe in his presence. 'It is to be done before the spit dries in my palm' was his favourite command, and he was always obeyed instantly by his followers. Mosheshe excepted, he was the most talented of the native rulers and came near to halting the Great Trek.

The migrants, the Voortrekkers, got off to a ragged start. There was little co-ordination among them beyond a common resolution to leave the colony and move up into the grasslands of the high veld. They did not travel as a mass but in small groups called trekkies, each following a particular leader. This arrangement had a patriarchal air which fitted in well with the Biblical interpretation that some of them put on their exodus. They felt they were Children of Israel leaving Egypt and its Pharaonic governor to look for a promised land in the high country, and a few took this theme so literally that they named one of the new rivers the Nile. In the autumn of 1836 and throughout the following year they set out by families: Potgieters, Liebenbergs, Smits, Bothas, and others, the names of later South African history. With the Krugers went a ten-year-old boy, Paul, later to be president of the republic. The majority of the trekkers were Dutch descended, but there were also ex-Huguenot families like the Cilliers led by Sarel Cilliers, a frightening figure with a chilling stare and the habit of preaching fire-and-brimstone sermons at awkward moments. For such scriptural-minded folk it was disappointing that the Dutch Reformed Church disapproved of their move, and that it should be an English Wesleyan, the Reverend Archbell, who first ministered to them at their rendezvous of Thaba Nchu on the far side of the Orange river.

The trek was an unhurried advance. Every morning half a dozen men from each trekkie would ride out to explore the day's trail, hunt for game and fix upon a campsite for the following night. The oxen were inspanned to their wagons, the Hottentot servants gathered the cattle and sheep, and when everything was loaded, the convoy sauntered forward at a gentle walking pace. Five miles a day was an average stage, and across the green expanse of the veld the availability of pasture and water was more important than distance covered. The trekkers were solid, steadygoing folk, the women in voluminous long skirts and prim bonnets known as 'kappies' with their twin flaps and careful rows of quilt stitching, the men in dark shades of moleskin and corduroy.

The Dappers, the strict Calvinists, were easily noticeable for the museum-like quality of their dress: knee breeches, broad-rimmed hat of plaited maize leaves, and a tight black jacket buttoned to the chin. Dapper jackets were cut so short that a fold of shirt often hung out at the back, and it was said that both Dapper and antelope could be recognized at a distance by the characteristic white flash of their rear view.

The centre of their life was the trek wagon. High sided, 3 or 4 feet wide, and 12 to 16 feet long, it was the convoy ship of the Great Trek. A triple roof, with two layers of canvas and one of reed mat, protected the interior. A chest served for a driver's seat, and the art of guiding the long line of a dozen or more oxen with light flicks of the whip was considered a great accomplishment. On each side dangled the many utensils of the owner, tar buckets, spades, spare harness and axle jacks; and the entire contraption rattled and swayed atrociously because it was constructed with loose joints so that it flexed and shivered over the ruts of the rough trail. Behind the iron-shod wheels on their spokes of assegai wood unrolled the blaze-mark of the trek – a ribbon of yellow soil where the wagons had passed and the cattle eaten down the vegetation.

It was the Matabele who first contested the Boers' path. Umzilikazi was by nature a marauder. He kept his warriors constantly in the field, making wide sweeps of his borders and terrorizing his neighbours. It was the Matabele custom to scout out the enemy's position, hide near his villages until a suitable moment, and then surprise the place with a massed charge. It was this technique which they used against the foremost Boer trekkies whom they caught in the open, strung out north of the Vaal river. In a series of lightning attacks by Matabele patrols the Botha trekkie was mauled; a party of ivory hunters pinned down, losing their servants and baggage; and the Liebenberg trekkie was virtually wiped out. Their leader, old man Behrend Liebenberg, refused to believe a hurried warning from an ivory hunter and in consequence was caught with half his men out of camp. He, his three sons, a daughter-in-law and

A Boer's wagon and oxen

Fording the Vaal river. Painting by Charles Davidson Bell

their companions were all massacred. The only survivors were the absentees and some children who hid or were overlooked by the Matabele. Fifty-three white men, women and children died before the Matabele withdrew.

Hendrick Potgieter, with the preaching Sarel Cilliers, was the senior leader in the region, and he ordered the advance parties of trekkers to fall back to a great laager at Veg Kop. There the Boers took up a strong position between the Rhenoste and Wilge rivers. Fifty wagons were drawn up in their classic laager ring, locked wagon tongue to wheel with the trek chains and the gaps closed with fascines of woven brushwood. In the centre were placed four wagons, their roofs reinforced with plank and rawhide. In them the women and children took refuge though several of the women and older children who knew how to handle weapons were allowed to join the defence while the camp prepared for a siege. Bullets were cast from melted down tableware, gunpowder distributed, and mounted patrols rode out to locate the Matabele.

In leisurely fashion Umzilikazi now sent down his senior general, Kalipi, with an army estimated at six thousand warriors. As far as Umzilikazi was concerned the earlier fighting had been little more than a skirmish. He bore no particular hatred for white men. In fact he was entertaining at the time an envoy from the Cape Governor and had recently shown similar hospitality to a passing big game hunter. The Matabele King failed to realize the seriousness of the

143

Boer threat and that they had come to stay. He thought that they needed no more than a bad fright to scare them off. Secure in the legend of Matabele prowess, he was sending Kalipi on what was really no more than a major cattle raid.

To this effect the Matabele column advanced quite openly. Cilliers, who had gone out with a mounted patrol, came upon them about an hour and a half's ride from the laager. To his astonishment the Matabele immediately formed ranks and sat down in orderly fashion, impassively allowing the white men to ride within fifty yards of them. But when Cilliers's Hottentot interpreter called out to ask why they had come to attack and despoil the Boers, the entire Matabele army jumped to its feet and roared out the one word 'Umzilikazi!' The Boers dismounted to fire their heavy guns but after a few discharges they fell back, seeing that the Matabele army was taking up its classic bull's-head fighting formation, with the two horns of the army curving out to encircle Cilliers's little force.

The battle of Veg Kop, which took place on 16 October 1836, was the first head-on collision between Bantu spearman and Boer musketeer, and it was clear from the start that the Matabele intended to fight in the open and with complete confidence in their own rules of warfare. After inspecting the laager and feasting on captured oxen, they divided into the three groups and patiently waited until the Boers had reloaded their guns and put their defences in order. Inside the laager Cilliers gave his usual oration; the entire Boer party knelt in a prayer for victory, and the women and children were sent to their central refuge. Only when the trekkers raised a white sheet as a battle standard did the Matabele advance, a mass attack which lapped entirely around the laager.

Their discipline and valour were remarkable. At thirty feet the Boers opened fire with slugs and ball. Despite enormous losses the Matabele kept steadily on, led by an enormous 'yellow Kaffir' leaping and gesticulating until Cilliers shot him down. Behind him came the full weight of the Matabele onset, experienced warriors and novice soldiers with long red feathers in their hair and clusters of black and white jaybird plumes falling over one eye. Their weapons were club, elliptical shield of dappled oxhide, and spears, both the lightweight throwing assegai and the shorter, broad-bladed stabbing assegai. As they pressed against the laager wall, some Matabele tried to crawl under the wagon beds, others laid shields against the thornbushes in an attempt to scramble over, and others tore at the fascines. The shock of their charge was so great that several of the wagons were wrenched six inches out of line. But the tightly lashed laager held, and the Boers poured a withering fire into the massed ranks at point blank range. It was, said one reporter, like 'shooting down sparrows'. The trekker women reloaded the heavy muskets with handfuls of buck shot sewn up in leather bags and handed them back to their men. By the third attack a ring of Matabele dead lay around the camp, watched by the younger Boers for bodies which sweated, for dead men do not sweat, and finished off with pot shots from their lighter weapons. Only when Kalipi had lost over four hundred men did his force make their orderly retreat. As far as he was concerned, he had won a notable victory, for he carried off the prodigious booty of some 55,000 head of cattle, sheep and goats to take back to Umzilikazi. As he withdrew, he sent a taunting message to the Boers, telling them that they were too cowardly to come out from behind their fortifications and fight properly.

Potgieter's trekkers were in an unhappy position. Although they had lost only two men killed, including Potgieter's son, and a dozen or so badly wounded, by their own standards they were ruined. Their wealth was in herds, and now they did not even have the necessary draught oxen to move their wagons. They had to harness horses to the trek chains in order to shift the laager a few miles back to get away from the stink of festering Matabele bodies. There they waited until help arrived from trekker parties farther back down the line, and especially from the Reverend Archbell who sent up his own oxen and a group of friendly Koranna to pull the stranded defenders of Veg Kop to safety.

The standard Boer retaliation to a native raid was the commando, a volunteer

The Battle of Veg Kop

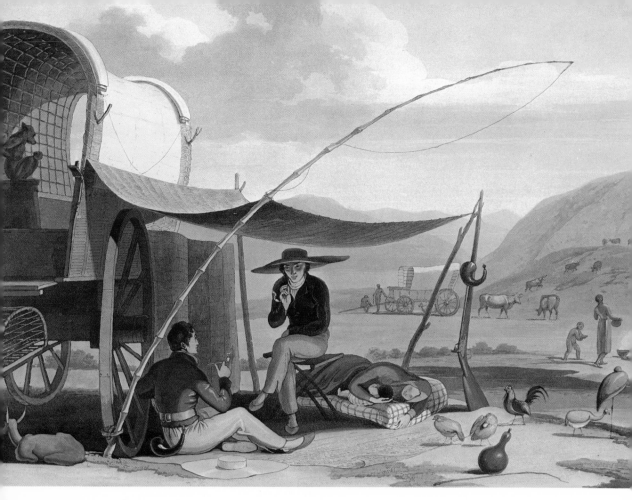

Boers resting after a day's trek

force under an elected officer which rode down and defeated the offenders and took retribution in the form of cattle and 'orphans'. It was a system which had been worked out very well in the Kaffir wars and against the Bushmen, the ill-fated and stubborn race of Aborigines who had suffered in turn from the incursions of Hottentot, Bantu and Boer. A few Bushmen, in fact, were to be found with the Trek, pathetic elf-like creatures with triangular-shaped faces and slant eyes that gave them a foxy expression. They were something of a status symbol for their Boer masters, a living trophy, and they were employed as domestics, though Bushmen had a habit of running away at the first opportunity and it was not unknown for them to be chained up at night. The Matabele attack, however, had been on a much larger scale than any Bushman raid, and so it was not until the flamboyant Gerrit Maritz came up with reinforcements of more than a hundred wagons that the Voortrekkers felt strong enough to take the field against Umzilikazi. With Potgieter as its captain, the revenge commando rode out on 2 January 1837, eleven weeks after Veg Kop. It comprised

107 Boers, 40 Griqua and Koranna allies, and 60 Barolong. The Griqua and Koranna were mounted and equipped with firearms, but the Barolong travelled on foot. They were to act as cattle herds for the expected booty and were as eager as the Boers to avenge past raids by the Matabele. Maritz's mounted squadron, taking its cue from their dashing leader, wore red emblems in their hats.

The speed of the Boer advance took Umzilikazi by surprise, for the Boers came down on his main settlements at Mosega to find the Matabele army utterly unprepared. Its senior induna was absent and Umzilikazi himself was some distance to the north. The conflict which followed was a one-sided affair. Led by a Barolong guide, the commando was able to enter the valley of Mosega unobserved and identify the military kraal where the local Matabele regiment was stationed. Splitting into two groups led by Potgeiter and Maritz respectively, the commando was able to launch a dawn attack from two directions. They caught the Matabele regiment asleep and never gave their enemy time to re-group. The commando swept through Mosega and broke the Matabele countercharge with musketry. After taking heavy losses the Matabele retreated in confusion. Behind them their attackers methodically put the fifteen Mosega kraals to the torch. Seven thousand head of cattle were taken, and the commando rescued the wagons which had been captured in earlier Matabele raids. As a sequel to Veg Kop, the defeat of Mosega was complete. Not a single Boer had been killed or wounded, though four of the Barolong had lost their lives. The Boers had out-classed the Matabele in every way. Without horses the natives could neither take the initiative nor close with their mounted opponents. Assegai and knobkerrie were no match for muskets loaded with shot or splinter slugs, nicked across the tip so that they disintegrated into minor shrapnel as they flew. Belatedly Umzilikazi had learned that the traditional pattern of raid and counter-raid between herding communities was finished. In their armoured laager the Boers were impregnable, while his own kraals were hopelessly vulnerable. Wisely he withdrew across the Limpopo, and under pressure from more commandos left the pastureland to the invader. But farther west, his arch enemy, Dingaan the Zulu, heard of Umzilikazi's defeat and realized that different tactics would be needed if he too was to try to stem the advancing trek.

Dingaan's territory at this time lay to one side of the Boer's main line of advance. Until now the Great Trek had been heading almost due north, following the line of fifteen-inch annual rainfall which dictated the grasslands they sought. Like stalks in a corn sheaf with its base resting in the old colony, the trekkie paths rose from Cape Colony, came together at the waist of the Thaba Nchu rendezvous, and began to splay out again north of the Caledon river. After the victory of Mosega, however, the trek split. While Potgeiter's followers continued to push into lands vacated by the Matabele, Cilliers, Maritz, and others, turned their wagons westward towards the Drakensberg mountains. Their leader was Piet Retief and their target was the rich lowland of Natal, the Meadow of Africa. Here, in a region of low hills, lush vegetation and fruitful soils, lay some of the best land in the continent. But it was also Dingaan's domain, and a Zulu prophecy had foretold that after Chaka's death the land would be crossed and re-crossed by swallows in every direction. To Dingaan the news of Boers descending over the wall of the Drakensberg with their multitude of cattle and horses must have seemed a fulfilment of the omen.

There was among the Boers, too, an air of high expectation to the descent of the Drakensberg. They had a feeling that once they had found a way down the great cliff, there was no turning back. To some it was the last great test, the crossing of Sinai with the Promised Land of Natal's green hills stretching out below. To take a wagon down the steep slope of the Drakensberg scarp, all but the two steadiest oxen of every wagon had to be outspanned. Women and children dismounted and walked alongside, and the men hung on to leather straps or operated wheel brakes to hold the vehicle back. On the more gentle gradients it was possible to transverse the wagon by switching the wheels, so that the two smaller front wheels were both on the uphill side and the wagon canted over. But for direct descents the rear wheels were removed altogether and replaced by logs to serve as drags. It seemed a miracle that during the entire operation, in which a thousand wagons were eased over the scarp, only a handful broke loose and crashed to pieces in the ravines. Then, spreading out from the front of the Drakensberg the trekkers quietly took up their positions along the deserted and apparently smiling vales of western Natal.

Retief, who had personally led the great descent, now went ahead to visit Dingaan and ask permission to settle. But to the Zulu King it must have seemed a little pointless. His spies were already reporting the steady encroachment of Boers on lands which were regarded as Zulu territory, areas which until now had been scarcely touched by the whites. It is true that at Port Natal there was a scrubby hut settlement on the coast, where a tiny community of traders and half-castes were led by Allen Gardiner*, formerly a captain of the Royal Navy but now with the Church Missionary Society. But Dingaan tolerated Port Natal as the entry point for European goods and his beloved mechanical novelties, and he kept the inhabitants in a constant state of alarm with his sudden demands for attractive gifts or accusations that they were harbouring runaways whom he wished to execute. Otherwise Dingaan permitted only an

---

* A remarkable man, Gardiner left soon afterwards and went as a missionary to Tierra del Fuego, dying there of starvation and exposure.

A treacherous ascent

Drawn & Engraved by C. Mitchell.

Dancing dress of Dingaan's harem and a Zulu woman of rank

occasional white trader at his court in Umgungundhlovu, a few half-caste interpreters and one important missionary, the Reverend Francis Owen. Although there were one or two other missionaries, chiefly American, among the outlying kraals, Owen's central position was crucial. He was, in effect, Dingaan's window on the outside world and, conversely, the most intimate foreign observer of the behaviour of this remarkable African potentate.

Owen had only recently arrived in Zululand and was still shocked by its savagery. A Cambridge man, he had graduated Senior Optime in mathematics from St John's College before taking holy orders. In 1836 he held a curacy in Yorkshire when he attended the anniversary meeting of the Church Missionary Society and heard Gardiner, lately back from Natal, deliver a passionate appeal for help. Owen volunteered forthwith. On Christmas Eve he sailed for Cape Town with his wife, a sister, and a female servant. By late summer he was installed in a leaky hut on the outskirts of the Place of the Elephant and quite out of his depth in Zulu politics.

He was, he found, treated like a combination of native soothsayer and foreign magician. Dingaan regarded him as more of a scientific oracle rather than a religious instructor. Owen had brought an encyclopedia in his baggage, and Dingaan cross-examined him on every subject from paper-making to the construction of a diving bell which was shown in a picture in the book. Above all, Dingaan wanted Owen to explain to him about the difference between foreign peoples, in particular between the Boers and the English, 'the children of George' as the Zulu called them. Dingaan had got the notion that the Boer trekkers were rebels against the English King and were fleeing his country just as Umzilikazi had fled from Zululand. He therefore expected Owen to help him in dealing with the Boers and, without revealing his plans to the missionary, persuaded Owen to conduct a correspondence with Retief on the King's behalf. Owen was already thoroughly disillusioned and suspected a trap, but there was little he could do. He wrote in his diary:

> The whole communication was indicative of the cruelty, artfulness, trickery, and ambition of the Zulu chief, who I have too much reason now to fear is induced by the example of the other native chiefs to make himself strong by the 'isabani' or musket, the power of which he dreads on the one hand but covets on the other. 'Tho he has not a horse in his dominions he will, if possible, be glad to train up a body of cavalry for occasions in which their service may be wanted.

Dingaan had gone straight to the heart of the matter. He saw that without guns or horses the Zulus would have no more chance of resisting the Boers than had the Matabele. The only way of obtaining these weapons was to capture them from the trekkers themselves. Accordingly he wrote to Retief agreeing to let him visit the royal kraal. As bait he told Retief that a Zulu impi raiding into Matabeleland had recovered a number of flocks of sheep which they recognized as being stolen from the Boers. He was, he told Retief, prepared to return these flocks to their rightful owners.

Even Owen was impressed by what he considered this fine example of Dingaan's honesty, and he was present on 6 December 1837 when Retief and four trekkers visited Umgungundhlovu where they were feasted and entertained to a dancing display by a Zulu regiment of novice warriors. An awed Owen wrote:

Dingaan in his ordinary and dancing dress. From drawings by the missionary A. F. Gardiner

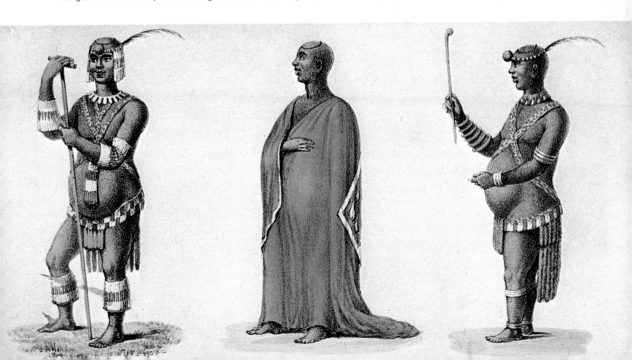

The regiment divided into companies, each soldier having a stick in each hand (or in lieu of a stick the horn or some bone of a beast, for very few had their shields, and no one his spear) with a sort of double quick march, performed various evolutions, exciting themselves to the supposed combat by some note of their voices, which could not be called a song, and by raising their sticks aloft in the air. Very soon 'tho it was not warm the wet ran down their bodies. On a sudden they gave a whistle, and forming into one large company they rushed furiously as if to charge down the open area of the town whistling as they ran. Some who had shields after this first essay, leaping aloft and kicking their shields cried out 'We are as hard as stones: nothing shall hurt us.' Presently the military divided into two parts and each dancing round the area on opposite quarters, they at last came within 20 yards of each other, when they made a tremendous rush as if engaging each other in close conflict.

This was Retief's first glimpse of a full Zulu regiment on exercise, and it must have been a sobering experience. The military machine of the Zulu nation probably had to no equal in Black Africa outside of Dahomey. Every adult Zulu male was expected to serve as a warrior and undergo a long and rigorous training programme. New regiments were constantly being raised from among the young men who went to special military kraals for their instructions. There they were toughened up by physical training programmes, which included long route marches over rough country and a variety of war dances like the one Owen had seen and several which involved the participation of herds of oxen specially drilled to manoeuvre in company with the troops. Under their officers, the indunas, the Zulu recruits were taught the use of club, throwing-spear and shield. Above all, they were trained to use the deadly stabbing assegai which had accounted for their success in all previous native wars. To lose one's stabbing assegai in battle was considered a final disgrace for a warrior. The whole aim of his instruction was to teach him to close within arm's length of the enemy, and there hack and stab until the adversary was either killed or lost his nerve and fled. Zulu morale was superb. Each regiment had its own name, such as the Buffalo regiment or the Elephant regiment, and was recognizable by the distinctive colours of its shields and accoutrements. Being based on age groups, each regiment was virtually the recruit's unit for life, and the older battle-tried regiments were regarded with considerable respect by the whole of Zulu society.

The dancing display by novice soldiers, which Retief was allowed to see, played an important part in Dingaan's over-all plan. It accustomed the Boer leader to this notion of Zulu behaviour, and it gave Dingaan an opportunity to observe his opponent at first hand. In a stroke of diplomatic genius Dingaan promised he would give the Boers a grant of land where they could settle, on condition that they captured and brought in Siyonkella, a Basuto chief who had been raiding the Zulu border. The cunning of his suggestion was that Dingaan knew that Siyonkella was one of the few native chiefs who possessed both horses and guns. This would give the Boers a considerable foe to deal with and they might well be defeated; and if victorious, they would be handing over to Dingaan the very weapons he wanted.

As it turned out, Dingaan's scheme miscarried due to the Boer's own double-dealing. Retief went back to the main trekker camps to raise a commando, and lured Siyonkella into a trap by asking him to a parley. While pretending peace, they managed to get handcuffs on the Basuto leader and seized him and his cattle. But then, instead of handing him over to Dingaan, the Boers ransomed Siyonkella back to his own people in exchange for a large levy of cattle. His guns and horses they kept for themselves. When he heard this, Dingaan was so furious that in an unguarded moment he let slip to Owen that he himself had never intended to keep his side of the bargain either. Now, however, there was news that Retief and a large party of seventy-one mounted Boers were on their way to the royal kraal to continue negotiations for a grant of land from the Zulus.

Owen was dimly aware that something was amiss. The day before Retief's arrival at Umgungundhlovu Dingaan summoned the missionary and told him to write out a message to Retief. He asked that the leader of the Boers should bring all his people to the kraal but without their horses. When Owen enquired how the Boers could be expected to travel without their horses, Dingaan hastily corrected himself and said he wanted to invite them to the centre of the kraal in order to see their display of horsemanship. Writing up his diary that day, Owen hoped that 'the Dutch will be too wise to expose themselves in the manner proposed, but I cannot conceive that Dingaan meditates any treachery.' That same evening he learned that large parties of Zulu in their war dress had been seen entering the town from the outlying kraals.

The Place of the Elephant was an ideal site for an ambush. The kraal was shaped like a huge oval. A thick fence of thorns formed the outer perimeter, and inside this ran concentric rows of straw huts, 1,700 of them according to one estimate, set out in orderly fashion and each serving as a barracks for 20 soldiers. Special platforms standing elevated on poles formed the Zulu armouries where the troops placed their spears and shields out of reach of white ants. At the centre of the oval was the 'Great Place', an open space used for parades and dances. Next to it, on the south side, lay the enclosure for the King's cattle and, beyond, the royal labyrinth. This was an area divided off by its own thorn fence and reserved entirely for the royal household. Its entrance was guarded by a sentry post, and no one was allowed inside except for royal wives and female servants. Over on the south-east quadrant stood Dingaan's palace or 'Great House'. It was built on rising ground so that the King could look out over the settlement which he himself had founded eight years earlier

SOUTH WEST

AFRICA

BECHUANALA

Kalahari Dese

Atlantic Ocean

Okavango

Lake Ngami

Molopo

Kolo

Kuruman ●

Griqualand

Orange

Namaqualand

Bushmanland

Cape Colony

Karroo

Graaf

Table Bay ● Cape Town
Table Mountain

Cape of Good Hope

THE GNOO.

0   100   200   300 Miles
0   100   200   300   400   500 Kilometres

Matabeleland

Mashonaland

Zambesi

Matopo Hills

Bamangwato

Limpopo

Limpopo

Mosega

Delagoa Bay

Indian Ocean

Vaal

Veg Kop

Wilge

Zululand

Blood River

Umgungundhlovu
(Place of the Elephant)

Modder

Thaba
Nchu

Basutoland

Seven
Fountains

Drakensberg Mountains

Natal

Port Natal
(Durban)

Caledon

BECHUANA HUNTING THE LION.

The interior of Dingaan's house

on a spot sacred as the birth and burial place of the Great Zulu, founder of the Zulu clan. Arranged to flank the King's house were command posts for his two chief indunas, the royal seraglio, corn stores and an abattoir. Surveying the orderly rows of beehive huts which formed barracks for the duty regiments, it was clear to any observer that Umgungundhlovu was much more of a military cantonment than a civil capital.

Piet Retief and his Boers rode up to Umgungundhlovu at about ten o'clock on the morning of Saturday, 3 February 1838. They came in column, two by two, firing off a salvo of muskets to announce their presence. They were not unduly suspicious even though Zulus could be seen hurrying into the royal kraal by all the surrounding tracks through the pleasant, undulating country-side. A Zulu herald who bore the title of 'Dingaan's Mouth' came out with a welcoming message from the King and instructed the visitors to camp just outside the kraal. He also asked them to lodge their guns and horses in the royal enclosure. In answer, Retief merely pointed at his own grey hairs and told the herald to tell Dingaan that he was not dealing with a child. The Boers would stay outside the kraal but keep their weapons with them.

That afternoon the Boers gave a cavalry display to a Zulu audience, and the next day, Sunday, Retief and five men went into Umgungundhlovu to parley with Dingaan and his councillors. During the lengthy discussion that followed, Dingaan appeared far more interested in learning just how badly the trekkers had hurt the Matabele and in a coolly bloodthirsty way, whether Umzilikazi was dead. Eventually he agreed to award a huge tract of land in southern Natal to the Boers in payment for their services against Siyonkella. A document was drawn up to this effect and Dingaan signed it with his mark. Then the Boers withdrew.

The rest of Sunday and all of Monday was spent peacefully. Owen, busy with his devotional work, saw little of the Boers. Dingaan, showing his most amenable face, arranged a particularly splendid display of military dancing in which two regiments of Zulus danced in formation with picked herds of trained oxen. One herd was composed entirely of black and white beasts, and the particular regiment involved in the performance, carried shields of matching colour. A second herd was all of white oxen, and its regiment bore white shields. To a knowledgable spectator, the colours would have had peculiar significance. The Black Shield regiment, the Ihlangu Umnyama, was normally stationed some distance out of town and must have been specially brought in. While the White Shields, the Ihlangu Inhlope, was Dingaan's crack battalion. Composed entirely of veteran warriors, they were the elite Zulu troops and wore the warrior's headring, a circlet of bark and grass stitched through the

Above Warriors of a Zulu regiment bow in homage to Dingaan as they file past him.
Below The Great Dance at Embellybelli

Overleaf The Battle of Blauwkrantz. Painting by Thomas Baines

scalp. Only Owen's interpreter, a white youth named William Wood, who had lived some time among the Zulu, grasped the full meaning of the preparations. On Tuesday morning he voiced his suspicions to some Boers who came to see Owen. But they ignored his warning. Exasperated, Wood told Owen's European servant 'You'll see that the Boers will be killed.'

Dingaan's preparations were now complete, hastened by the news that the Boers had inflicted yet another defeat on the Matabele on the high veld. At eight o'clock on Tuesday morning the Zulu King sent word to Retief to bring his men down to the kraal for a final ceremony. The invitation was cleverly timed. The Boers were on the point of departure. They had their treaty; their horses were saddled; and their equipment was packed. They were completely off guard. The Zulu messenger insisted that they should see this final display, but regretfully announced that it was a strict rule that no stranger was allowed to carry weapons inside the royal kraal. Rather than depart and leave their host offended, the Boers stacked their arms and, leaving their horses in charge of native horseholders, went down on foot to the Zulu camp. There they found Dingaan seated on his throne with his indunas at his side. To his left was the colonel of the Black Shields and on his right the induna of the White Shields. Both regiments were drawn up by the throne. Dingaan welcomed Retief warmly and invited him to sit near him. The rest of the Boers were shown to an open space where they would have a good view of the dancing. Beer was distributed among the guests and as they relaxed, the performance began. For Retief it was at least the third time he had been entertained in this fashion, and his men had seen a similar spectacle only the previous day. Therefore they were unworried when the dancers surged close in front of them, and probably did not even notice the armed Zulu regiments quietly coming round behind them. Suddenly jumping to his feet, Dingaan roared 'Kill the Wizards!', and the warriors pounced. Springing forward, they seized the dazed white men.

There was virtually no resistance at all. Retief's interpreter, a man from Port Natal, had understood the King's shouted command and cried out 'We are finished!' In Zulu he begged 'Listen, let me speak to the King.' But Dingaan silenced him with a wave of the hand. Pulling out a knife, the interpreter slashed at his first two attackers but was then overpowered. Only one Boer broke free. Hurling himself out of the mêlée, he made a dash for the gate. A dozen Zulu warriors leapt after him and brought him down. Elsewhere there was scarcely a glimmer of a fight. Any white man who struggled violently was clubbed down; the others were hurried out of the kraal towards a low hill, the Zulu execution ground known as Hlomo Amabata, the Place of the Skull. There, at Dingaan's command, the prisoners were killed by the traditional Zulu method of beating their brains out with a knobkerrie.

Meanwhile, quite unaware, Owen had been at his quarters outside the kraal.

He was quietly sitting in the shade of his wagon and reading the Testament, when a royal messenger came running up. The tense expression on the man's face told Owen at once that something unusual was happening. To his horror he was informed that Dingaan wished him well and sent to reassure him that there was no need for alarm. Only the Boers, the King said, were to be killed. Owen was still recovering from this appalling news and wondering what he should do when, in his words,

> I was released from this dreadful dilemma by beholding an awful spectacle! My attention was directed to the bloodstained hill nearly opposite my hut and on the other side of my wagon, which hides it from my view, where all the executions at this fearful spot take place, and which was now destined to add 60 more bleeding carcasses to the number of those which have already cried to Heaven for vengeance. There (said someone) they are killing the Boers *now*. I turned my eyes and behold! an immense multitude on the hill. About 9 or 10 Zulus to each Boer were dragging their helpless unarmed victims to the fatal spot . . .

The unhappy missionary was so overcome that he lay down on the ground. Then he, Mrs Owen, and his sister together read the 91st psalm. Later, through his telescope he could see Dingaan still sitting at the parade ground and before him swarmed the several divisions of a Zulu impi. 'About noon', he wrote, 'the whole body *ran* in the direction from which the Boers came. They are (I cannot allow myself to doubt) sent to fall or to join others who have been ordered to fall unawares on the main body of the Boers who are encamped . . .'

The operational efficiency of the Zulu war machine now revealed itself. The main body of the trekkers were strung along the watercourses about a week's journey to the west. Travelling across country by forced marches, and linked by runners, the indunas of Dingaan's army swung their impis into position for a combined assault. Three Zulu regiments closed with the main trek camps unnoticed and, in a brilliantly coordinated attack at one o'clock on a moonless night, burst down on the whole trekker line. The Boers had no warning. Young Daniel Bezuidenhout heard his camp dogs barking. He went out to investigate, and by the time he got back, found his family's wagons overrun with Zulu. They hacked and stabbed and killed any living thing. Small groups of settlers were swamped. Blood-stained survivors staggered over to their neighbours who, hearing the far-off shooting, had laagered in time. A few mounted patrols managed to rescue outlying groups, and at one point a mounted Boer bravely galloped through the Zulu siege ring to bring ammunition to a beleaguered party on a hill top. But in general it was a massacre. Three hundred Boers died, over half of them children, and two hundred and fifty coloured servants. The canvas tent sails of some wagons were soaked with blood. Then, just as suddenly, the Zulu assault groups withdrew.

Now there was total war. The anguished Boers, led by Cilliers and Maritz, fell back to three main laagers. Potgieter and his veterans of the Matabele campaign came across to help them. Mounted patrols hunted Zulu and, if they got the chance, shot them out of hand. But for a while the whole future of the trek into Natal was in doubt. Supplies ran low; fever broke out in the laagers; and the Zulus controlled the countryside, making communication difficult. The lowest point was when a strong commando met up with a Zulu army in broken, rocky country. Stupidly the Boer leaders tried a mounted action. Unable to manoeuvre properly and attacked on all sides, the commando was lucky to break out of the Zulu ring intact. They lost their commander and galloped for safety, a deed for which they became scorned as the Vlug Commando, the Flight Commando. From Port Natal came news that an expedition launched by the white inhabitants had failed miserably. Dingaan's troops retaliated by sweeping into the settlement and razing it to the ground. The inhabitants, including the Owens who had fled Umgungundhlovu, evacuated to a ship anchored in the bay and for some days watched the Zulus sack the town, dancing and feasting by the light of the burning huts.

There was much coming and going among the Boers; fainthearts packing up and leaving Natal, and reinforcements arriving. Among them was Andreus Pretorius, under whose leadership the Boers reverted to the tactic which had been successful against the Matabele at Veg Kop. A new commando of 500 men went out to strike directly at Dingaan's capital, and instead of mounted attack, they relied on the armoured laager, even taking along four small cannon. Advancing with great care, they encamped on the night of Saturday, 15 December 1838 on the banks of the Incomi river. Lanterns were hung out on whipstocks to guard against surprise attack, and next morning, which dawned bright and calm, the defenders heard the extraordinary sound of a full Zulu army advancing, a rushing noise like wind over the grass or a river in spate. By five o'clock the Boers estimated they were facing a Zulu army of between nine and twelve thousand troops.

Pretorius had picked the position well. The laager was arranged in a tight quadrant between the Incomi river and a dried up watercourse. Two of the cannon pointed forward from the wagon arc, one covered the river which was deep enough as to be virtually uncrossable and the fourth cannon had as its field of fire the dried up watercourse. All four guns were loaded with grape shot. The commando's horses and cattle were collected in the middle of the laager, and the usual wagon wall was reinforced with gates and hurdles over which the Boers stretched rawhide. The Zulu were obliged to attack across a level plain extending over 800 yards, swept by musketry. As with the Matabele, the courage of the Zulu impis was unquestioned. An early, lucky, cannon shot landed amongst a staff conference of indunas killing several of them outright. Undeterred, battalion after battalion ran the gauntlet to try to come to grips with

W.C.Harris

the enemy, but all failed. They were stopped by a hail of slugs and ball, and fell in waves. The guns of the defenders grew so hot that they became dangerous to reload, and on that windless day the smoke from the black powder they used rose in a choking cloud over the laager. At one moment the cattle threatened to stampede and break the laager, but an order was given for general volleys on all sides so that the terrified beasts retreated shivering to the centre. The Zulus never had a chance. The first two charges were pressed home with great bravado, but were so badly shredded that the captains and lieutenants could be seen lashing their men back into line for the next assault. There were two more charges before the native retreat began. Only the White Shields, the blooded veterans, rallied for a final time, but they too were smashed. The Boers, making a sortie from their position, turned it into a general rout. The dried-up water course they found packed with warriors, and there was a carnage as they were shot down in it point blank. Scores of Zulu hurled themselves into the river to escape, and Boer hunting parties walked the banks with muskets to flush them out or pick them off as the desperate warriors rose to breathe from where they had been hiding with only their nostrils above the water. After the killing the name of the stream was changed to Blood river, and in Cilliers's gloating phrase, the dead Zulus 'lay on the ground like pumpkins on a rich soil that had borne a plentiful crop'. The Boers had suffered only three wounded and not a single man killed.

Blood River broke the back of the Zulu nation, and turned Dingaan into a fugitive. A Boer commando sacked Umgungundhlovu and auctioned off Dingaan's hoard of novelties. On the Golgotha outside the town they came across the corpses of Retief and his men, still bound at wrists and ankles with leather thongs. These bodies they buried, recovering from Retief's leather pouch the land deed by which Dingaan had granted Natal to the trekkers. It was a grant which they now took up, elevating Dingaan's half-brother, Panda, to the status of puppet king to give the whole affair an air of legality. By right of conquest, too, they seized the Zulu cattle, leaving Dingaan discredited and dispossessed. Shortly afterwards came news that Dingaan was dead, assassinated, it was claimed, in Swaziland by a disgruntled servant. Of the Boers' major antagonists only Umzilikazi was still alive, carrying on a rearguard action across the Limpopo. Defiant to the last, he was buried by his followers in the Matopo hills, an example later copied by Cecil Rhodes. The new pastoralists had taken over the south of the continent by virtue of the gun and the wagon, and were there to stay.

A Naturalist's Paradise

CHAPTER SEVEN

One afternoon in 1722, when the Cape of Good Hope was still in Dutch hands, a thin-faced Swede could have been seen near the summit of Table Mountain, standing on the shoulders of his French companion. With a long stick, the Swede was trying to keep his balance and at the same time to beat down a clump of blue flowers which bloomed from a crevice in the rock face above him. The Swede was Carl Peter Thunberg. Twenty-eight years old and already a Doctor of Physic from Uppsala University, he had studied under the 'Father of Botany', Linnaeus, and the plant he was trying to dislodge was the blue orchid, *Disa longicornis*. In the end he succeeded in knocking down exactly five blooms, the only ones he was able to acquire while in Africa, and these he added with great delight to his unique collection of rare African orchids and bulbous plants. His companion was making his first botanizing excursion up Table Mountain and managed to collect in one day no less than three hundred different species of plant, most of which he had never encountered before. In doing so, he was happy to sacrifice three pairs of thin shoes, ripped to pieces as he scrambled eagerly over the rough ground to gather up his spoils.

Carl Peter Thunberg

To the botanist, Cape Province was indeed a treasure trove. Scarcely larger in area than the Isle of Wight, it possessed a greater variety of unknown plants than any comparable region in the world. There were orchids and arum lilies, regal plants with brilliant ruffled petals, ixias and heaths and Cape pelargoniums – a species of wild 'geranium'. The local 'honeysuckle' attracted swarms of brilliant hovering sun birds, and at a little distance inland one found exotic fuchsias, tree aloes sprinkled with yellow and orange buds, and proteas whose petal display radiated from a central boss in a blaze of scarlet, yellow-orange, or deep purple lined with pink. Some flowers looked like stones; others seemed to be a licking mass of coloured tongues, or sprang from strange stunted cones. There were blossoms which stank of carrion to attract pollinating insects, and a night-flowering gardenia which was to be named in honour of Thunberg himself. Their popular names indicated their splendour – Belladona lily and Peacock flower, Tigers' Jaws, and above all the Bird of Paradise flower. The latter, growing to a height of about four feet, produced a single stiff spike

GERANIUM.

Nova Species.

in a green and pink sheath, from which rose the flowers in slow formal succession, vivid orange mingled with blue.

The enormous profusion of plant forms almost surpassed belief. Within a few yards the skilled eye could detect a dozen or more different species, and a trained botanist like Thunberg was unable to keep pace with the flood of new plant types which revealed themselves. The Province was one vast reliquary of the last surviving offshoots of the archaic plant associations of South Africa, and in the Colony's *blomtyd*, the bloom time, whole areas of land outside Cape Town were carpeted with daubs of blue, white and yellow. And because the plant displays changed with the seasons, even the regular collector could never be quite sure what new species he might not uncover on his next walk.

Only Linnaeus's new system of classification, worked out in the second quarter of the eighteenth century, was able to make sense of this botanical luxuriance; and suitably, it was two of Linnaeus's own pupils – Carl Thunberg and Anders Sparrman – who played the leading roles in bringing the splendours of South Africa flora to the attention of the outside world. The two men were remarkably similar in the boyish enthusiasm with which they went plant hunting, usually armed with nothing more ferocious than a large knife to dig up roots, a few collecting boxes, and a light lunch of biscuits and sugar sweets. 'Perhaps none but a lover of natural history can imagine what pleasure we enjoyed together among the herbs and flowers', wrote Sparrman. 'At first almost every day was a rich harvest of the rarest and most beautiful plants, and I had almost said, that at every step we made one or more new discoveries.'

Sparrman and Thunberg made only a few excursions together before the former was lured away by the offer of a place as naturalist aboard Captain Cook's *Resolution*, which called at Cape Town on her voyage round the world. But twenty-eight months later he came back with his enthusiasm undimmed. When *Resolution* anchored in Table Bay after the first eastward circumnavigation, Sparrman and the rest of the ship's crew celebrated one extra day of the calendar (21 March) to make up for the day lost on the voyage, and then he came ashore eagerly to take up his plant hunt once again. In the meantime Thunberg and a Scots gardener named Masson, who had been sent out from George III's private estate at Kew, had begun the great work of cataloguing and collecting specimens from the floral riches of South Africa.

Their rewards were immediate and spectacular. Masson caused a sensation when he sent back to England the first specimens of ixias with soft pale blue-green flowers. There were also the pink and white flowered heaths, and over fifty varieties of *Pelargonium* which soon gave rise to the lavish displays of 'geraniums' in Georgian London. Some plants were unsuited or difficult to raise in European conditions, so the collectors had to be content with taking specimens and seeds; drying, labelling, and cataloguing them; and then shipping them off in boxes all pressed and glued to sheets of imperial paper. But the reaction which flooded back from Europe was uniformly enthusiastic. The plant hunters were encouraged to press farther inland for their collections and so, loading their wagons with reference books and botanical presses, they creaked into the backlands with a dedication that took the Dutch by surprise. The authorities at Cape Town were worried that the botanists were military spies preparing maps for an invasion. Boer farmers thought them mad to be chasing after *bosjes*, mere 'bushes', and suspected that they were secretly after gold mines. One of Sparrman's hostesses came near to hysterics when she found his hat brim covered with a frieze of impaled insects, skewered there when his collecting box was full.

To all this the collectors reacted with a delightful lack of self-consciousness. Thunberg strolled through the woods unconcernedly shooting at tree tops with his musket to cut down high flowering branches. He and Sparrman on separate occasions swam across rivers to wander happily on the other side, stark naked, with nothing but a handkerchief to hold any plants they had found and, in Sparrman's case, his wig still perched on his head. They seemed to be protected by a charmed ingenuousness which allowed Thunberg to leap cheerfully down a thirty-foot cliff to gather plants below, trusting only to the bushes to break his fall, or to slide across rock faces on the seat of his breeches in order to explore a mysterious cave in the rocks. All he found was a dead swallow. He organized a light-hearted competition with Masson to see who could collect the most plants in a day; and when they sat on the ground for lunch, contentedly let unknown snakes slither across his outstretched leg so as to observe them better.

Undoubtedly their researches were attended by some risk. Riding through a wood, Thunberg's party was attacked by a rogue buffalo. One horse was gored to death and everyone, including the escort – a sergeant from the Cape garrison – was chased up a tree. As usual Thunberg himself had lagged behind the main party because he was constantly stopping to pick plants. He rode unawares into the scene to find his wagon abandoned and no sign of his companions. He too was charged by the buffalo, and only escaped with his life by dismounting and leaving his horse as a target. The buffalo's assault was so furious that one of its horns passed clean through the saddle and the horse was knocked down and died of its wounds within the hour. At night time when they camped, the naturalists were obliged to tether their draught oxen within a circle of fires to discourage attack by lions or cattle-rustling by marauding bands of Bushmen and Griqua natives who raided the outlying Boer farm-steads. On the whole, though, the travellers got on easily with the natives who were flattered and pleased when the scientists carefully measured and examined them, dutifully bought artifacts, and struggled to compile vocabularies of their strange languages. The natives took to hanging hopefully round the wagons like jackals, waiting for the naturalists to shoot their zoological specimens. Once the skin and head of the animal had been removed, the hangers-on rushed in to devour the carcass raw.

The travellers' native servants were far more of a nuisance. They were constantly disappearing on errands of their own invention or failing to turn up when wanted, and they had an almost superhuman ability for getting at the casks of liquor which the naturalists carried for preserving small animals entire. Eventually, Thunberg had to recourse to placing a live snake in his liquor cask in front of his servants, and telling them that anyone who drank from it would certainly be poisoned.

The zoology of South Africa was, of course, as intriguing as its botany. Astonishingly little was known about African wild life, and much that was believed was erroneous. It was said for instance that lion bones were so hard that they could be used instead of flint to strike sparks; that the unicorn might live beyond the Orange river; and that the rhinoceros killed men by knocking them down and then licking the flesh from their bones with a rasp-like tongue. Many of the animals of Africa seemed monstrous, altogether too bizarre and too awkward to be absolutely genuine. They appeared as caricatures of other known animals. The gnu had the head of a bison and the hindquarters of a deer. The hump-shouldered hyena, believed to be a hermaphrodite, was a similar mongrel but with a dash of leopard to give it spots. The great French

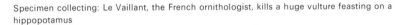

Specimen collecting: Le Vaillant, the French ornithologist, kills a huge vulture feasting on a hippopotamus

The sassaby and hartebeest

naturalist Buffon had put forward a theory to explain these anomalies. Many of the African animals, he claimed, were the result of cross-breeding. In times of drought the different species were obliged to gather around the surviving water holes, and under these crowded circumstances miscegenation took place. In Buffon's time the hippo was still known as the Behemoth, and it was said that, before drinking, elephants stirred up the water with their trunks because they could not abide to see their ugly faces reflected. Because they were so strange, African animals were also very valuable. A Mogul of India had paid two thousand ducats for a zebra to add to his private zoo, and the most famous rhinoceros in Europe (an Indian one) had been painted so often that, for generations afterwards, many naturalists considered that the calluses on its skin, raised by rough handling during shipment, were normal excrescences to be found on every rhinoceros in natural conditions.

Obviously there was much to be done in the study of African zoology, and once again it was 'Linnaeus's men' who tackled the job with their usual gusto. Rushing up to his first dead rhinoceros, Sparrman thrust his hand into the

Hunting at Meritsane. Views by the big game hunter Cornwallis Harris

animal's mouth to feel its tongue, and was mildly disappointed to find it quite smooth. Told that rhino-horns would shatter into pieces if brought into contact with any poison and that for this reason the Boer farmers made their drinking goblets of them, he spent hours filling rhino-horn cups with different poisons. The effect, he noted carefully, was negligible. Only in one case did a few bubbles rise to the surface and these probably because of air trapped in the cavity of the horn. Obtaining specimens of African animals was such a lucrative pastime that, stuffed and shipped back for display in European cabinets, they brought good prices from wealthy collectors and this helped to pay for botanical work. Later, as the naturalists moved father inland and the variety of plant life dwindled, the attraction of the fauna increased until it was zoology rather than botany which drew visitors even deeper into Africa.

The greatest prize was the giraffe, still known as the cameleopard. Sparrman and Thunberg both wrote descriptions of the animal, but it was left to a French ornithologist, Le Vaillant, travelling in the interior ten years later, to collect a giraffe skin and send it back to Europe in first-class condition. Le Vaillant was

Le Vaillant's 'giraffe camp' beside the Orange river. The giraffe skin is drying on its frame

a swashbuckling figure who pursued his researches with a considerable panache. Son of the French Consul at Paramaribo in Guiana, he had learned to use both bow and arrow and blow-pipe when young, and he arrived at the Cape with the confident ambition of being able to travel the entire length of Africa collecting birds and animals. Undeterred by the destruction of all his equipment when the ship carrying it blew up in an explosion, he borrowed a large tent from the army stores at the Cape, stocked up with a supply of gunpowder and preserving equipment, and so overloaded his wagon that it collapsed in a rut within half a mile of Cape Town. Patiently he put everything back together again and proceeded in a wide circuit that led him to Namaqualand and into the fringes of the Kalahari.

With a tame baboon named Kees for company, Le Vaillant kept himself in considerable style. He ate elephant's foot baked in embers, put hippo milk in his coffee, handed out grenadier caps (also begged from the Cape garrison) to native chiefs who were very taken with the crowned lions of Holland on the gilt-copper badges, and flirted with native women to whom he distributed quantities of snuff. Several of Le Vaillant's zoological claims were equally extravagant. He insisted that he caught, saddled, and rode a zebra without difficulty; and that the rhinoceros habitually ran across the countryside like a juggernaut, ploughing up a furrow with its horn, throwing its urine a great distance behind it, and always kicking to pieces its excrement. On the other hand he also witnessed and wrote a first-class description of a fight between a snake and a secretary bird, and wrote a brilliant book on African birdlife which was based on his observations. His giraffe he considered the prize of his collection. He spent nine days flaying, cleaning and tanning the skin, carefully preserving it with an ointment of ashes and tobacco so that its original colours would not fade before he brought it back to Europe where it was set up on a frame for public exhibition in Paris. The exhibit was to influence Lamarck in his theory that short-necked leaf-eaters evolved into long-necked animals by constantly stretching for their food, and caused a minor revolution in women's fashion as the style *à la girafe* became popular.

The untapped wealth of the South African plants and animals was even more forcefully illustrated a few years later by the return from the interior of William Burchell, an English naturalist. After a journey up-country in 1811–12 he brought back news of a new species of rhinoceros, the 'white rhino', and of a new type of zebra which had brown shadow bands between its black stripes and was duly named in his honour. Moreover he had seen and identified the blue wildebeeste and the sassaby, and brought back in his wagons no less than 63,000 objects of interest, including 40,000 botanical specimens, 120 skins of quadrupeds, and 265 different skins of birds. It was a haul which was to keep him busy cataloguing and commenting for virtually the rest of his career, as well as making him the first man to import live hyenas to England.

William Burchell. Drawing by J. Sell Cotman

Burchell's life had an element of personal tragedy hanging over it. A nurseryman's son, he had been well educated and then spent some time at Kew before being sent out to St Helena as a government botanist. There he had arranged for his fiancée to follow him and marry him on the island. But on the voyage out she fell in love with the captain of the ship and married him instead. Desolate, Burchell threw up his post and shipped for South Africa where he hoped to make a living by collecting specimens of natural history and selling them in Europe. 'All that I had pictured to myself of the riches of the Cape in botany',

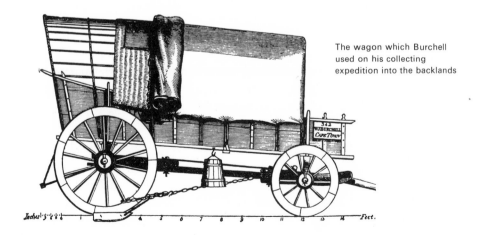

The wagon which Burchell used on his collecting expedition into the backlands

'Driving in an eland'. The technique was to run the animal until it was exhausted and then herd it on the hoof right up to the cooking pot. *Below* Return from the chase. Painting by Thomas Baines, pioneer artist who travelled with Livingstone's Zambesi expedition. *Opposite* Andries Africander, professional huntsman

he wrote after his first excursion and in a manner very reminiscent of Thunberg, 'was surpassed by what I saw in this day's walk. At every step a different plant appeared; and it is not an exaggerated description, if it should be compared to a botanic garden neglected and left to grow to a state of nature, so great was the variety to be met with.' He confessed that he was almost frightened at times to walk on, for fear of treading on and destroying some rare plant, and in four and a half hours he managed to collect over a hundred distinct species until forced to stop when his collecting boxes were full.

Like the Swedish collectors, he was astonished at the disinterest of the Dutch settlers in the natural world around them. Sparrman had once showed a book of four hundred plant specimens to a local doctor, and found that the man was scarcely able to recognize a third of them. Burchell observed that the Dutch gardeners were far more proud of growing ordinary carnations, tulips, and hollyhocks – all of them foreign imports – than in collecting any of the splendid African species. The government garden had only vegetables in it,

W.C. Harris delt

and the Cape menagerie possessed merely a lone gnu, some ostriches, a lion and lioness, and – of all things – a Bengal tiger.

Burchell was perhaps the most meticulous of the naturalist travellers. He set out for the interior in a Cape wagon containing a library of some fifty volumes, nearly all reference books to help him identify and catalogue his finds, and he kept a massive geographical daybook in which he noted the time, place, and character of every single specimen he procured. His chagrin can therefore be imagined when, years later, he visited the British Museum to view his finest animal specimens which he had sent them. Only a handful had actually been put on display. Several had been mislaid, and his rarest skin, that of a new antelope, was missing.

> At length an old packing case was found, which had been nailed up in a manner which evinced that the preservation of its contents had not been the purpose for which it was intended; and on its being opened I discovered the skin of my *Antilope lunata*, together with another undescribed species, of which that also was the only individual ever shot or seen, and six others, all swarming with live moths and maggots, and the hair dropping off.

It was true to say that Burchell lived for his animal and plant collections. After bringing back to England an even vaster array of specimens from South America, he became a recluse and virtually vanished from society while he devoted himself to the labour of arranging and classifying them. At eighty-two, when he finished his mammoth work, he committed suicide because, it was said, he felt that his task was done and that he was too old to begin a new project.

But it was when the travellers pushed out ahead of the line of the farthest Boer settlements and beyond the Vaal river that popular interest in African wild life was really aroused in a spectacular fashion. The travellers found themselves in a landscape which was unequalled since the last Ice Age in the teeming numbers of game it supported. Enormous herds of browsing animals lived mingled together in open parkland. It was a scene which many visitors compared to a vast zoo which stretched as far as the eye could see. Flesh-eating beasts, natural disasters, and the puny efforts of native hunters kept the numbers of herbivores from increasing out of all proportion, but even so the numbers were stupendous. It was estimated that there were over five hundred million springbok between the Karroo and the Kalahari, and a single herd would contain several thousand. On their great migrations the hills and kloofs were literally black with them, and they stripped the pasture as effectively as any swarm of locusts. Boer farmers spoke of losing flocks of sheep swept away in the torrent of animals, and how a large herd of springbok might take four or five hours to pass a single observer. Larger animals were also found in abundance. Across parts of Bechuanaland it seemed that a rhinoceros head was projecting from every bush of wait-a-bit thorn, and it was a foolish trekker who did not guard his cattle against nocturnal attack by lions. The echoing report of a heavy musket would set the entire veld alive with a moving carpet of frightened animals, galloping wildly in all directions until enveloped by a low fog of dust, kicked up by their thundering hooves which one observer said was like the distant sound of a massed charge of heavy cavalry.

News of this incredible abundance was surprisingly slow in coming to the ears of the European big game hunting fraternity. Scraps of information were gleaned from the reports of missionaries and from wandering naturalists like Burchell; from remarks in the official volumes of the government surveyors sent inland after the British took over South Africa; and in person at the Cape where Boer ivory hunters sent down huge tusks for sale. The first hunting enthusiasts to take advantage of this mouth-watering situation were Indian Army officers. Not only were they by far the most enthusiastic and experienced in big game hunting, but they called at the Cape as a matter of routine on their voyages to and from the Orient. It was one of their number, Captain William Cornwallis Harris of the East India Company's Engineers, who really brought the matter to general attention and unleashed a flood of eager Nimrods, as they liked to call themselves, to ride out into the tawny plains of South Africa.

In many ways Cornwallis Harris was typical of his army fellows, though he was much luckier than most of them in being so early on the scene of African big game frenzy. From childhood he had been afflicted with 'shooting madness' as he put it.

> My first essay in practical gunnery was made at the early age of six, by the discharge of an enormous blunderbuss, known to the inmates of my paternal mansion by the familiar soubriquet of 'Betsy'. A flock of sparrows perched upon the corner of a neighbour's pigstye were the only sufferers; but information was maliciously laid against me, and I underwent severe corporal chastisement. Almost a year afterwards, I took ample revenge on my ill-natured neighbour by *pinking* his ducks and geese with a crossbow of my own construction; but my catapult was unfortunately discovered, seen, and confiscated. I next clubbed my Christmas capital with that of two sporting confederates, and raised a sufficient joint stock to purchase a condemned musquet (sic), with which during the holiday vacation we shot. . . From this time, I date my rapid improvement in the noble science of projectiles.

It fell to Harris after some years of soldiering and shikari in the Indian Army to be sent to the Cape of Good Hope for two years for reasons of ill-health. There, advised the Bombay Medical Board, he was to help recruit his strength by undertaking some travel. Scarcely believing his luck, Harris sailed from Bombay on 16 March 1836 in a large Indiaman and during the voyage laid his plans for a great hunting excursion. He persuaded a fellow passenger, a Mr Richardson of the Bombay Civil Service, to join him; and in May, when he reached Simon's Bay, Harris immediately went off to interview Dr Andrew

Smith, leader of a government scientific expedition but lately returned from Matabeleland. Harris wanted to know what he should take with him for a prolonged shooting trip in the interior, and in particular, what would make a suitable present for Umzilikazi, King of the Matabele. On Umzilikazi's goodwill the success of the expedition would ultimately depend, as it was in Matabele territory that Harris coolly proposed to hunt, having heard that it was virgin territory for the big game shot and swarming with elephant.

Harris had arrived at a crucial moment in South African history. Even as he was assembling his own expedition, many of the Boers were preparing their equipment for the Great Trek. In fact Harris had the greatest difficulty in obtaining sufficient wagons for his party because all available transport was being bought up and refitted by what Harris called 'the emigrant farmers'. Eventually, and at a price, Harris managed to buy suitable wagons and oxen, and to engage the drunken Hottentot drivers who came with them. For his camping equipment he had brought along all his Indian gear, including a tent, chairs and crockery – and expecting to be away for a considerable time, he laid in an enormous supply of munitions, including 18,000 bullets together with spare pigs of lead. There was a store of wine and brandy for himself and Richardson; 'inferior spirits' for the hired Hottentot servants; and a mass of beads and trinkets, geegaws and ropes of tobacco as presents for the natives. On Dr Smith's advice, a greatcoat was specially tailored in Cape Town as a present for Umzilikazi. The main body of the coat was of duffel, surmounted by six capes and ornamented with huge bone buttons. Its lining and trimmings were all of scarlet wool, and in front the coat was held together by a ponderous brazen clasp in the shape of a crest. This unique garment, Dr Smith assured the captain, would make a perfect gift for the King of the Matabele.

On 1 September the party was ready to set out from the farming centre of Graaf Reinet. It comprised Harris himself, Richardson, and Richardson's Parsee manservant, Nasserwanji Motabhoy. Harris's own Indian attendant, a Muslim, had refused to accompany his master from the Cape as soon as he learned that he was liable to be contaminated by association with Kaffirs and unbelievers. For their chief huntsman the expedition hired a villainous looking, one-eyed, pensioned private of the Cape Rifle Corps named Andries Afrikander. According to his high recommendations, Andries was a crack shot, had visited the Matabele country before and could act as an interpreter. As it turned out, he was both a braggart and a coward, and his company proved more of a nuisance than a help. Some idea of the travellers' future problems was swiftly gained from the discovery on the day of their departure that all six of their Hottentot servants were dead drunk. Three had pawned their new muskets to buy liquor, and all of them had to be bundled by hand into the wagons before the expedition could set out.

On its first stage Harris's party was moving through the outlying districts of Boer farm settlement. It was an area which had virtually been shot out by the Boer farmers using their heavy *roer* guns, and there were few animals to be seen except when they ran into a minor springbok migration near the district of Seven Fountains. 'Even so', Harris wrote, 'the face of the country was literally white with spring bucks, myriads of which covered the plains, affording us a welcome supply of food.' Crossing the Orange river, Harris met up with another sporting enthusiast, Captain Sutton of the 75th Foot, 'a mighty nimrod' who was on his way back from 'a successful expedition against the elephants'. Feeling greatly encouraged, Harris pushed on briskly for the missionary outpost of Kuruman, at that time run by Robert Moffat, a veteran missionary who was later to become Livingstone's father-in-law.

Kuruman really marked the limit of previous large scale hunting activities. Between the missionary post and Umzilikazi's capital at Mosega lay almost two hundred miles of virgin plains, literally seething with game. It was an area visited by an occasional party of Boer ivory hunters and shot over by bands of Griqua, armed with cheap trade guns obtained from the white settlements. But their depredations had scarcely scratched the surface of the game reserve. To Harris, armed with a modern double-barrelled rifle, it was a sportsman's Mecca. He was utterly unperturbed when Moffat warned him that Umzilikazi's Matabele were on the march against the vanguard of the Boer trekkers and had already attacked their outposts. Harris's party would be travelling across the fringes of the battle zone and could easily be mistaken for a Boer advance party and wiped out. Nor, Moffat pointed out, was there any guarantee that Umzilikazi would welcome the Englishmen at Mosega. The Matabele King could well have decided to exterminate all white intruders regardless of their origin. But Harris found such risks mere trifles. He felt that dispute over the ownership of the veld was a matter between the Matabele and the Boers. He himself was confident that Umzilikazi would recognize the neutrality of an English officer and sportsman who was only there to find the best shooting possible. Between the two sides, black and white, Harris honestly did not have a preference. He admired Moffat for his dedication and understood him as an Englishman, but Boer or Matabele were equally foreign. Sport was the only thing which mattered, and Harris did not intend to let a native war stand in his way.

His audacity soon paid off. Leaving Kuruman, Harris established camp on the Meritsane river, where he settled in for some serious hunting. The country-side was covered with waving grasses interspersed with low shrubs bearing a profusion of yellow flowers. Umbrella-shaped acacias, the favourite food of herds of giraffes, afforded a degree of shade and also gave off an aromatic and overpowering perfume. Amid this landscape, which reminded Harris of a luxuriant country park, moved an immense variety of animals. There were troops of quagga, similar in size and related to the zebra but of a pale red colour and striped only on the head and neck. Soon to be extinct, the quagga were seen in company with numbers of brindled gnu which provided the hunting party with a convenient source of meat. Riding out one morning to shoot for the pot, Harris and Richardson saw an extraordinary sight as the whole plain came alive with moving animals. Harris wrote:

> I could not estimate the accumulated numbers at less than fifteen thousand, a great extent of the country being actually chequered black and white with their congregated masses. As the panic caused by the report of our rifles extended, clouds of dust hovered over them; and the long necks of ostriches were also to be seen, towering above the heads of their less gigantic neighbours and sailing past with astonishing rapidity. Groups of purple Sassabys, and brilliant red and yellow hartebeests likewise lent their aid to complete the picture which must have been seen to have been properly understood, and which beggars all attempt at description.

At the insistence of their servants and a band of Bechuana camp followers, the two hunters galloped wildly through the fleeing herds, shooting from the saddle. As animals fell wounded, the Bechuana rushed up to dispatch them with a thrust from an assegai, and immediately began disembowelling and butchering the carcasses for meat. There was no need for marksmanship. Repeatedly firing both barrels into the packed mass of animals, the hunters would drop several animals at a time. Two bull eland were seen standing under a tree and amid excited cries of 'impoofoo! impoofoo! eland! eland!' Harris and his companion spurred off in pursuit. After a short gallop, they caught up with the fleeing eland who were so fat and sleek that they had soon become exhausted. Their skins turned first blue and then white with froth, and their pace slackened to a walk so that a single ball at close range was enough to bring them down. Later Harris learned that it was possible to save even the labour of carrying the carcass of a dead eland back into camp. Instead one could run the animal until it was jaded, and then herd it at a walk back to the wagons like an old cow to the slaughter yard.

The haul in raw meat from a single day's hunt was enormous. The Bechuana gorged themselves on flesh until they groaned with bulging stomachs, and then carried off what they could not eat immediately as bloody strips hung around their necks. Harris and his party ate only the choicer meats, preferring the eland flesh as it resembled the finest beef, marbled with streaks of fat and possessing a delicate game flavour.

By mid-October Harris reached the Matabele capital of Mosega. There he found that Umizilikazi himself was some distance to the north, prudently awaiting the return of his impi under his general Kalipi who had gone to attack the leading groups of Boer trekkers at Veg Kop. Still determined to have Umizilikazi's permission to hunt elephant on the Vaal river, of which he had heard such glowing reports, Harris boldly pressed forward. After some thirty miles he was met on the road by the King's official herald. This huge brawny warrior, who was over six feet tall and stark naked, approached the wagons roaring and charging in frantic imitation of a lion. Placing his arm before his mouth, he then swung it about rapidly like the trunk of an elephant, throwing it up above his head to trumpet shrilly. Next, he ran on tiptoe like an ostrich, and lastly fell on his face in the dust weeping like a baby. At each interval of the performance he shouted out the matchless prowess and enormous victories of his master, while the sweat poured from him and the spittle foamed on his lips.

On the 24th the expedition arrived at the kraal where Umzilikazi was staying, and tactfully fired off several salutes of musketry in his honour. The King had already been informed that the white men were bringing special presents for him; and a page, who had the widest mouth Harris had ever seen, promptly came out to inspect the wagons and their contents. This he did in absolute silence and withdrew without uttering a word. Harris sent a message after him to say that he was extremely anxious to pay his respects to the King, and a few

Praisers of Umzilikazi. Painting by Charles Davidson Bell

Cornwallis Harris's wagon at Mosega

minutes later a loud shouting and yelling announced Umzilikazi's arrival. A squad of equerries preceded the King through the crowd of onlookers, brandishing their sticks to clear a path. Next came two more heralds, crying his praises in a string of unbroken sentences and whirling their batons. Finally, to a great shout of congratulation from the crowd, the King himself appeared, dressed in a girdle of leopards' tails, with a bunch of animal sinews around his left ankle, and his three famous parakeet feathers thrust into the issigoko, the warrior's ring of twisted hair on his scalp.

Relations between the English captain of engineers and the King of the Matabele soon reached a remarkably informal level. At their first meeting Harris handed over the special scarlet-lined cloak, some brass wire, a two-foot-square mirror, and two pounds of extremely ferocious Irish Blackguard snuff to which the Matabele were very partial. More important, he added fifty pounds of blood-red beads. At the sight of these last, the King showed every sign of immense gratification, putting his thumb between his teeth, opening his eyes to their widest and exclaiming 'monante! monante! tanta! tanta! tanta! – good! good! bravo! bravo! bravo!' It later turned out that the feared warlord of the Matabele was badly henpecked by his harem of heavily built women. In Harris's opinion some of the wives were positively obese. They had enormous pendant bosoms and wore their hair in a single upright tuft decorated with feathers. Their only garment was a short leather kilt, but this and their bodies were overlaid with layer upon layer of coloured beads arranged in fanciful patterns so that some of them appeared blue, or red, or parti-coloured from head to toe. Of course their demand for these decorations was insatiable.

Interviews with Umzilikazi were expensive affairs for the visitors. On the first occasion Umzilikazi put on his cloak, admired the clasp's crest of a hand clutching a spear which Harris tactfully said was in honour of the King's illustrious victories, and climbed into a pair of tartan trousers specially sewn for him by Mrs Moffat. He was not so carried away, however, that he did not insist in drinking from Harris's cup when invited to take tea, for fear of being poisoned. Later meetings became mere raiding forays as Umzilikazi visited the wagons to carry off any odds and ends which caught his fancy. He acquired Harris's shooting boots, and the Parsee's red braces and multi-purpose pocket knife, and while scrambling about inside the wagon, succeeded in unearthing the bead chest which had unwisely been left unlocked. Plunging both arms into it, he gave a great smile of delight and would not be put off until Harris gave him the entire contents.

Such informality contrasted sharply with the rigid discipline of life in Umzilikazi's own kraal. There he was treated with a respect which bordered upon dread. He was in effect the absolute despot of his people, officially owning all the tribe's cattle and with the choice of any of its women for his own seraglio. Every day long files of women could be seen coming from the outlying kraals, singing as they walked and carrying bowls of malt beer on their heads as tribute. Sweat-soaked messengers would arrive running at top speed from the neighbouring pastures to drop suddenly on their hands and knees and crawl the last fifty yards to the King's feet. There they blurted out reports of cattle deaths and calving among the herds. If the King had no questions, the man would

Head, paws and tail of a Lioness, and the two herd boys reputed to have killed her in defence of the cattle, being presented to Umzilikazi. Painting by Charles Davidson Bell

spring to his feet, give a great yell of congratulation, and sprint back to swoop down and pick up his weapons and then race back to his post. When they passed the royal presence, all but the most important courtiers were obliged to bend over double, and maintain this obsequious posture for several paces before and after passing the King.

By the costly gift of his own tent which he erected in front of the King's hut, Harris finally managed to get permission to return to the Cape by way of the hunting grounds of the Vaal river. This was the goal for which he craved. After tactfully making a detour to call on Umzilikazi's son at his own kraal and present him with, among other things, a gross of gilt regimental buttons and a brown toby jug for his beer, Harris and his party found themselves in what he called 'a fairyland of sport'. He shot lions without having to leave his wagons, and with his pocket telescope he selected herds of elephant before sending his men to drive them past while he picked off the finest specimens. On one occasion matters got out of hand and the enraged herd stampeded right through his camp, luckily without doing any damage. He found rhino so numerous that within half a mile he counted twenty-two and complained that they became a dreadful nuisance by charging him while he was taking aim at a different target. When his white turban, which he wore wound round his hunting cap, was torn off by a branch, he looked back to see no less than three irate rhino sally forth from the bushes to attack it. On the Limpopo he shot hippo, and from the large herds of eland he now killed animals only to take their tongues for salting. He bagged a type of water buck which no white man had ever killed before, and his greatest prize – like Le Vaillant's – was a cameleopard. With almost mystic reverence he told how he rode alongside a great bull giraffe at full gallop and poured in shot after shot until, after the seventeenth bullet, the towering beast tottered and fell with 'the tears trickling from his full brilliant eye'.

His party also had a frightening encounter with Kalipi's impi which was showing scars of its fight with the Voortrekkers. Wounded warriors were carried past on shields, and others were bearing home the weapons of the dead which would be ceremonially placed before Umzilikazi. The Matabele were in ugly mood, and, seeing the white party, mistook them for Boer sympathizers. Swarming round the travellers, they called on them to halt and with every sign of hostility began to plunder the wagons. The position looked so grim that Harris's Hottentot driver actually fainted with terror and it was not until Andries Afrikander was actually seized by a Matabele soldier that he managed to blurt out that Harris had been a guest of Umzilikazi. The mere mention of the King's name took instant effect. The Matabele immediately became respectful, clambered down from the wagons, and began to beg rather than demand presents. The narrowness of their escape was brought home to the

Harris in hot pursuit of giraffe

travellers some time later when they stumbled across the site of an old battle ground where Umzilikazi's troops had wiped out a raiding force of a thousand mounted Griquas. Taking advantage of the fact that Umzilikazi's regular army was occupied in the north, the Griquas had ridden across the Matabele border and lifted cattle. They were making their way home when a scratch force of Matabele levies, not their full warriors but trainee youths hastily summoned for the emergency, had struck their camp. Scarcely a Griqua had survived, and the base of the hill where they died was thickly strewn with the whitened bones of men and horses, broken guns and tattered relics.

In the new year the growing scarcity of game animals along their path indicated to Harris that he and his party were once more approaching the fringes of white settlement. By that time their wagons were already so full of trophies that they were having to leave behind the tusks of the last elephants they killed. In his personal collection Harris now had two complete skulls of every game quadruped to be found in South Africa and a huge portfolio of drawings of animals and peoples, including a portrait of Umzilikazi himself. For the last third of his journey his cot had been reserved for the skeleton and skin of the hitherto unknown Sable antelope, which was to be named in his honour. He declared himself perfectly satisfied. The entire venture had cost £800, and there had not been a single day when he had not been able to go out of camp at dawn, weather permitting, and spend the entire time until dusk in his favourite hobby of hunting. 'I can safely aver', he announced, 'that some of the happiest days of my existence have been passed in the wilds of Africa. They form a passage in my life which time can never erase from the tablet of my recollection – a green spot in memory's waste, to which, in after years I shall revert with intense and unabating pleasure.'

Harris's enthusiasm was to be taken up by an increasing number of sportsmen. Many of them had read the captain's book of his adventures, which was printed up for him by the American Mission Press in Bombay and intended 'for the perusal of some of my brother officers in India.' They saw an added attraction in the fact that Harris had made a profit from the sales of his book and of his African portfolio. An expedition after African big game, it now seemed, could be made a paying proposition, and more and more sportsmen travelled through the Boer settlements and crossed the frontier into unknown native lands to try their luck with rifle, gun, and note book. In so doing, they made a special contribution to African exploration by filling in the gaps between the routes of the major explorers. It was a vital role, for it brought them into contact with unknown native tribes as well as revealing the land much more thoroughly than the isolated traverses of the earlier explorers. Sometimes too, the hunter-travellers found themselves well ahead of the line of exploration, being the first to penetrate into Mashonaland and many parts of the Kalahari. Equally, they were of inestimable help to the more famous explorers, lending them both support and materials. Livingstone owed the success of his first trip to the assistance of William Cotton Oswell, a well-to-do Indian civil servant who was known as 'the Nimrod of Africa'. With a friend, Oswell not only paid for all the expenses of Livingstone's trip, but accompanied it as campmaster and hunter to look after the wagons and the feeding of the expedition. This left Livingstone free to attend to his survey programme, his note taking, and his anthropological and geological work. Oswell was something of a *beau idéal* of a Victorian traveller, having been educated at Rugby under Arnold and passing out first in his year from the East India College at Haileybury. He was to remain one of Livingstone's few close friends – the missionary named a son in his honour – and helped to bring Livingstone's work to the attention of powerful supporters in England, while remaining very much in the background himself.

By complete contrast was an old Etonian, Roualeyn Gordon Cumming, who also passed through Livingstone's missionary station several times. Livingstone called him 'a mad sort of Scotchman' and there was much truth in the adjective. Second son of a Scots aristocrat, Cumming had tried all sorts of adventuring before he finally became a South African hunter. He served a spell in the Madras Cavalry; joined the Royal Veteran Newfoundland Companies as an Ensign but found it too tame; and in 1843 transferred to the Cape Mounted

Rifles. A year later he resigned his commission and taking out his two cavalry chargers as shooting horses, announced his intention of travelling beyond the frontier to shoot game. He then set out with 4 Cape wagons; 3 hundredweight of lead for making bullets and 50 pounds of pewter to add to the mixture when preparing for thick skinned animals; 2,000 gun flints and 50,000 percussion caps made up his armoury, and he had a cockney ex-cab driver for a servant.

Cumming's trail into the heart of South Africa was so ferocious as to make Captain Harris's efforts seem gentle by comparison. He was so keen to get started that he went out shooting by moonlight and killed a Boer's string of saddle horses in mistake for quagga. While Harris had killed for food or for trophies, Cumming shot for a sensual enjoyment which verged on the lunatic. According to Murray, the contemporary travel writer:

> The whole country figures in his narrative like an immense zoological garden, with all the dens broken up and all the menagerie set free. Springboks, gemsboks, blesboks, wildebeests, oryxes, gnus, buffaloes, antelopes, giraffes, rhinoceroses, lions and elephants, to say nothing of smaller gentler creatures . . . Mr. Cumming ran riot among them all as freely as they ran riot among one another. He gave chase to everything which could rouse his blood or put him in peril. He fought many a duel with the biggest monsters of the forest. He became as familiar with lions as ordinary British sportsmen are with moor fowl; and often ran after elephants as dauntlessly as ploughboys run after hares; and generally 'imbibed' the terrific gigantic 'game' quite as numerously as they had been partridges or trout. His perils, of course, were constant and awful; many of his escapes were hair's-breadth and wonderful; and while all proved to him to be one of the bravest of mortals and as mighty a hunter as Nimrod, some excite sickening horror, and provoke sharp questionings as to the moral character of such *sport*.

'A Waltz with a hippopotamus'. Determined to save his trophy, Gordon Cumming 'a mad sort of Scotchman', plunged in after a wounded hippo, cut handholds in its hide with his hunting knife, and steered the beast ashore

Murray had good reason to question Cumming's behaviour in the field. The Scots hunter lived more like a savage than many of the natives he described as uncouth. His normal attire was to go bare armed and bare legged while wearing only a shirt, and either a kilt or a pair of leather breeches. His shoes were made of various bits of animal skin: the soles of buffalo or giraffe; the front of kudu or hartebeest; the back was taken from the hide of a lion, a hyena, or Sable antelope; while the thread consisted of a thin strip off the skin of a stienbock. Dangling all over him by 'rheimpys' or thongs of leather, were his hunting accoutrements, as many as possible – such as powder-horn and hammer – being manufactured from animal horns and hoofs. Even his fishing bag, which he had bought from the family estates at Altyre, was still filthy inside with fish scales and blood-stained grouse feathers, much to his pride. His behaviour matched his dress for eccentricity. He was the least squeamish of any African explorer. Hungry, he milked straight into his mouth the warm breast of an antelope he had just shot. Cold, he skinned a dead animal and used the pelt as a blanket and the carcass as his pillow. When excited by the chase, he spoke rapturously of the smell of trees and grass exuding from a dead antelope, and of the 'perfume' when riding among frightened giraffe, which reminded him of the smell of a hive of heather honey in September. From experience, he could differentiate between the various screams and moans of the larger species of African game as they died; and not surprisingly, he confessed to having terrible nightmares in which he was attacked by legions of wild beasts.

Yet for all his brutality Cumming was not only an explorer in his own right, but probably did as much as anyone to attract English gentry to African exploration. Riding with his Hottentot hunters, he penetrated new territory for almost three hundred miles beyond Kolobeng, examined the Limpopo valley in detail, and was the first to enter the country of Bamangwato. Like Harris, he also showed that African adventuring could pay for itself. With ivory fetching up to £40 a hundredweight and a good pair of tusks weighing perhaps 300 pounds, he made as much as £1,000 on each trip, returning five times in five years of hunting to the frontier towns in order to dispose of his wagon-loads of booty. In exchange he picked up cases of cheap muskets and sold them for tusks at three thousand per cent profit to the natives. The income paid all and more of his ferocious expenditure in ammunition and equipment, which used up a string of 45 horses dead of tsetse and murrain, 70 draught cattle, and 70 hunting dogs, variously gored, trampled, clawed, or bitten to death by his quarry.

But most of all, Cumming published the excitement and thrill of Africa. When he came home in 1848, he shipped with him his Bushman after-rider, and almost thirty tons of souvenirs including his Cape wagon, native bric-a-brac,

Cumming beset by wild dogs while shooting at night from a 'grave' by a waterhole

and a superb collection of skins and stuffed animals' heads hermetically sealed in tins. Much of it went on display in the Great Exhibition of 1851. When his book of adventures was published, he was lionized in London and the provinces, and made a large amount of money by giving lectures on Africa. He was quoted everywhere as an authority on Africa, and generally known as the 'Lion Hunter'. Eventually Cumming proceeded in a blaze of publicity to Scotland where, at Fort Augustus, he set up a permanent exhibition of his African collection. There the curious, including the Nile explorer John Hanning Speke, could inspect for themselves the marvellous fauna of Africa.*

Inevitably the effect of men like Cumming and his imitators on African wild life was catastrophic. At the apex of the pyramid the finest game animals all fell to the traveller-hunters, who formed an unbroken line of succession from Cornwallis Harris to such great names of big game shooting as Baker, Selous, Millais and President Roosevelt. At the base of the pyramid, the destruction of the wild life was even more depressing. Among the grazing animals the natives of the area, armed with weapons provided for them by hunters and traders, wreaked fearful execution. In a temporary burst of success, they slaughtered thousands of the less spectacular animals to feast themselves and their families. The symbiotic relationship between man and African wildlife, unstable at the best of times, was broken, and for a zoologist at least, the land never recovered.

* Cumming died of drink in 1866 after, according to his memorialist: 'a Scotch premonition of death, for he ordered his coffin and made his will just before he died.'

Victorian Lions

CHAPTER EIGHT

On the day the Light Brigade charged the Russian batteries near Balaklava, the six greatest heroes of Victorian exploration in Africa could be found spread across half the globe. Richard Burton and John Hanning Speke, soon to go looking for the sources of the Nile, were both in Aden preparing for their first trip together. It was to be an excursion into Somaliland, and Burton was already wandering about the town dressed up in Arab clothes and indulging his hobby of investigating bizarre native sexual habits. James Augustus Grant, Speke's later and more sober-sided companion, was out in India with the Bengal native infantry and in his spare time painting in water colours and going on shikari. Another sportsman-cum-explorer, the wealthy Samuel Baker, was tramping about Ceylon, thinning the elephant population of the island. While at the other end of the social scale a thirteen-year-old illegitimate waif, later Sir Henry Morton Stanley, was shut up in St Asaph Union Workhouse in North Wales. There Stanley was suffering appalling miseries from a crippled brute of a work-master who later went insane. Only David Livingstone was actually in Africa. He read of the Charge of the Light Brigade, 'the terrible affair of the Light Cavalry' as he called it, in a copy of *The Times* sent up to him at the last Portuguese outpost in Loanda before he plunged back into the interior and was lost from view.

On that same day only two of these six Victorian lions of Africa had anything of a reputation. Livingstone was beginning to be known in well-informed circles as the man to whom the Royal Geographical Society had awarded a prize of twenty-five guineas (Silver Chronometer) for finding a shallow lake on the north side of the Kalahari Desert. His dramatic appearance at Loanda, emerging from the mysterious hinterland, would soon elevate him to the Society's gold medal and make his name a household word. The *enfant terrible* Richard Burton, by contrast, boasted a certain notoriety. Senior officials of the East India Company's army still smouldered over his scathing exposé of life in the brothels of Karachi, while a more lenient public was looking forward to his new book of how, disguised as a Pathan, he had penetrated to the forbidden cities of Mecca and Medina and made drawings of the Kaba'a, the sacred stone of Islam. But apart from these glimmerings of fame there was

David Livingstone.
Portrait by General Charles Need

little indication of the heights to which the six explorers would quickly rise. At the same time that the Light Brigade's blunder was being transmuted into a deed of heroism, a similar paen of Victorian congratulation would be lavished on her explorers. In a sense England was ready for her explorer-heroes. Confident and expansionist, she needed a handful of outstanding geographical adventurers on which to hang her laurels and identify her achievements. British gentlemen were travelling to the ends of the earth, in the Polar wastes, in the mountains of Tibet, and in the Australian desert. But these were, in the main, sparsely inhabited places. They lacked the colour and glamour which Africa and her tribal peoples could provide. So it was hardly surprising that it was Africa which, above all, caught the public's imagination and the African explorers who won the greatest acclaim. Between them the six great Victorian lions carried off three knighthoods, numerous lesser decorations, and every geographical honour on offer.

All this was made possible, in the words of the citation for Baker's knighthood, by 'laborious research in Africa'. Excepting Burton, who was a brilliant orientalist in his own right, there was no reason why Speke and Grant should not have remained obscure career officers in the army, Stanley a minor newspaperman, and Baker a dilettante big game shot. Equally, David Livingstone might well have spent his entire life as an unknown missionary labouring among the Chinese millions, as was his original intention.

That part of Africa which gave the Victorian lions their chance was, roughly speaking, the middle third, the great tropical belt lying between the deserts in the north and the white settlements in the south. By good fortune it also offered some of the most spectacular country in Africa – immense river basins clothed in dense jungle; plateaux overlooked by mountains and inhabited by exotic peoples; great valleys cradling magnificent lakes. It was the last and most tempting slice of the continent yet to be explored, and it lay very vulnerable and enticing. On every side were ideal launch-points – Zanzibar on the

View of Gondokoro

east coast where the British maintained an anti-slavery squadron and a consul; the Portuguese outposts at Loanda and the lower Zambesi; and Gondokoro, an Arab trading station on the upper Nile. It was possible, if one had the inclination and the right contacts, to go by Arab river-boat to Gondokoro, stay there with the Austrian missionaries or with a certain Circassian ivory hunter who lived in some style with cases of sparkling wines brought specially up river, and then set out to follow the Nile to its unknown source. No one had yet done so, and looking at the blank spaces on the map, it seemed as if Africa had saved her most coveted prizes to the last. Both the Nile and Congo obviously rose in this region, and there were additional rumours of the Mountains of the Moon, of lakes known to the Romans, of pygmy people, underground tunnels and rich mineral deposits. Darkest Africa, as the blank space was promptly called, was a very obvious target for Victorian energy.

Of course there was never any doubt in the Victorian mind that darkest

Africa would be successfully illuminated. A formidable range of equipment was now available for the traveller, and he was expected to use it to advantage. Indeed Africa was regarded as an excellent place to test some of the more practical inventions like tarpaulin, mackintosh and tins. Livingstone was to use an inflatable rubber boat, and Burton one of corrugated iron. Speke took out a special photographic developer formulated for him by an East India Company chemist, and Grant made stereoscopic pictures with his new-fangled camera. Expeditions were expected to be technological exercises, examples of scientific and inventive superiority. In weaponry alone the visitors had made immense gains. The percussion cap had replaced the flint, and even the peaceable David Livingstone brandished an enormous six-barrelled Colt revolver under the noses of hostile chiefs, and wrote home asking to be sent the recently developed explosive rifle bullet cased in gutta-percha. Designed for the whale fishery, Livingstone intended to use it against elephant. Burton was himself the inventor of a carbine pistol, and sporting Samuel Baker was perhaps the leading authority of his day on the design and use of firearms. While still in his teens, he had made drawings for his own masterpiece, which later evolved into a massive weapon nicknamed 'the Baby'. This fired a half-pound exploding shell with twelve drachms of powder. Baker was constantly experimenting with different mixtures of zinc, lead and tin for his bullets; and he held strong views on the right weapons for the hunter-traveller. 'The size and weight of guns', ran his dictum, 'must depend as much on the strength and build of a man, as a ship's armament does upon her tonnage.' Fortunately in his own case he was built to heavy metal standards, and his battery consisted of four matching guns with platinum sights by Beattie of Regent Street. Using a heavy steel-tipped conical ball he reckoned he could knock down six to eight men in a row with a single well-placed shot.

Well armed, the explorers were as well fitted out. The list of equipment which Grant published in the appendix to his book indicated what an experienced two-man expedition took with it. Most of the kit was supplied by Grindlay's and included 2 iron beds weighing 28 pounds each, serge sheets and hairpillows, 2 tents, 4 packs of playing cards, 4 pairs of glass and wire eye preservers, 2 green veils, and a couple of pounds of mustard and cress seeds. This was in addition to the more humdrum paraphernalia of guns, cooking equipment, tarpaulins, and so forth. By the end of the trip all that was left to him and Speke were the clothes they stood up in, a rifle each, and a handful of bullets. Yet without a trace of humour Grant assured anyone who cared to follow in his footsteps that the iron beds had been excellent value; Crimean blankets, sheets and waterproofs were essential; and that everything had best be packed in japanned trunks because they stood up to wear and tear better than wood or leather. It was hardly surprising that when expeditions came to repeat the same routes they found themselves following a trail of litter from boots to bed frames which had been discarded by their predecessors. As early as Grant's day there was a native rumour that spare white men were carried in the square tin boxes on their porters' heads. Like their portable beds, these white visitors were supposed to be reassembled in sections at their camp sites.

Naturally this quantity of equipment needed a matching commissariat to transport it, and few expeditions could have started without the help of the Royal Navy. Time and again naval units were dispatched to drop off explorers and their baggage, or stood by for weeks watching over desolate river mouths in hopes of retrieving the adventurers. Naval cutters ran ashore on inhospitable coasts to off-load reinforcements or pick up mails, and naval lives were sometimes lost in the process. In 1856 the commander, lieutenant and five men of a brigantine were drowned on the bar of the Zambesi while trying to get through to Livingstone. It was all seen as part of the technological exercise, and it was fortunate that while Victoria's navy commanded the oceans darkest Africa lay with her two flanks exposed to the sea.

On shore, of course, the explorer had to rely on native man-power to shift his baggage tail. So there was the hiring and organizing of porters, guards, cooks, gunbearers, valets, guides, and canoemen. Stanley was undoubtedly the best at it, wielding huge marching columns over three-quarters of a mile long and composed of up to a thousand men. Livingstone proved a poor hand, depending instead on the loyalty of a few trusted servants and keeping his gear to a minimum. The military contingent – Speke, Grant, Burton – were unexpectedly clumsy. Grant had so little rapport with his men that when he was sick he could not stop them from carrying his litter head foremost so that all he saw was a rear view of the explored country unrolling behind him.

Inevitably a semi-professional corps of expedition porters soon evolved, particularly at the favourite base of Zanzibar. When Stanley set out from there for the Congo, he found he had men in his party who had travelled previously with Livingstone, Speke, Burton, and Grant. Speke's own veterans had been issued with their photographs at the end of their trek so that they could be more readily identified on future occasions. One Zanzibari, Sidi Bombay, accompanied so many white expeditions that he became something of an explorer in his own right and could demand, as he did, to be paid in advance. Burton, who gave praise grudgingly, agreed that Bombay was the gem of his party and remarkably lively at the end of the hardest day's march. Grant put Bombay in charge of the stores depot and relied on his ability as a forager to turn up a brace of chickens in the most desolate spot; and Speke sent him huge distances by himself, using him as a messenger and a scout. By the time Bombay died in 1886 aged sixty-two or sixty-three, he had seen as much of Africa as any of his employers.

Hoisting the foremost section of the steam launch Ma Robert from on board the Pearl. — West Luabo River, a.m. 16 May 1858.
G. Baines

Livingstone (foreground) supervises the hoisting of the foremost section of the steam launch *Ma Robert* from his supply ship *Pearl* at the mouth of the Zambesi — a.m. 16 May 1858. Pencil drawing by Thomas Baines

Medicines and the skill to use them were the weakest feature of any explorer's equipment. Not until his last trip did Livingstone take the precaution of boiling his drinking water, and instead he placed much faith in his ferocious 'Rouser Tabloids' composed of jalap, rhubarb, calomel, and quinine in equal parts. Both he and Stanley so overdosed themselves with quinine that their ears buzzed and they sometimes fell unconscious. Speke's medicine chest, though it weighed thirty pounds, was so useless that he could not shake off a bad cough, went delirious, and temporarily lost the use of an arm. His companion Grant was crippled by a poisoned leg which swelled up despite all efforts at poultices and gunpowder treatment. Both men, as a matter of course, suffered from fevers and eye inflammations of the type which nearly blinded Speke from seeing Lake Tanganyika.

Almost in desperation explorers turned to native nostrums. They potioned and plastered themselves with every medicine short of fetish charms, and seldom noticed any improvement. Only Livingstone experimented on a scientific basis. He intended for example to test Bechuana arrow poison as a cure for rheumatism. The catalogue of fevers, paralysis, blindness, sunstroke, and weight-loss was endless. Malaria was known simply as 'African fever'. Burton thought it was something to do with sleeping in the moonlight, and Stanley associated it with ozone in the air. Livingstone wrote:

> Very curious are the effects of African fever on certain minds. Cheerfulness vanishes, and the whole mind is overcast with black clouds of gloom. The countenance is grave, the eyes suffused, and the few utterances made in the piping voice of a wailing infant. At such times a man feels like a fool, if he does not act like one. He is peevish, prone to find fault and contradict and think himself insulted; he is in fact a man unfit for society.

Diarrhoea brought on piles, and marching caused ulcers. Whatever afflicted the white man, afflicted his porters even worse. On the Speke expedition Bombay vomited up a tape worm six to nine inches long, and the day's march of an expedition usually began with a sick parade which turned up anything from gangrene to cholera.

Yet it was noticeable how rarely an explorer was injured in a normal accident. There were the occasional sprains and bruises. Livingstone broke a finger, and Stanley was laid up with a strained leg after he fell off some rocks. But on the whole the explorers were remarkably accident-free. Mishaps tended to be as exotic as Livingstone's famous mauling by a lion. The beast seized him as a

'The missionary's escape from the lion'. Livingstone's arm was broken in the attack

cat picks up a mouse, and its jaws broke his upper left arm. Afterwards he could never raise the arm above the horizontal and suffered from a false joint in the humerus if he put too much strain on it. He owed his life, he thought, to the prompt action of his native attendant who distracted the lion's attention, and to the fact that he was wearing a tartan jacket which wiped the virus from the lion's teeth before they pierced his flesh. After his death, his corpse was identified by his father-in-law from the distinctive fracture in the bone. Speke, by contrast, was badly stabbed in a Somali spear attack, but he healed so quickly that, in Burton's phrase, 'the wounds closed up like pricks in a rubber ball made with a sharp knife.'

David Livingstone, of course, was the example to dominate his successors. Among the African heroes he was a giant among giants, as much to his contemporaries in Africa as to the public at home. His expeditions became the gauge by which all later journeys were planned, judged, and criticized, even though the comparison was not always fair. It was often overlooked that Livingstone's second trip, a large-scale expedition to the lower Zambesi, was a failure which had to be cut short by the home government. Livingstone set out with six assistants, including his brother Charles, a small river steamer, and £5,000 worth of equipment. By the time he came home, he had alienated all but his brother; the steamship was a wreck; and Livingstone's wife, who had gone out to help him, was in a fever grave, as were other missionary reinforcements.

In point of fact Livingstone was a virtuoso solo traveller, the prime exponent of the small overland party rather than a captain of complex expeditions. Nowhere was this more evident than on the great trans-African journey of 1853–6 when he delighted his admirers by crossing Africa from side to side with only a few natives to help him and a minimum of equipment, though he did take along a magic lantern for slide shows in chiefs' huts. 'The art of successful travels,' he wrote afterwards, 'consisted in taking as few "impedimenta" as possible, and not forgetting to carry my wits about me, the outfit was rather spare . . . ' A good part of the journey was performed on the back of his ox, Sinbad, of whom Livingstone wrote:

> He had a softer back than the others, but a much more intractable temper. His horns were bent downwards and hung loosely so he could do no harm with them; but as he went slowly along the narrow paths he would suddenly dart aside. A string tied to a stick put through the cartilage of his nose serves as a bridle. But if you jerk this back it makes him go faster, if you pull it to one side he allows his nose and head to go, but keeps the other eye on the forbidden spot and goes in spite of you. The only way in which he can be brought to a stand is by a stroke of a wand across the nose. Once when he ran in below a climber stretched across the path, so low that I could not stoop under it, I was dragged off and came down on the crown of my head. He never allowed a chance of this sort to pass without trying to inflict a kick, as if I neither had nor deserved his love.

In the best missionary tradition, Livingstone was the all-round practitioner. He was doctor, mechanic, gunsmith, engineer, architect and farrier rolled into one. He possessed, too, an extraordinary patience which gave him that rare quality of the lone traveller who could undertake a team endeavour. His style was to travel slowly, make friends with the tribes, and burrow forward by sheer persistence. This combination of dedication and versatility partially explained the charisma he had for the public at home. It was felt that Livingstone was the perfect ambassador of civilization, the man bringing the gospel to the chiefs by the force of his character, and the benefits of outside contact by his example. His claim that legitimate trade followed the explorer and ousted slavery was a righteous motive, and his public image of the self-effacing martyr rubbed up a glow of public satisfaction. The public spoke warmly of a man who had been away so long helping the Africans that when he came home he failed to recognize his own son.

But in making him so stalwart, his admirers made Livingstone dull. They weighed him down with high motives and leaden piety. It was an image which Livingstone himself despised, the vision as he put it of 'the dumpy sort of man with a bible under his arm'. In fact he was rarely meek, and at times could be violently self-opinionated and cantankerous. He was so stubborn that he nearly failed his medical examination by quarrelling endlessly with his examiners over the uses of the stethoscope. Livingstone's portraits – dour, forceful, and more than a little pugnacious – reinforced the impression of his career. Vindictive in his grudges, he was quick to condemn a man on scanty evidence, and for someone so patient with Africans he was remarkably testy with Europeans. He castigated the builder of his unsatisfactory Zambesi steamer as a rogue and fool, and he accused Thomas Baines, artist with the Zambesi expedition, of misappropriating expedition stores. With utter lack of tact he ordered two junior colleagues to search Baines's boxes, and though they found nothing incriminating during this unpleasant task, Livingstone nevertheless drove Baines from the expedition. In short, Livingstone was a bad man to cross, and a worse one to get on with; and as a hero he was easiest at long range.

A similar misconception was the public's idea that Livingstone epitomized the church's missionary effort in Africa. In fact he was a very unusual missionary, and early in his career lost the sponsorship of the London Missionary Society which had first sent him to Africa but could no longer reconcile his activities as an explorer with his duties as a missionary. The Society thought in terms of a slow advance into the interior, saving souls rather than mapping geography. Their ideal missionary was a man like Livingstone's father-in-law, Robert Moffat, who ran the Mission Station at Kuruman for half his life and laboured over the translation of the bible into Sechuana. On the other hand Livingstone resented being ordered about by the directors of the London

Missionary Society, and early in his African career was denounced by his fellow missionaries as over-ambitious. They failed to realize that Livingstone was a genuine wanderer. He loved to travel, and revelled in the idea of any new journey. He once wrote:

> The mere emotional pleasure of travelling in a wild unexplored country is very great. When on lands of a couple of thousand feet elevation, brisk exercise imparts elasticity to the muscles, fresh and healthy blood circulates through the brain, the mind works well, the eye is clear, the step is firm, and the day's exertion makes the evening's repose thoroughly enjoyable.

These words were written at the outset of his last and most famous journey which brought out all his personal strengths and weaknesses very clearly. The venture, which began on his fifty-third birthday, 19 March 1866, was a modest affair, financed partly by the government and partly by private donation. One of Livingstone's traits was his sure touch with men in authority, an ability which contrasted strangely with his coolness towards his more immediate circle. Thus he had been able to raise sufficient funds and official backing for his trip, including a firman from the Sultan of Zanzibar. But by common agreement he set out without a single white assistant. Instead he took along forty-seven Negro porters and a squad of marine sepoys under their havildar. Within six months he had proved once again his inability as a commander and, by comparison, his extraordinary magnetism. The sepoys had been led in such vacillating fashion that they became insolent and lazy, all discipline had ebbed and Livingstone had been forced to give the worst offender several smart cuts with his cane before he sent the entire detachment back to the coast. As for the porters, only eleven of them remained after all the others had deserted or asked to be discharged. Yet of these eleven, Susi and Chuma would stick with him throughout the frightful difficulties of the next seven years and be with him at the end. It was a brand of loyalty which no other African traveller could evoke.

As always, Livingstone kept up his correspondence on this last trip while he was wandering in a complicated path around the lakes of southern Tanganyika territory, attempting to define their limits. He was a letter-writer by nature, a correspondent of prodigious energy whose circle ranged from the President of the Royal Geographical Society to James 'Paraffin' Young, a philanthropist whose fortune rested on an invention of petroleum purification. Even Queen Victoria, it was said, asked to be kept informed of Livingstone's dispatches, and Prince Albert took a close interest in his movements. On every possible occasion Livingstone would sit down to write, cajoling, amusing, occasionally pompous, seldom giving a mere report of his progress. When he ran out of paper, he used the backs of proof sheets or other surplus scraps he could salvage. When he finished his ink, he substituted a concoction squeezed from berry juice which hagiographers quickly claimed was his own blood. An intricate system of runners and letter-carriers took his letters down to the coast and forwarded them to Zanzibar, where the steamers carried them to places as far apart as England and Bombay. In the end it was the long silence without any letters from Livingstone which led outsiders to fear he was dead, and Bennett of the *New York Herald* to send Stanley to find him. As it turned out, Livingstone had been writing his letters all along, but they had failed to reach the coast. He was not 'lost' so much as silent.

Pettiness, technical competence, and his characteristic persistence were equally well represented on the last journey. He accused Kirk, consul at Zanzibar, of mismanaging the arrangements for supplies; he made brilliantly detailed observations of the drainage areas around Lake Mweru; and he spent, in total, over seven years on the endeavour. But it was impossible to ignore the fact that he carried out his programme only with the help of Arab merchants, many of whom were connected with the slave trade. He was escorted by them, protected, and sometimes succoured by them. It was an obvious contradiction of his entire mission, and not until he witnessed a terrible massacre at Nyangwe, a town on the Lualaba river and his farthest west on the trip, did he resolve to sever his connection with the traders. Even then, it was impossible. Destitute, he depended upon Arab help until Stanley brought him badly needed supplies.

The story of Stanley's arrival at Ujiji, the incidents of their four months together, and Livingstone's last march into the morass of Lake Bangweolo, all became part of the Victorian legend of Africa. The image was of the ageing missionary in his faded naval cap with its band of gold braid, walking, riding, and finally being carried into the swampy wastelands. Stanley had already

Livingstone on his last foray in the swamps near Lake Bangweolo

given the world a microscopic description of the explorer's ill-health – his emaciation, the stooped shoulders and exhausted tread, a mouth full of gaps and broken teeth after years of inadequate foods and the usual scourge of fever reinforced by recurrent pneumonia. But it was not until later that it came out that Livingstone had been cruelly unlucky. His own sketch maps of the lake area were wrong. His original observations to the south of Lake Mweru had been dislocated by a damaged chronometer. His chance to rectify the error was lost through a fault in the reflector of his sextant. For the first time on the expedition Livingstone was, in effect, lost. For days he wandered in the swamplands, his journey making a futile circle while he steadily weakened. Still he kept up his letters: to James Young dwelling gloomily on the possibility of death; to a missionary colleague asking him to speak to a dentist about the speedy fitting of false teeth, and to arrange rooms near Regent's Park. By the end of April it was clear that he was dying. The servants had to help his every movement, even holding his watch while he wearily turned the key. Finally, at 4 am on 30 April, they found him dead, kneeling by the bedside as if in prayer.

The circumstances and aftermath of Livingstone's death only added to the momentum of his fame. There was a macabre splendour to the way in which his attendants cut out his heart and buried it in Africa. His mummified body was then carried to the coast, cocooned in bark and sailcloth and slung, like a big game trophy, on a pole between bearers. From there it went by P. & O. liner to Southampton. On 18 April, almost a year after his death, Livingstone's desiccated remains were buried in Westminster Abbey after a funeral service that bordered on the imperial.

Left Jacob Wainwright accompanies Livingstone's coffin on its journey to England for burial.
Right Stanley, far left, is one of the pall bearers at the funeral in Westminster Abbey

It was fitting that Stanley had the place of honour – first on the right – among the pall bearers. Stanley, for all his brashness, was one of Livingstone's most ardent disciples. He revered the older man and, though he had known him only four months at Ujiji, fondly imagined a father-son relationship. It was an affection typical of Stanley's impetuous pace through life. He picked up Livingstone's unfinished African programme and, despite the sneers of detractors, pushed it through to a rapid conclusion. He was blamed for causing African deaths, for rushing through the countryside like a whirlwind, and for glory seeking. But in the final analysis he did exactly what Livingstone had wanted; he opened up the interior on a scale which had scarcely been dreamed of. He managed this huge programme because, in the Victorian mould, he knew how to wield the technical advantages of his day. He, alone among the Victorian lions, was a big-expedition man.

His great Congo expedition, which left Zanzibar on 12 November 1874, less than seven months after Livingstone's funeral, numbered 224 assorted porters, askaris, gunbearers, and camp followers. It was being paid for by *The Daily Telegraph* and by Gordon Bennett, Stanley's former patron from the *New York Herald*, and so struck out under the resounding title of 'The Anglo-American Expedition for the Discovery of the Nile and Congo Sources'. Its intention was equally massive, being 'to solve if possible the remaining problems of the geography of Central Africa, and to investigate and report upon the haunts of the slave traders.' To do this, Stanley took along 3 white assistants, 5 dogs, and a portable boat. His choice was a typical mixture of sense and sentiment. The boat, which he designed himself, was 40 feet long, 6 feet wide, and 30 inches deep. Built of cedar wood by a Thames boat builder, it came apart into five sections, each intended to be carried between four strong porters. At the last minute the sections proved too heavy and modifications had to be made; nevertheless the *Lady Alice*, as his vessel was christened, was a brilliant success. Riverworthy and stable, she circumnavigated two major African lakes and sailed nearly the whole length of the Congo, including several hair-raising passages of cataracts. Packed with Snider-wielding marksmen, she was as formidable among African canoes as an ironclad among wooden frigates.

Stanley's three European assistants were a less logical choice. Two brothers, Frank and Edward Pocock were somewhat reminiscent of the Lander brothers in West Africa (Edward Pocock, like Richard Lander, was an amateur bugle player). They were taken along because their father had been recommended to Stanley by Edwin Arnold of *The Daily Telegraph* on the slight grounds that he had once looked after Arnold's private yacht. At least the Pococks were experienced in boat handling, whereas the third member of the team was a complete greenhorn. He was Frederick Barker, a clerk at the Langham Hotel until Stanley abruptly hired him. Both Barker and Edward Pocock were to die early on the trip, as did the dogs. Two mastiffs had been sent as presents to Stanley just before he left for Africa but to obtain the other three animals he had to make a special trip to Battersea Dogs' Home.*

Stanley's handling of his unwieldy African column was masterly. He lined up all the porters and graded them by size and age. The tallest and strongest men carried the heavy cloth bales; shorter men had sacks of beads. The older and steadier walkers were given the fragile loads such as photographic equipment, boiling thermometers, and chronometers wrapped in balls of cotton wool. The valuable coils of wire, used to pay *honga*, the native chiefs' transit tax, were slung on the shoulders of armed askaris. Edward Pocock taught the column, which extended over half a mile in length, to obey the call of his bugle, and Stanley vaccinated every man who had not had smallpox.

A thrusting brusqueness characterized Stanley's progress. On Lake Victoria the *Lady Alice* was nearly lost when a hoard of angry Bumbireh seized her and dragged her bodily up the beach with Stanley still sitting in the sternsheets uselessly waving a brace of revolvers. He and his crew got the boat away while the Bumbireh were deciding whether to ransom or kill them, but in Stanley's opinion such 'insolence' could not go unpunished. He came back with a flotilla of Waganda and Wangwana canoes, and, putting a rifleman in each boat, advanced in line abreast to within fifty yards of the Bumbireh landing place where an armed mob rushed to meet him. Then he gave them a broadside 'with tolerable good effect'.

Stanley's harsh methods aroused a storm of criticism at home. The Society for the Protection of Aborigines, churchmen and philanthropists all condemned his tactics. A faction within the Royal Geographical Society tried to have him publicly censured, and the consul at Zanzibar was instructed to hold a secret enquiry into the affair. But Stanley was quite unrepentant. Indeed his own rather Wild West descriptions (he had once been a reporter on the American frontier) of native battles gave his critics their own sort of ammunition. Stanley always maintained that the traveller had 'the privilege of self-defence', and it is true that he never opened fire on peaceful peoples. The difference between him and Livingstone was that Stanley had neither the time nor inclination to soothe a hostile mob. Where Livingstone trod cautiously and spoke gently until the spears were lowered, Stanley took no risks. In a threatening reception he levelled his guns, asked for safe conduct, and if denied, pulled the trigger. Livingstone had been known to fire on natives waiting in ambush but Stanley made a habit of it. Unfortunately it was not always clear whether

---

* The idea of taking a dog on East African exploration was not new. On his last journey Livingstone started out with a poodle which later drowned at a river ford.

Stanley and his retinue in Africa

the natives were capering from real animosity or just bravado. Even Richard
Burton, who had a sardonic view of the Africans, referred to 'Stanley, who still
shoots Negroes as if they were monkeys. That young man will be getting into
a row – and serve him right.'

In fairness to Stanley, though, it should be said that Central Africa was in
far greater turmoil than in Livingstone's day. Guns and commercial slavery had
arrived; and the white man was no longer protected by his novelty or good
intentions. The old fabric of kingships and tribes was in ruins. Even Mtesa,
Kabaka of Buganda and generally considered the most powerful sovereign in
the area, was caught up in a full-scale war against the rebel Wavuma tribesmen
of Lake Victoria. Considering how widespread was the bloodshed and treachery, it was extraordinary that Stanley's column, with its valuable guns and
trade goods was not annihilated. Straggling porters seldom re-appeared, and
their corpses were found stabbed and mutilated at the side of the trail. When
the expedition approached a village, whole populations either fled screaming
with terror into the bush or circled around behind the visitors to attack them

in the rear. At its worst, Stanley wrote, 'they considered us as game to be trapped, shot, or bagged at sight.'

It said something of Stanley's own reputation and the fighting ability of his Zanzibaris that even the most predatory of the roving brigands of Central Africa preferred to negotiate with him rather than fight. The most notorious freebooter was Mirambo, a Negro war captain who had set out to corner the ivory market. With an armed column he ranged about the area south of Lake Victoria, seizing all stocks of ivory for himself and forcing the natives to pay a tithe on food and lodging. He had been so successful that even the Arab slavers did not dare attack him, and he had managed to treble the price of ivory. Stanley heard the advance of Mirambo's column a day's march in the distance by the thud of their Brown Bess muskets and the terrified shouts of a native messenger calling upon the local population to produce food for the raiders. Face to face with the dreaded Mirambo, Stanley was astonished to discover a mild-mannered, handsome young Negro, about thirty-five years old and without a trace of arrogance or brutality. Only his eyes were remarkable. They 'met your own and steadily and calmly confronted them'. He was, said Stanley 'a thorough African *gentleman*'.

Stanley's ability to impress the condottieri of Africa was one of his great assets. Without their active help he could never have moved so far nor so swiftly across Central Africa. Mirambo made him a blood brother after a crude ceremony which involved mixing blood from incisions in their legs and taking a ferocious oath; and with Mirambo's Arab equivalent, the slaving pasha Tippu Tib, Stanley became an active collaborator. Tippu was the most ambitious of the many remarkable Arab traders and adventurers who had penetrated inland to live among the Negroes. Himself part Negro he had built up a thriving trade empire on the innermost fringe of Arab activity in Africa. Stanley, working his way steadily west, found Tippu Tib living in the luxurious style of a Zanzibar merchant prince. Immaculately dressed in dazzling white gown, and with a retinue of servants, a travelling harem, and a small private army, Tippu Tib was a vision of elegance and cultured hospitality. Yet the foundation of his wealth was a horrendous trade in slaves, the cheapest crop, as one of his lieutenants aptly put it, because it did not need to be grown, only gathered. Either because Tippu Tib was genuinely curious or, more probably, because he wanted to extend his slave-catching trawl, he struck a bargain with Stanley. For $5,000 he agreed to escort the Anglo-American Expedition westward for sixty marches from the town of Nyangwe into the Congo basin.

Nyangwe was a watershed for Stanley. It was where Livingstone had turned back, and in practical terms it stood virtually at the geographic centre of the continent. To an explorer it marked the great divide between known and unknown Africa. As far as Nyangwe Stanley had been filling in the gaps left by earlier travellers. Now, however, he was about to commit himself to the supreme test. Every step he took from Nyangwe would carry him farther from his base in Zanzibar, and in theory make it more sensible for him to continue right across to the far side of the continent. But the difficulty was that no one knew where this course might lead him. The only highway for the *Lady Alice* was the Lualaba river which flowed past Nyangwe. Livingstone had thought it might prove a source of the Nile; others believed that it joined the Congo or the Niger. Quite literally Stanley did not know whether he would emerge at Cairo, the mouth of the Congo, or in the Bight of Benin. All that was certain was that the Lualaba led straight into some of the worst country in equatorial Africa – dense tropical forest shunned by the Arabs as the haunt of cannibals and pygmies. Even Livingstone had described sailing down the Lualaba as a foolhardy venture, and shortly before Stanley arrived, another British explorer, Lovett Cameron, had sheered off even though his column was armed with Snider rifles.

Tippu Tib

This, then, was the challenge Stanley accepted with the *Lady Alice* and his Zanzibaris. Of his white companions only Frank Pocock was left, the other two having died of typhus and fever. Tippu Tib promised an escort of musketeers, but it was evident that he would only go as far as conditions suited him. It was entirely up to Stanley to press forward the venture, and see it to its conclusion. In his narrative (though there was no mention of the incident in his diary of the trip) he gave a romantic picture of the fateful decision. Calling Pocock to his tent, he told him of the choice: to risk the river, or to detour like Cameron to the south. Pocock suggested they toss a rupee coin to decide, and six times in succession the coin fell indicating the detour. Dissatisfied, Stanley tried drawing long and short straws, and again the indication was for the detour. Finally he gave up the charade and said firmly – 'It's no use, Frank. We'll face our destiny, despite the rupee and the straws. With your help, I'll follow the river.'

The expedition bolted together the *Lady Alice* on 19 November 1876, in an atmosphere of considerable nervousness. The local Wagenya natives were hostile, and there was a bad moment when the travellers mistook chimpanzee skulls, which lined their village streets, for human heads. But the Wagenya had no knowledge of firearms, nor of portable boats, and became more cooperative at the sight of the *Lady Alice* floating on the water. Even with an additional flotilla of dug-out canoes, there was not enough room for the entire caravan on board, so while Stanley went ahead with the water-borne section, Tippu Tib marched parallel on the bank. News of such a large force naturally travelled on ahead, and it was another indication of the savage state of the country that most villages were promptly evacuated. On the 22nd Stanley's advance guard floated quietly up to the village of Makula. It was a busy market day, and they

207

'Heads for the north and Lualaba; tails for the south and Katanga'

came within two hundred yards of the beach before a child noticed their approach. He told his mother who, looking round, screamed with terror. At once there was pandemonium. The market dissolved as merchants, women, and children ran off into the bush. Even the goats which had been quietly grazing nearby, said Stanley, fled for safety.

Despite the reluctance of the natives to contact the expedition, Tippu Tib's land force somehow picked up an infection of smallpox. Soon it was crawling along, while Stanley had to hang back and take the sick aboard his boats as hospital ships. Progress was barely three miles a day. The Arabs were disheartened; food ran short; and sporadic native attacks, using poisoned arrows, had to be brushed off. Stanley proudly picked off a marksman hidden in a tree top. By the end of the year Tippu Tib had had enough. The expedition had gone less than 200 miles and his contract was only half complete, but he asked to be released. Stanley knew he could not force him to go on, so agreed to pay him a draft of $2,600. On Christmas Day they held a farewell feast; a lighthearted interlude with canoe and foot races and a challenge sprint between Frank Pocock and Tippu Tib down the three-hundred-yard length of the village street. To the delight of the Arabs Tippu Tib won by fifteen yards.

On the last day of 1876 Stanley reviewed his much depleted force. Slightly more than half the original men who had started from Zanzibar remained. Out of a total of 143, including women and children, only 48 had guns, mostly Sniders and percussion-lock muskets. The formula for survival was whether Stanley's supply of guns would outlast losses to the river. Each time one of his canoes capsized, a few precious weapons sank and were lost. Reserves of cartridges, spare bullets and powder were dwindling, and yet it was increasingly evident that the expedition would have to fight its way through. The riparian tribes of the Congo either failed to understand that the white man and his followers were on passage and had not come to despoil them, or they considered him and his small force an easy prey. Their reaction varied from the pathetic to awe-inspiring. Stanley had to meet onslaughts from yelling and drunken natives, some of them wearing strange white hats that looked like university mortar boards, and others with filed teeth or brandishing huge shields as large as doors. In one camp site the natives, pygmies most probably, set up nets around the camp as if the visitors were a species of wild game to be snared.

At the confluence of the Aruwimi, named Battle river by Stanley, his party were attacked on two sides by a huge fleet of forty-four war canoes, some of them so immense that they seemed capable of carrying five hundred men. The flagship of this fleet was the most impressive vessel Stanley had seen. Propelled by sixty chanting paddlers, this huge canoe carried a jutting platform on the bow, on which pranced half a dozen picked warriors hideously painted and wearing feathered head dresses. Behind them stalked the ship's commander, like an admiral on his poop deck, supervising the efforts of his crew. Even at a distance Stanley could distinguish the superbly barbarous fittings. Every

Stanley's lecture slide showing the *Lady Alice* in sections

Stanley and his party fight off an attack by Congo war canoes

paddle was surmounted by an ivory ball, its shaft wound about with copper and iron wire, and at the prow streamed, like a battle standard, a thick fringe of the long white fibres of palm frond.

Stanley's river tactics were well rehearsed. At the first sight of a serious attack, he would cajole his Zanzibaris' canoes into line and order them to drop overboard their stone anchors. He himself then took up position in the centre of the line with the *Lady Alice*, slightly in the van, where his followers could see him. Standing up so as to be clearly visible, he opened fire at long range with his elephant gun, aiming at the waterline of the leading enemy canoe. The effect of a direct hit on a large canoe foaming downriver with a disciplined crew of paddlers was dramatic. The bows disintegrated and the vessel ploughed steeply forward as the water rushed in. Within seconds the boat would founder, leaving a line of bobbing, wailing heads. Even a heavy rifle ball placed squarely among the paddlers at long range was enough to stop an attack. The men who were hit were knocked to the bilges or into the water, and the rest of the crew, after a moment of appalled silence, broke rhythm and, as likely as not, abandoned ship.

Yet it was the river itself which provided the worst danger. Day after day was spent floating downstream with no more than an occasional glimpse of a native face peering from the forest, or the distant, mournful, booming of drums and ivory war horns. But as the river curved from north to north-west, and then around to the west it dawned on Stanley that the Lualaba had to be the Congo, and that in all likelihood there would be cataracts in his path. Captain Tuckey, a thwarted up-river explorer, had reported them years earlier and, 'Tuckey's Farthest' was an impassable cataract on the lower river. Now, the slope and height of the land, the immensity of the river, and the distance it had to run to the sea, made it obvious that severe cataracts, if not major waterfalls, were to be expected.

They came in two widely separated groups which, like the falls of the Nile, proved to be fearsome obstacles. Arranged like treads in a flight of stairs the upper group, renamed Stanley Falls, were negotiated in January 1877, and the lower or Livingstone Falls were crossed during March and April. Stanley had the choice either to portage his boats overland or, at far greater risk, to shoot the rapids. In a blaze of energy he built brushwood tramways around the worst sections, hacked pathways through the jungle and dragged the heavy dugouts by brute force. At Inkisi, where the lower river ran boiling between high cliffs, he astounded the hopeful native spectators, who had come to see the expedition drown in the over-falls, by ordering his men to carry the boats up a fifteen-hundred-foot mountain, a feat that was accomplished between dawn and dusk. But usually Stanley preferred to shoot the rapids or to lower his boats through them on hawsers. It was excruciatingly delicate work, and accidents were depressingly frequent. The Congo's current was deadly. On 28 March his convoy was hugging the bank to avoid the worst of the flood when the canoe *Crocodile* strayed into the mainstream and was swept away. On board was Kalulu, a young African who had been with Stanley on the trip to find Livingstone and then accompanied him to London. Stanley thought of him almost as a son, and now watched in horror as the *Crocodile* hit the lip of the falls, tilted, and plunged over into the maelstrom. Kalulu and seven men were dragged under and drowned.

A greater tragedy came on 3 June. Stanley had gone on ahead and was sitting on a rock watching the river through his field-glasses when he saw a canoe in difficulties. Capsized, it was being swept down from the Massassa ledge towards the Zinga cataract. At the very last moment he saw nine of her crew abandon the canoe, and swim ashore while the vessel swept on to destruction. Then a runner came stumbling up to tell Stanley that Pocock had been in

Death of Kalulu

the canoe and was missing. Little by little, the story came out. Pocock, a strong swimmer, had decided to take the canoe to a point halfway between the rapids, and station her there as a rescue boat for the rest of the convoy. Perhaps influenced by the fact that his feet were ulcerated and he found it painful to walk, he decided to shoot the upper rapids rather than lower the boat through on lines. Unfortunately the vessel was caught in an immense back eddy, spun round three or four times, and sucked downwards like an arrow. Pocock, Stanley could only surmise, had struck his head and had drowned. Five days later the natives of Mbelo saw a white man's corpse floating on its back in the river. They did not try to recover it but told Stanley that the shirt was torn away, and below the pantaloons, they could see the shape of the bandages which Pocock had worn on his injured feet.

Pocock's death very nearly demolished Stanley. His field-book broke down into a long, rambling, incoherent entry, filled with remorse and grief. The writing was so shaky as to be almost illegible, the phrases of mourning tumbling out in a chaotic flow of sorrow; and Stanley, for the first time made notes for his executors in case he should die and the expedition fail. He and Pocock had often discussed the death of one or the other, but the sudden shock exposed the

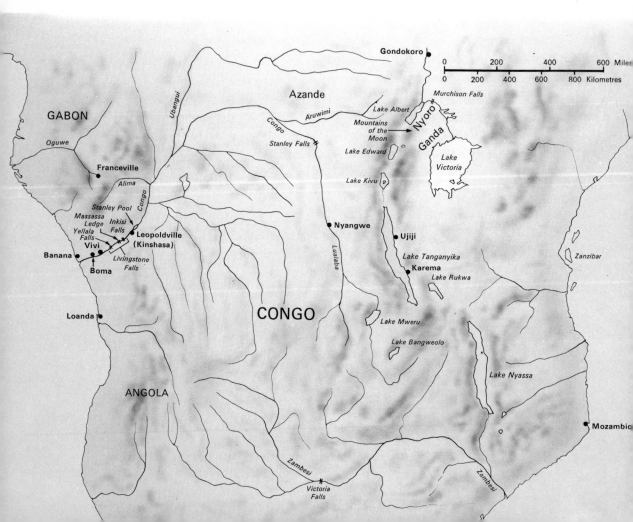

Opposite Central Africa of the Victorian explorers.
'Along the rivers': *above* Livingstone almost sunk by a hippo;
below missionary support party resting on the river bank

raw, desperately lonely core of the man who had attached himself so immediately to Livingstone and treated Kalulu like a son. Stanley had built Pocock
into the notion of a faithful acolyte, and, far more than Livingstone mourning
the loss of a colleague in Africa, he gave vent to his grief over Pocock's death.
He referred in his diary to 'the long, long companionship in peril thus abruptly
severed, his piety, and cheerful trust in a generous Providence suffuses my
heart with pity that he departed this life so abruptly and unrewarded for his . . .'
Thereafter, like his syntax, Stanley's writing became undecipherable with
emotion.

Nothing underscored the tragedy of Pocock's death more than the fact that
on the very same day the expedition came across its first signs of European
contact. The natives of Zinga knew the distinctions between Portuguese,
English and French, and one man wore a jacket. Stanley needed every straw of
encouragement to coax his Zanzibaris forward. Numb with exhaustion, disappointment and malnutrition, they were dispirited and mutinous. One man
was caught stealing and was abandoned in the wilds; another, Safeni, the staid
coxswain of the *Lady Alice* on Lake Victoria, went stark mad and rushed off
into the jungle, screaming 'We have reached the sea! We are home! We are
home!' Thirty men deserted, and only the terrifying hostility of the jungle
brought them cringing back. Finally Stanley had to leave the river and cut
overland in a desperate attempt to reach Boma the nearest European outpost.
Scarred and leaky, the *Lady Alice* was hauled out and left to rot and the column
reeled forward. On 4 August Stanley sent a messenger ahead to Boma with
a note, begging the white men at the outpost to despatch supplies. Fearful
that they would not respond, he scribbled a postscript – 'You may not know
me by name; I therefore add, I am the person that discovered Livingstone in
1871. – H.M.S.' On 9 August, the relief party found him. It was exactly 999
days since he had set out from Zanzibar and his shoes were so dilapidated that
they were held together with spare trunk hide and gutta-percha.

Stanley's monumental Congo voyage placed him on a level with Livingstone
as a traveller. There would be nothing quite like it again in African exploration.
He and Livingstone were established as the outstanding long-distance African
voyagers of the age, and there was an air of finality to their efforts because, in
effect, there were no more such vast rivers to explore. Yet there were other,
more intimate, similarities between the two men. Of the six Victorian lions,
only Stanley and Livingstone came of genuinely humble birth, Livingstone a
cotton worker's son and Stanley from the Welsh working class. Their back-
grounds may well have contributed to the unease they shared in the admiring
society which their efforts attracted round them. It was an important similarity
between the two men. Livingstone, after clearing a *cordon sanitaire* around
himself, allowed very few close friendships to pierce the barrier. His emotions

Livingstone and Stanley on the Rusizi. The two men spent four months together after their meeting

seemed to operate best at one remove. It was said, for instance, that he got on well with all children but his own; and certainly there was an essential remoteness about a man who made a point of giving little black dolls to Scots children and who invariably signed his letters, even to his wife, with his name in full. This isolation, self-imposed in Livingstone's case, affected Stanley differently. Desperately lonely and insecure, as he had every reason to be after such an appalling childhood, he was rashly affectionate and easily rebuffed. His frenetic energy, his tendency to bully, and his longing to be accepted by society, were attempts to balance this emotional isolation. Many people, especially of the English upper middle class, found his manner off-putting, but Livingstone did not. It is revealing that for four months these two men, whom some believed to be the very antithesis of one another, lived side by side in Africa with no other white man to dilute the contact. Yet it is clear from Livingstone's letters, and from Stanley's journal, that they got on very well. The roles of teacher and disciple pandered to Livingstone's self-esteem and to Stanley's tendency to hero worship; but at the same time it is clear that Livingstone liked Stanley and admired his brisk manner. It was a judgement soon forgotten by Stanley's detractors who, often as not, were Livingstone admirers. What they failed to recognize was the inevitability of the succession. Had Livingstone lived another twenty years, it is doubtful that he could have accomplished much more than he did. Alone and unsupported in the field, as he wished to be, he could only be the symbol. Already the slave traders were leapfrogging his discoveries and bringing the worst elements into primitive Africa. It was left to Stanley to introduce the techniques, manpower, and colonial ambitions which were Europe's response. Livingstone's goal had been to direct people's attention to Africa; Stanley, whom he had liked, put the attention into practice.

Pride and Prejudice

CHAPTER NINE

> These were the days when the Society in question [the Royal Geographical] could not afford to lack its annual lion, whose roar was chiefly to please the ladies and push the institution – *Burton*.

In gold letters on discreet olive green the names of four of the Victorian lions march together on the honours board of the Royal Geographical Society. Between 1859 and 1865 Burton, Speke, Grant and Baker all received the Society's most coveted medal, and all four lectured to public meetings of the Society or wrote articles for its prestigious *Journal*. They had just come back from investigating the sources of the Nile, and were the leading players in an African game, which, though neither as solemn nor as political as the 'great game' on the North-West Frontier of India, had its own rules, spectators and heroes. Livingstone and Stanley, whose names also appear on the honour roll, were players too. But whereas they were the professionals, the other four Victorian lions rejoiced in being amateurs.

Their amateur status could be recognized at once by a curious social geography of its own. A map drawn before any of the four men ever went exploring in Africa would have shown that they had already followed the same well-beaten and socially acceptable path. They had all been to the Orient: Burton, Speke, and Grant as officers in the Indian Army;* Samuel Baker to his family estates in Ceylon. Except for Grant, who stayed on in India and was wounded at the relief of Lucknow (where Speke's brother was also), they then all moved on to the Black Sea. There Baker built railways near the Danube and went shooting in Asia Minor. Speke was attached to a regiment of Turks in the Crimea; and Burton got himself a staff officer's post in the Dardanelles with a colourfully extravagant body of irregular cavalry known as the Bashi Bazouks, commanded by a fiery general from India. To Burton's acute disappointment the Bashi Bazouks never saw action while he was with them, though they almost came to blows with their Turkish allies.

Only in Britain did the paths of the four men really diverge. Baker and Speke

---

* Grant and Speke first met while on service in the second Sikh War.

were both from the West Country, being country-house gentry keen on field sports and invested in rolling acres. Baker was much the wealthier man, his family having made a fortune in West Indian plantations, and his father holding a directorship of the Great Western Railway. Grant was a clergyman's son from Rosshire in Scotland; and Burton, whose parents had wandered all over Europe during his childhood and entrusted his education to an unpredictable series of tutors, tended to pick up rooms casually in London whenever he happened to be there. Nevertheless Burton, like the others, belonged by background and inclination to the Victorian upper middle class which regarded a European tour and the army's posting list as the normal scope of travel. Africa, in the beginning at least, was a detour.

By some accident of nature – or by clever artwork – the faces of the four men projected their personalities very neatly. Burton had his famous 'gypsy

Speke (right), Grant and Bombay, their African assistant, in 1863. Painting by Henry William Phillips

eyes', bold forehead, jutting jaw, and a striking black moustache that carefully failed to hide the scar on his cheek where a Somali spear point had gone through into his palate, knocking out four back teeth. The deliberate effect was a raffish, devil-may-care swagger, a pose which went with the sinister character he liked to assume at every opportunity. It was said that at house parties he would even seize upon unruly children and terrify them by grimacing horribly into their faces until they fled screaming from the room. Bluff Samuel Baker, on the other hand, so full of bonhomie and booming goodwill, was everyone's image of a favourite uncle. He sported a huge bush of a beard which fell down to his chest like an Edward Lear illustration and seemed as if it might harbour some small species of wildlife. At hunting parties in the Highlands or partridge shoots in Somerset, Baker always threw off an air of rubicund goodwill and sturdy energy. Speke, also well bearded, aspired more to the noble brow, the lofty glance and soldierly bearing which he felt was commensurate with his dignity. His companion Grant, the member of the group most frequently overlooked, had a thin face and a rather startled expression, underscored by a sparse beard and moustache which at times gave him some semblance to a questing sheep. Such superficial impressions were, of course, deceptive. Grant was a difficult man to overlook as he stood 6 feet 2 inches tall and was broad in proportion. Burton, despite his nonchalance, was desperate for an audience to impress, and spent a good deal of his time concocting suitable scandals, whether a hare-brained scheme to abduct a nun from her convent or the rumour that he was a cannibal.

To all four men the Royal Geographical Society was the pivot of their careers as explorers and in this way they differed once again from Livingstone and Stanley who departed for Africa on errands which at first did not concern the geographers. The amateurs, however, needed the Geographical. It gave them the approval of their colleagues and the learned guidance which made their African trips more than mere tourist ventures. In a sense the Royal Geographical Society was both umpire and rule-maker in the game. Its exploration committee approved the traveller's plan before he set out, often helped him raise funds, and then judged the merit of his efforts when he returned home. It was a convenient arrangement which maintained the player's amateur standing, put the seal on his intentions, and at the same time provided him with a gentlemanly platform from which to celebrate his achievements – perhaps at one of their 'African nights' which were so popular.

The Society's offices were in Whitehall Place until 1870 when they moved to new premises just off Regent Street at 1 Savile Row, an impressive plaster-swagged building in whose map room Livingstone's body was deposited for the night prior to his funeral. Its President for many of these years was Sir Roderick Impey Murchison, a man whose character reflected the nature of the

organization he controlled. Murchison was in many ways a latter-day Sir
Joseph Banks. Methodical, meticulous and with a splendid private income, he
wielded great influence as a leading light of the scientific establishment in
Victorian England. His house in Belgrave Square was a meeting place for
politicians and savants, in much the same fashion as Banks's home in Soho
Square had been a gathering place for the gentlemen of the Enlightenment.

Left Sir Roderick Impey Murchison, President of the Royal Geographical Society for fifteen years.
Right Sir Samuel Baker addressing a meeting of the Royal Geographical Society

Like Banks too, Murchison was overshadowed intellectually by several of his
contemporaries. His forte was observation and practical organization rather
than original science. A tall wiry man, he had been in the Army and served
under Sir John Moore at Corunna before resigning his commission and taking
up the expanding science of geology. At the age of thirty-three he was elected
a Fellow of the Royal Society, though more for his social eminence than his
academic brilliance, as he had written as yet only one paper on his subject and
was better known as a fox-hunter of terrific enthusiasm. In 1843 he became
President of the Royal Geographical Society, a post he was to hold for fifteen
years.* His personal interest as a geologist and topographer was to spur on the

* When Murchison was first elected president of the R.G.S. there was a rule that the president had to be
  changed every second year. But after Murchison had held six alternating presidencies, the Society gave up.
  It amended the rule to allow Murchison to continue in office for nine consecutive years until his death in
  1871.

Nile quest and to be remembered, among other honours, in the Murchison Falls, named after him by Baker and described as 'the greatest falls of the Nile'.

Sir Roderick was at nearly every turn of the Nile quest. He persuaded Lord Clarendon to put up £1,000 of Government money for Burton's trip; introduced Speke to Prince Albert; and arranged the meeting between Grant and Palmerston at which the Prime Minister made his famous remark, 'You've had a long walk, Captain Grant.' More sourly, when Murchison wheedled another £2,500 of Government funds for Speke by personal application to Lord John Russell, a Treasury official grumbled, 'I must say the Geographical Society draw largely on us.' Increasingly narrow-minded and arrogant as his prestige mounted, Murchison also represented the weakness of the Society. Both he and the Geographical could be stuffy and intolerant of opposition, and to the amazement of foreign observers spent a good deal of time and energy in useless squabbles which involved personalities and favourites rather than scientific facts.

It was with Murchison's blessing that two of the gentlemen-explorers, Burton and Speke, started inland from Zanzibar in 1857 to investigate the mysterious 'Sea of Ujiji' reported by the Arab traders. The Nile, Murchison believed, took its course either from this lake, or from a lake very like it, or it rose in the Mountains of the Moon mentioned by the classical scholars. In any event the expedition's task was not believed to be a difficult one. With Burton as leader the two explorers were to follow the Arab trails down which slaves were regularly brought to the Great Market at Zanzibar. On the main-

Below Explorers setting out into East Africa. *Opposite* Feasting on 'the choice bits' — the trunk and feet — of an elephant. Watercolour by Thomas Baines

land was a mission station where Burton and Speke could pick up advance intelligence about conditions in the interior, and in Zanzibar itself they could easily hire experienced guides who had travelled all the way to Ujiji. What made the project awkward, as every Fellow of the Royal Geographical Society would soon know, was the simple fact that the two explorers were thoroughly incompatible. The difficulties of their journey lay as much in themselves as in Africa, and they should never have been members of the same team. Yet this was a problem which had nothing to do with Murchison. It was after all a basic assumption of the African Game that the gentlemen-explorers had the good taste and judgement to pick their own companions.

At first glance it certainly seemed that Burton and Speke should get along well. They had much in common. They were both Army officers with equal rank of Captain; they shared Indian experience, and in the days when East Africa was treated as a political and practical appendage of India, this was considered very useful; and they had already travelled together on their previous expedition to Somaliland. Yet it was precisely these similarities which bedevilled their relationship. In almost everything they had done together, the two men pulled in opposite directions. Speke saw an Indian Army career as a gentlemanly vocation, but to Burton it was only a temporary interest. Speke's behaviour in India had been the orthodox attitude of the white officer commanding native troops, while Burton had spent his time studying oriental languages, dressing up as a native, and generally earning his soubriquet of 'the White Nigger'. Nor was their Somaliland trip a happy memory. The whole episode had ended with the Somalis attacking their camp, Burton and Speke being wounded, and mutual recriminations of cowardice and incompetence. Moreover Speke rankled with the impression that Burton had creamed off most of the publicity from the expedition and failed, in Speke's opinion, to give his companion due recognition. In view of all this it was, perhaps, more remarkable that they should have agreed in the first place to go out to East Africa together, than that they should have come to loggerheads once they were there.

Their only real link was a disastrous once: the shared desire for public acclaim. No other motive for going to Africa was quite so strong for a gentleman-explorer. Both travellers had small private incomes, so financial rewards were welcome but not essential. Both had superior interests and careers, whether in the Army or in oriental studies, and they could have satisfied their wanderlust equally well in Tibet, South America or wherever they wished. Neither man had the driving conviction of a Livingstone nor the deliberate editorial instructions which set Stanley on the road to Africa. In fine, Burton and Speke looked for the sources of the Nile not so much to advance science as to advance themselves.

Of course there was nothing new about the injection of private ambition into African exploration. Mungo Park had sought his fortune in the same way, so too had Gordon Laing. But in the Victorian era the opportunities were much greater and the expectations higher. The public lovingly anticipated the flavour of success, and for the explorer there was a delicious sense of immediacy to the notion that he need go no farther than the nearest telegraph office to broadcast his good news. Knowing their readership, the newspapers and magazines were poised to trumpet the announcement by 'Special Submarine Cable' or 'Dispatches from Bombay'. *The Times*, *Blackwood's Magazine*, *The Daily Telegraph*, *The Athenaeum*, were heavyweights, all keenly interested in Africa. So too was the *Illustrated London News* and, in a smaller way, *John Bull* and *Good Words*, a magazine specializing in edifying missionary memoirs.

What made the Burton–Speke expedition doubly newsworthy to any discerning editor was the fact that the two men were aiming at pre-eminence by very different routes and towards slightly different destinations. On the one hand there was John Hanning Speke, a man with whom many of his contemporaries could easily sympathize and identify the popular notion of the patriotic

Englishman. Indeed if Sir Roderick Murchison was the paragon of the successful Victorian, Speke was his faithful apprentice almost to the point of caricature. Speke saw himself as the archetypal sporting Britisher, upright and manly, a fellow who did quite well at whatever he cared to try, and who enjoyed African tramping mixed with a spot of African exploration. He was deeply influenced by the current vogue for big game hunting, and could easily have been another Cornwallis Harris. In fact at times his expedition journal read almost like a game book. With typical solemnity he announced that he proposed to find the source of the Nile because it was only right that England should have the glory of solving a problem 'which it has been the first geographical desideratum of many thousand years to ascertain and the ambition of the first monarchs in the world to unravel.' It was an extremely orthodox motive, and indeed there can seldom have been such a conventional – yet so ambitious – person in the annals of African discovery. Nowhere was this more evident than in Speke's writing. He was entirely at ease with the ideals and clichés of his generation, a fact which Burton was quick to ridicule:

> Speke really believed that 'the interests of Old England were at stake', and his literary style showed the pedestrian qualities of his mind. A mass of foul huts is 'a village built on the most luxurious principles'; and a petty chief is a 'king of kings'; whilst a 'splendid court' means a display of mere savagery, and the 'French of those parts' are barbarians somewhat livelier than their neighbours. 'Nelson's Monument at Charing Cross' is a specimen of what we may expect from Central Africa. . . Not less curious is the awkward scatter of Scriptural quotations and allusions that floats upon the surface of his volumes. It looks as though some friend had assured the author that his work would not 'go down' without a little of what is popularly called 'hashed Bible'.

Burton was being cruel but there was no doubt that he was right in finding that Speke carried the commonplace to its extreme. From India Speke shipped back consignments of stuffed animal heads to decorate the walls of the family mansion, and in Africa he refused to dress up as an Arab because he felt it would 'demean' him to their level. His ambition was a K.C.B.; his literature *Blackwood's Magazine*; and his obsession was physical fitness. He even practised walking barefoot while on shikari and made a point of eating the foetuses of animals he had shot. To his very core Speke believed that he possessed the qualities his countrymen held most dear, and that in Africa he could prove them.

But harnessed to him was Richard Burton, a man who, as irony had it, went to Oxford with the author of *Tom Brown's Schooldays* but deliberately mocked everything that Speke and the conventionalists stood for. Burton's chosen route to eminence was to play the maverick, the critic-proved-right. Not excluding James Bruce, Burton was the most provoking man in the entire African adventure. As a child he had been an imp, smashing shop windows and

223

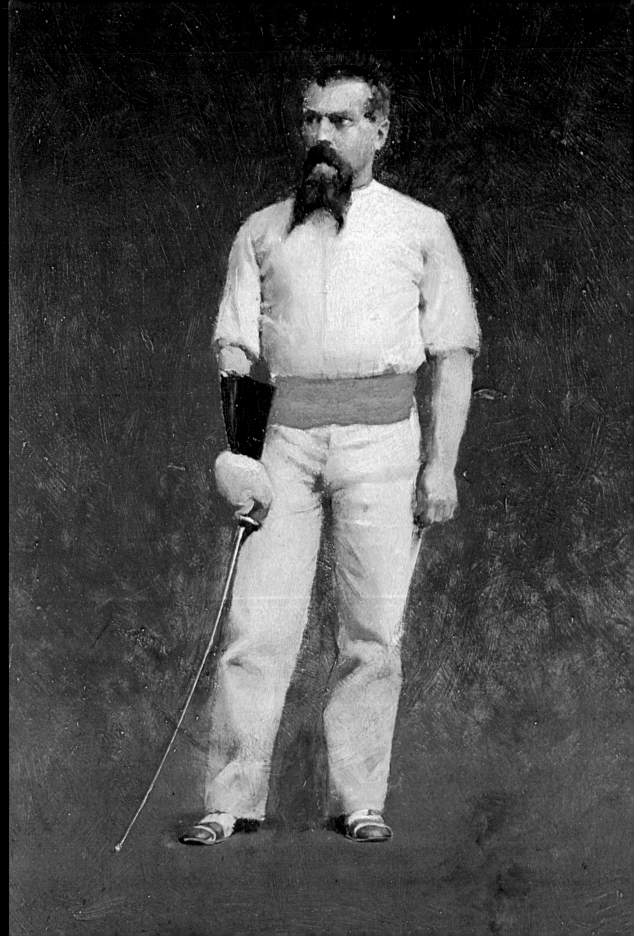

spinning wild yarns about nannies horribly done to death. As an under-graduate he had been sent down from Trinity College, Oxford for consistently making a nuisance of himself, and as an Indian subaltern he infuriated his messmates by lampooning his colonel and keeping a troupe of monkeys dressed in clothes and attended by servants, with the notion of compiling an index of monkey talk. Yet it was obvious to all but his most bitter enemies that Burton was more than an eccentric gadfly. He undoubtedly possessed enor-mous, if diffused, talent. With his flair for languages and a system of his own invention by which he could acquire reasonable fluency in a matter of weeks, he was already well on his way to acquiring over forty languages and dialects in his lifetime. With them he was constantly making significant contributions to oriental studies, social and physical anthropology, and comparative literature. To some observers Burton with his wild schemes and murky pastimes was too clever by half. Yet few dared laugh openly at his extravaganzas, his posturings as a hedonist or his blatant cloak-trailing because, again like Bruce, he had a reputation for violence. It was known that he was an expert with the bayonet and had written a manual on its use, and that he was a *maître des armes* in fencing, with two new sword strokes of his own creation. In the Victorian context Richard Burton therefore represented the darker genius of his age, the shadowy and unpredictable cast which threw into relief the more familiar efforts of men like Speke and sometimes made them look absurd.

Burton and Speke spent almost two years together on the East African mainland. In that time, from June 1857 to March 1859, they successfully located two of the greatest lakes of the interior. In Lake Tanganyika they identified the Sea of Ujiji of the Arabs and the object of their mission; and while the expedition was heading back for the coast, Speke took an independent detour to the north and made the discovery of his lifetime when he glimpsed Lake Victoria, the largest body of water in Africa and, as it turned out, the main source of the Nile.

By any standards the expedition had done remarkably well. Each man could claim a new lake for himself. Burton as leader of the expedition had Lake Tanganyika; Speke had his Lake Victoria. Yet because neither lake had been properly surveyed – in particular their northern shores were still unknown, from whence theoretically would flow the infant Nile – the supreme accolade of the discovery of the Nile source hung in doubt. It was this squabble over prestige that became the notorious 'Nile duel' which reverberated far beyond the Council Room of the Royal Geographical Society and obscured the truth about the Nile source far longer than necessary. On their return to England the explorers could easily have been reconciled, for in a spurt of tact the Royal Geographical Society engineered a very decent compromise: they gave Burton a Gold Medal for leading the expedition, but they elected Speke to command a new venture to verify Lake Victoria. There the matter could have rested. But it was too late. The whole complicated machinery of Victorian controversy was meshed into gear and careering to a grand finale.

Undoubtedly it was Burton who locked the machinery on course once Speke had set it in motion. Burton was indignant when Speke published independently in *Blackwood's Magazine* an account of the discovery of Lake Victoria, followed by the forthright claim that the lake was the source of the Nile. Until that moment the conflict could have been salvaged. Previously Speke had expressed his notions semi-privately; and Burton had gone out of his way in his speech of thanks for the Gold Medal to refer to the contribution made by his companion. Even John Blackwood was cautious. Before he published, he asked Speke to clear the text with Burton. This of course Speke failed to do. Once the article was out, Burton not only counter-attacked but pressed home his rebuttal with such vigour that a major uproar was inevitable.

Burton's fusillade was contained in a brilliant, hastily written book, *The Lake Regions of Central Africa*. In it, for the first time in African exploration, the popular image of the gallant English gentleman-explorer was torn to shreds. It was the sort of attack which Burton always relished and in which he was well rehearsed. Speke was referred to obliquely as 'my companion' and reduced to a minor anonymous helpless nuisance. In his preface, written at the East India and United Service Club of which both he and Speke were members, Burton wrote:

> I could not expect much from his assistance; he was not a linguist – French and Arabic being equally unknown to him – nor a man of science, nor an accurate astronomical observer . . . and as may be imagined amongst a party of Arabs, Baloch, and Africans whose languages he ignored, he was unfit for any other but a subordinate capacity.

Having thus indicted Speke as an ignoramus, Burton went on to demolish him in his role as the sporting traveller. The alleged crack-shot was depicted as stumbling about Africa peering hazily through watery eyes; the physical fitness enthusiast insisted on staying overnight in a leaky tent thereby 'laying the foundations of his fever' and became liverish from 'over devotion to a fat bullock's hump'. Hunting trips were fruitless; Speke could only converse in debased Hindi with the servant Bombay; and he returned from one expedition 'moist, mildewed and nothing done'. The cruellest descriptions were of Speke's fever attacks. According to Burton they had permanently damaged Speke's brain. Once Burton had to disarm his half-crazed companion, and on another morning he found Speke –

> . . . sitting or rather lying upon the chair, with limbs wracked by cramps, features drawn and ghastly, frame fixed and rigid, eyes glazed and glassy, he began to utter

a barking noise, and a peculiar chopping motion of the mouth and tongue, with lips protruding – the effect of difficulty of breathing – which so altered his appearance that he was barely recognizable, and completed the terror of the beholders.

Logically Burton's campaign against Speke should have collapsed as soon as Speke returned, in 1863, from his second expedition to Lake Victoria and confirmed that the Nile did indeed issue from the lake. Taking Grant as his companion, Speke had travelled to the north end of the Lake, identified the Nile exit, and as a bonus brought back intriguing descriptions of life in the splendidly barbarous kingdom of Ganda. Yet Burton refused to give up. He supported the accusation that Speke's new map of the Nile made the river flow uphill – in fact a careless error on Speke's part – and he pointed out that Speke casually moved mountain ranges about the map as if they were chess pieces. Naturally Burton had done exactly the same thing, calmly raising the elevation of Lake Tanganyika because, he pleaded, his boiling thermometers were wrongly calibrated, in order to provide sufficient head of water to reach the Nile. Far more important was the personal clash between the two men. There was accusation and counter-accusation of faithlessness and dishonesty as Burton called Speke a fraud and hypocrite, and Speke denounced Burton as a libertine and a man who had adopted all the worst vices of the Orient. Officers in their respective regiments, it was said, were urging a duel between the two rivals in order to satisfy honour.

Yet nothing of the sort was ever really feasible. The entire affair was a *cause célèbre*, a creation which could have stopped the moment that either partner wished to call a halt. Burton had most to gain from the furore, as it kept his name in the public eye despite his lesser discovery of Lake Tanganyika. Speke, anxiously writing up two books about his travels, also profited from the publicity. Then too there was the whole impetus of public involvement. The Burton–Speke feud would never have been sustained nor reached such heights had it not been for the public's delight in taking sides in such controversies. In smoking rooms, London clubs and country-house parties, a feeling of vicarious satisfaction was derived from fighting the explorers' battles for them. There were academic arguments over this or that notion of African geography, but far more vindictive were the clashes of the leading personalities. Like kings fighting through champions, the Victorian explorers were represented by surrogates whose wild blows knocked the scabs off old wounds and laid on fresh infusions of personal animosity.

One storm centre was the Council of the Royal Geographical Society. There Murchison started out, naturally enough, as an ally of Speke against Burton. 'Speke, we must send you out there again', he had told the ambitious young explorer when he called at Murchison's house to press his claims for Lake Victoria. But after his second trip, Speke rashly threw away this most powerful supporter by taking his story straight to Blackwood and not to the Royal Geographical for publication. Once again it was a question of publicity. Murchison was at first piqued, and then positively angry when Speke began to put it about that he thought the Geographical too inefficient and slow to publish the results of the expedition properly. Fortunately for Speke, Murchison's disillusionment was partly compensated by the staunch support the explorer received from another Council member, Christopher Rigby.

An orientalist of orthodox methods and considerable ability, Rigby had been accounted the most brilliant linguist in the Indian Army, and was very proud of this reputation. Then Burton showed up, beat him in a competitive examination in Gujerati, and carried off the official prize and congratulations. Thereafter Rigby was an implacable enemy, and, being appointed consul at Zanzibar, was in a good position to damage Burton. He wrote to a friend:

> Speke is a right good, jolly, resolute fellow. Burton is not fit to hold a candle to him and has done nothing in comparison with what Speke has, but Speke is a modest, unassuming man, not very ready with his pen. Burton will blow his trumpet very loud and get all the credit for his discoveries. Speke works. Burton lies on his back all day and picks other people's brains.

Burton, never inclined to let enmity fade, made a point of baiting Rigby. On one occasion they nearly came to blows on the stage of a Royal Geographical Society lecture, and in his narrative Burton confessed to preferring Bombay's face – which was notoriously gap-toothed and ugly – to Rigby's.

Nor were the explorers' friends necessarily all they seemed to be. The British geographer James M'Queen actually damaged Burton's cause when he overstepped the mark and published a scurrilous attack against Speke, accusing

Photograph of Colonel Rigby, H.M. Consul at Zanzibar, taken by Grant with the new fangled stereoscopic camera

him of dishonesty, shabby treatment of friends, and sexual adventures with African women. M'Queen's book, to which Burton lent his name, was scalded by the literary critics who considered the whole affair to be in very bad taste and a poor reflection on both its authors. More insidious were the machinations of one of Speke's false friends, Laurence Oliphant, the private secretary to Lord Elgin. Oliphant was a family acquaintance of the Spekes and happened to be aboard H.M.S. *Furious* when she took Speke home from his expedition with Burton. Oliphant was a mischief-maker of serpent-like ingenuity and during the voyage established a powerful influence over Speke. He prompted Speke to claim the Nile source, to go straight to *Blackwood's* with his story, and to press ahead with reducing Burton's prestige. All this advice was harmful to Speke, and even as the quarrel festered, Oliphant was taking care to keep Burton informed of Speke's increasing bitterness.

With Oliphant's help, matters came to a head in September 1864. Suitably it was Sir Roderick Murchison who reappeared in his role of umpire. He arranged a climactic meeting at the Mineral Water Hospital, Bath, where Burton and Speke were to engage in a public debate over the relative merits of Lake Tanganyika and Lake Victoria as the Nile source. The occasion was the annual convention of Section E 'Geography and Ethnology' of the British Association, and though the savants grumbled about vulgar public spectacles, a packed audience had assembled to witness this gladiatorial contest. Burton, with his wife, was actually seated on the platform holding his notes when Murchison appeared from a private meeting with members of the Committee, including David Livingstone. Addressing the audience, Murchison announced the stunning news that Speke was dead, killed in a shooting accident on the previous afternoon while walking up partridges on his uncle's nearby estates.

Speke's death, better than anything else, demonstrated that the African Game had its own particular decorum. Burton, who had been poised to cut his rival to pieces in public, went white with shock, stumbled through a hasty speech on another subject, and left the auditorium visibly shaken. According to his wife he wept bitterly when he got home and was in a state of great emotional distress for days afterward. When invited, he agreed to contribute to a Speke memorial fund. Speke's former companion, James Grant, heard the news of the tragedy while writing his own book of the expedition. At his special request the pages on which he was working at the time were enclosed within a black border of mourning. Murchison himself proposed to the Royal Geographical Society that 'a monumental pillar should be erected in some happily chosen spot', and a shaft of red granite was duly put up in Kensington Gardens, near to where the Society would later transfer its premises. Murchison, Livingstone, and Grant, all travelled down to Somerset to attend Speke's funeral in the little church of Dowlish Wake; and, to complete the circuit, the Speke family directed that royalties from the dead explorer's book should go to assist David Livingstone in his work.

Death on a rough shoot, though premature, was not altogether an unsuitable demise for Speke. He died in his role of the sporting gentleman and, significantly, when *The Times* published an editorial on the subject, it fretted as much over safe gun handling as over the loss of so distinguished a traveller. Yet it was not Speke, but Samuel Baker who fitted the image of a sportsman-explorer most closely. Baker was everything that Speke had strived so hard to be: well regarded, influential, manly and a superlative shot. Burton had slyly remarked of Speke that he was not in fact a very good marksman and often came back from the hunt empty-handed. Baker, by contrast, seemed to hit most things he aimed at, whether with his ferocious 'Baby' and its exploding shell or his favourite light-weight double-barrelled Fletcher rifle, with which he jubilantly bagged a crocodile at the foot of Murchison Falls on the moment he discovered them. When he had expended his bullets, Baker thought nothing of firing coins as slugs, and, shaking with ague, he sat up all night in a 'grave', a hunting pit, on the off chance of ambushing an elephant. Where other explorers were bogged down in bitter controversy, Baker rarely made an enemy or created a rival. According to Stanley, he had 'a good word for any explorer who happened to be an object of attack at the time', and he was not averse to showing his approval of their efforts. Thus he was genuinely pleased when, in 1863, he met the successful Speke and Grant at Gondokoro as they were coming downstream from the Nile source. Baker recalled:

> My men rushed madly to my boat, with the report that two white men were with them who had come from the *sea*! Could they be Speke and Grant? Off I ran, and soon met them in reality. Hurrah for Old England! . . . they were walking along the bank of the river towards my boats. At a distance of about a hundred yards I recognized my old friend Speke, and with a heart beating with joy I took off my cap and gave a welcome hurrah! as I ran towards him.

Baker's admiration and delight were completely unfeigned. He gave Speke and Grant all the equipment that they wanted from his private stores, loaned them a boat to get to Khartoum, and went out of his way to thank them for the advice which led him in the next few months to discover Lake Albert, the consort lake-source to the Nile.

But there was more to Baker than the bluff, good-hearted English gentleman. Alongside his high patriotism and huge love of sport, Baker was at heart something of a swashbuckler. He had a sense of style which led him to put his gunbearers in livery, design his own hunting costume, and carry around full highland dress from bonnet to sporran for wearing when he called on important

Tea at Gondokoro – Speke and Grant are entertained by the Bakers

chiefs. At a later date he also trailed the delicious rumour – true or not – that his beautiful blonde-haired wife had originally been purchased in a Balkan slave market. Because he was so thorough-going and able to pay for his whims, Baker was the most self-confident of the Victorian lions. When he lost his trail, he simply started a bush fire to burn off the vegetation and see his horizon; if threatened by a mutiny of porters he marched up to the ringleader and knocked him to the ground. Utterly fearless, Baker found the presence of danger to be merely exhilarating. He never faltered whether confronted with a charging rhinoceros or fencing off an enraged Arab swordsman with an umbrella and his Turkish pipestick. His composure was so unshakeable that he saw nothing ridiculous in conducting his first interview with the King of the Nyoro, lying on the ground because he was so weak with fever. Baker's arrival in Nyoro had been a sensation. Unlike Speke and Grant who had turned up in rags, Baker appeared with his wife, whose golden hair was amazing to the Africans, a personal gunbearer, 112 porters and askaris, a mass of souvenirs

Samuel and Florence Baker

and animal trophies, and a brace of pet quails. Viewing this cortege Kamrasi, the King of Nyoro, was worried lest Baker intended to seize his kingdom and, with Florence Baker's help, breed a new royal dynasty.

Kamrasi's reaction was significant, for he and Mtesa were the two African monarchs who saw most of the white explorers, and their behaviour was a guide to the African view of the newcomers. By tradition the entire health of his State depended on Kamrasi's personal well-being, so he was naturally reluctant to meet the strange visitors face to face. He fobbed off Speke and Grant with a wild story that they were said to be cannibals who ate men's

The Bakers watch a dance of welcome

flesh three times a day and drank the rivers and lakes dry. An unhappy incident soon after Speke's party left his court fully justified his caution. A gang of slavers appeared from the Gondokoro direction and gained entry to Nyoro by claiming to be friends of Grant and Speke. They then attacked the Nyoro villages, killing three hundred men, and carried off slaves. Therefore, when Baker appeared with a similar introduction from Speke, Kamrasi sent a deputation to the border to interview Baker, examine the whiteness of his skin, and make absolutely sure that he was 'Speke's brother'. Even then Kamrasi kept his distance. A 'double', posing as Kamrasi, conducted the early interviews with the Bakers, and Kamrasi quietly arranged that Baker's considerable force of riflemen was left stranded without canoes on a swampy island.

In most matters Kamrasi was more than a match for his uninvited guests. Both Speke and Baker loudly denounced him for a grasping and supercilious despot, and it was evident that Kamrasi was in no way abashed by their bluster. Shrewdly he saw at once that the best tactic to use on them was not physical threat but procrastination. The explorers were in such a hurry to reach the lakes and rivers they sought, that they would hand over valuable items of their equipment as a bribe to be on their way. Kamrasi got from the Speke and Grant expedition a tent, chronometer, sketching stool, and Speke's own Blissett rifle. He suggested that Baker should present him with his wife, a request that led to angry gun waving by Baker and a scorching speech from Florence. Clearly Kamrasi knew the value of his loot for when Baker, hoping for an interesting souvenir, offered to exchange back Speke's Blissett for some

Speke and Grant give Kamrasi his first bible lesson

muskets, Kamrasi flatly refused the trade. He suggested instead that Baker might like to assist him against Rionga, the rival claimant to the Nyoro throne. Rionga's rebel army was encamped nearby and Kamrasi's idea was for Baker to take up a sniper's position on a high cliff overlooking the camp and assassinate Rionga and all his people.

The suggestion was uncharacteristically bloodthirsty, as Kamrasi was by nature an easy-going monarch. He burst into roars of laughter when a salute from Baker's gun sent the onlookers tumbling over themselves like frightened rabbits, and he was very mild in his justice. Capital punishment in Nyoro was officially by breaking a man's neck with the edge of a sharp club and then throwing the body into a lake. But it was very rarely done. Kamrasi preferred to order a whipping or a reprimand, and when a man had to be killed, the execution was carried out by a foreign mercenary. As Speke pointed out, Kamrasi's leniency was in direct contrast to the next door kingdom of Ganda where the entire structure of tribal society was based on the predatory autocracy of the young Kabaka, Mtesa. Speke found the Ganda court to be a nightmare complex of strange customs and rivalries, where Ganda nobles with pet cocks and dogs in their arms sought to curry favour and catch the attention of the young Kabaka, or to arrange the deaths and humiliation of their opponents. The royal capital existed in a state of semi-hysteria. Its approaches for a considerable radius had been eaten bare of provisions by visiting embassies. The royal audience chamber was thronged with sycophants and petitioners who periodically fell face down on the ground 'to flounder about like fish on land' calling out '*tweanze*!, *tweanzege*!', literally 'we have received it; we thank you for it'. Here and there darted like demonic imps the royal pages, some wearing manacles as they were of royal blood. At the centre of this confusion stalked with his famous lion's gait the young and capricious Kabaka, accompanied by his royal symbols of white dog, shield and spear.

To Speke, with his mechanical contrivances and guns, Mtesa quickly awarded a favoured position. Speke had only to fire three shots before the royal gates and he was allowed into the enclosure. With childlike delight the Kabaka took him on walks and eagerly asked him to use his wonderful weapons to pick off vultures or cattle. He sought to please him by dressing in ill-fitting trousers, and flew into a tantrum when Speke devoted his attention to the Queen Mother. But nothing succeeded in hiding the brutality of the Ganda regime. Speke saw men and girls dragged away for execution at the slightest breach of the rigid etiquette, and even the royal executioner came to beg his help in reprieving the executioner's own son from death. Through the thin walls of their hut Speke and Grant daily heard the sounds of floggings, and when he first presented Mtesa with a gun, Speke was disgusted to see the Kabaka hand it to a page and tell him to run outside and test the weapon by shooting a man.

Left Mtesa, with his symbolic white dog at his feet, reviews his troops while Speke looks on.
Right Grant dancing with Ukulima, the Bugandan Queen Mother

With similar disregard for the lives of his people, Mtesa loaded a double charge of powder and casually fired a bullet through a tethered cow and the adjoining palace wall so that the bullet went whizzing across the compound.

To Mtesa, who lacked Kamrasi's experience as a diplomat, the white visitors were little more than strolling magicians with strange taboos and customs. Speke's presents had their spells removed by being rubbed against the face of a native, and although he was willing to try a blistering compound, Mtesa insisted that Bombay was treated in similar fashion. Seeing that Grant had lost the index finger of his right hand (actually a wound from Lucknow), Mtesa casually asked what crime he had committed, as in Ganda the amputation of a finger was a punishment for theft.

In their own way, the white men's idiosyncrasies were no more explicable than native habits. Speke made a great fuss when he presented his gold ring to the Kabaka and gave him a lecture to the effect that gentlemen in England would think it a great honour, and they never wore brass or copper as they considered the metals to be demeaning. For much the same reason he refused the Kabaka's request to take pot shots at some vultures in a tree, because English gentlemen never shot sitting targets, and he preferred that the natives should throw stones to make the birds fly.

Undoubtedly the Victorian explorers were actors, playing and dressing for roles which had audiences at home as well as in Africa. Speke's refusal to sit on the ground before the Kabaka and only to doff his cap in salute was good publicity as well as good politics. Mtesa was intrigued by his visitor's audacity, and Speke's English readers felt he had preserved his status. Even the explorer's costumes had the dual purpose of inspiring the natives and giving an air of individuality to the wearer. Baker, besides his highland dress, usually wore in

235

Africa an over-sized kepi with an enormous sun flap. Livingstone's famous gold-braided naval cap eventually became official consular garb; and Speke and Grant insisted on muffling themselves in tweed waistcoats to demonstrate that the clothing of a Victorian sporting household was quite suitable for tramping in Africa. Even Stanley abandoned his renowned but commonplace solar topi, which he raised to Livingstone at Ujiji, in favour of a high-crowned cap with brass-lined air holes which became known as his 'Congo hat'.

Nor were the explorers averse to turning the newspapers' interest to good account. Their preferred paper was *The Times*, then at the height of its reputation as a news-hunting paper. Baker referred jokingly to his camp gossips as being as good at gleaning news as a *Times* reporter. Burton and Baker both made regular use of its correspondence columns to forward their own opinions, and Livingstone had copies sent via the Governor of Cape Town to the mouth of the Zambesi. His other favourite was *Punch*, copies of which he took into the interior with him; and in his letters he had a habit of referring to well known cartoons from the magazine. Stanley himself was a *Daily Telegraph* man, a compliment the paper's proprietors duly returned by helping to finance his Congo trip. However much the explorers ranted and raved about the inaccuracies and nuisances of the reporters, they were well aware of the value of publicity. Livingstone, in particular, was a habitual critic of the newspapers. He complained that he could not go to church without being pointed at, and that he was mobbed by the crowd in Regent Street and had to escape in a cab. Yet without the active help of the press his campaign to send missions to Africa would have been severely curtailed, and years before he became famous he was trying unsuccessfully to sell articles on missionary life to uninterested editors.

Vanity also played its part. Speke carefully arranged with John Blackwood that copies of his own articles were sent out to Africa when he went back there on his second trip; and his cable 'the Nile is settled' was a masterpiece of self proclamation. Sent from Khartoum to the Royal Geographical Society, it gave ample time to prepare a splendid home-coming. The Khedive's own paddle steamer was sent to bring Speke and Grant down from Aswan, and at Cairo they put up at Shepheard's Hotel. So much public enthusiasm was whipped up in England that Speke came home to a band playing 'See the Conquering Hero Come', and the local town of Taunton voted him a pair of presentation vases in gold, decorated with Nile flowers. Prince Albert himself attended a private lecture on the results of the expedition, and so many visitors attended the Special Meeting of the Royal Geographical Society to greet the two explorers, that it was held across the road in the larger capacity of Burlington House. Despite this precaution, the crush was so great that several windows were broken by the press of bodies.

Yet the book, even more than the magazine and newspaper, was the explorers' medium. They were note-takers of phenomenal dedication, clutching sheaves of blank paper to record their adventures and drawing pads on which to capture the exotic scene. Everything was done with an eye to the eventual book of the expedition. One reason why Speke selected Grant was that he could draw and paint; Burton, who made notes on every book he read, calmly set up a card-table in the execution square of Dahomey so as to take notes of a mass butchery; and Livingstone in the pitch of exhaustion still found time to transfer his notes fair hand from scraps of paper to a large stiff-bound journal carefully fitted with lock and clasp. These diaries and field-books were by far the most precious items of baggage. Stanley levelled his revolver at the head of the wretched porter carrying the tin box containing Livingstone's notes which Stanley had promised to take safely to the coast. The porter was wading unsteadily across a ford, and Stanley called out that if he slipped and dropped the box, he would be shot forthwith.

Publishers as well as authors were fiercely eager to see the expeditions in print for an enthusiastic public. John Murray's corner in Africana was strong, partly because he had been so quick to sign on Livingstone as an author at fifty per cent of the profits. But the Blackwood family made a serious attempt to breach it. Not content with publishing articles about rambling in the Rockies or hunting in the Himalayas, John Blackwood made Speke a handsome offer for the narrative of his second Nile trip. As Murray had already suggested £2,000 and a share of the profits, Blackwood matched the bid, invoked his personal friendship with Speke – he had earlier provided him with Grant's address when the expedition was being planned – and threw in the bait of a quiet room in his own house near St Andrews where Speke could work up his manuscript. Speke accepted, but the book itself received a roasting from the critics and undersold its print run. Undeterred, Blackwood approached Grant to recast some of his experiences as a parasite publication entitled *Camp Life*.

Part treatise, part travelogue, the explorers' books were more than library staples or presentation volumes. They were essential items in an explorer's baggage. Stanley carefully read up on Burton, Speke and Grant before he went off to look for Livingstone. Livingstone had Baker's *Albert Nyanza* with him on his last trip, and his own *Missionary Travels* were packed in the trunks of James Stewart, another missionary-pioneer who went out to the lower Zambesi to carry on the Doctor's work. By his own confession Stewart was so disillusioned by the realities of what he found that he took pleasure in hurling the *Travels* into the muddy depths of the river. Even the native rulers were included in the audience. Kamrasi had Baker's pictures sent to Nyoro and the *Illustrated London News* portraits of Speke and Grant lecturing the Royal Geographical Society were despatched up the Nile while Baker was still there.

One reason why the explorers were such inveterate authors was that, with the exception of Burton, they were indifferent public speakers. Burton was actually better on the podium than in print. He had a commanding presence, a clear voice, and a flair for repartee. By comparison his writing seemed confused and prolix, clouded by his love of foreign languages. In a single sentence he was capable of including words from six different foreign languages and then confusing the sense even further by inventing Englishisms of his own. So when Murchison invited him to the public debate against Speke, Burton was undoubtedly at an advantage. Compared with Burton and his forceful delivery Speke was a turgid and stiff lecturer, and he would have had no help from Grant, who was self-effacing to the point that he refused to attend the debate.

Baker, of course, preferred to go off shooting with friends in Scotland rather than stand up and lecture audiences. Livingstone was handicapped by a deep-rooted shyness coupled with what his tutor had called 'a heaviness of manner'. As a trainee missionary giving his first sermon, he had entered the pulpit to find that every word of his prepared speech had vanished from his head. Scarlet with embarrassment he turned and fled the congregation. Years later and after hundreds of sermons, lectures, after-dinner speeches and public breakfasts, he was still a weak performer, disjointed, stumbling, and difficult to follow. Only once was it recorded that a public address by Livingstone really struck fire. The occasion was a lecture in the Senate House at Cambridge to an assembly of dons, civic dignitaries and undergraduates. Livingstone had just completed a long lecture tour of Dublin, Glasgow, Edinburgh and the big industrial cities of England, and he was extremely tired. Very likely it was this tiredness, helped by the thought that he had finished his round of commitments, that made him relax. At the end of a dull and rambling talk he remained standing for a moment of silence, still facing his audience. Unexpectedly he told them that he would shortly be returning to Africa and that he expected to die there. Then with his voice rising to a shout he called out across the hall 'I go back to Africa to make an open path for commerce and Christianity; do you carry out the work which I have begun. I LEAVE IT WITH YOU!' The effect of this abrupt appeal was astonishing. According to the university registrar, 'there was silence for a few seconds, and then came a great explosion of cheering never surpassed in this building.' It exceeded anything he had ever heard in the Senate House, though he had attended four university installations including Prince Albert's and had been present at announcements of great victories over Napoleon.

It was Stanley's misfortune that by the time he too came to give public lectures about Africa, the public mood had changed. Audiences had grown apathetic, and in their boredom found diversion in ridiculing this earnest little man with his self-conscious attempts to imitate his predecessors. A subdued campaign of disparagement began gnawing away at Stanley even before he arrived back from finding Livingstone. There were letters to the papers saying he was a humbug. A Mr Gray writing from the British Museum raised doubts about the authenticity of Stanley's claims, but was promptly rebuked by a member of the Savage Club. Another writer thought he had detected a tell-tale flaw in Stanley's story. The Doctor, according to Stanley's account, had looked pale and wan at Ujiji. But, said the correspondent triumphantly, it was well known that on his last visit home Livingstone's complexion had been deeply tanned and 'it is difficult to conceive by what process it could have become blanched'.

Naturally there was a streak of national pride in these aspersions, as indeed there was throughout the lionization of the African explorers. 'It is with some regret', wrote the *Daily Telegraph*'s man from Marseille 'that I must commence by saying that Mr Stanley is not an Englishman or rather a Welshman, but an American citizen.' After one or two false starts including a Gallic rumour in *Le Soir* that he was the grandson of Lord Stanley and heir to the Earl of Derby, a Caernarvon newspaper ferreted out Stanley's true parentage, variously locating his mother as the innkeeper of the Cross Foxes in St Asaph or the Castle Arms in Denbigh. The *Pall Mall Gazette* grumbled that Stanley's story, exclusive to the *New York Herald*, was being 'doled out to us in driblets from the columns of an American newspaper'; and Sir Henry Rawlinson injudiciously wrote to *The Times* that Stanley had not found Livingstone, but Livingstone had found Stanley. His statement, though palpably untrue, was widely quoted, for there was a patriotic notion that Central Africa was somehow reserved for British explorers and that Stanley had been trespassing.

Two weeks after he arrived in London Stanley delivered his first serious public speech on the Livingstone rescue. It was an event full of ill-augured coincidences. The speech was made to Section E of the British Association, the same assembly to whom Speke's tragic death had been announced eight years before. Once again the Association was holding its summer meeting in a spa, this time at Brighton, and the presence of James Grant in the audience made a personal link with the earlier *débàcle*. Three thousand people including the ex-Emperor and Empress of France had come down to hear speeches on Africa, and yet Stanley himself arrived expecting that a short paper about his travels in company with Livingstone would suffice. Instead he found himself called upon for a complete account of his trip, and he proceeded with appalling clumsiness to trample upon the sensibilities of his listeners. Believing that they wanted to hear a eulogy of Livingstone and not a scientific summary – of which he was incapable anyhow – Stanley began a speech which blended mannered humility with gauche bravado. His first line was 'I consider myself in the light of a troubadour, to relate to you the tale of an old man who is tramping onward to discover the sources of the Nile.' Thereafter his speech lurched inexorably downward. Livingstone's friends in the audience were appalled to hear of their hero from the mouth of a man they thought so crass; the geographers were annoyed at what they felt was a wasted lecture; and the entire audience was embarrassed as Stanley grew near maudlin in his adulation of Livingstone. Even when Grant rose to put a serious question on problems of African drainage, he was put down with a renewed encomium of the great doctor. By the end of Stanley's lecture his listeners were half stunned and half amused by the grotesqueness of their chief speaker; and at dinner that same evening, under the onion domes of the Royal Pavilion, there were snickers from some of the diners when Stanley responded to the toast Health of the Visitors. Mortified, Stanley broke off his speech, announced that he had not come to be mocked and stalked furiously from the Banquet Room. Scarcely believing their luck, the newspapers seized on this new explorer scandal with gusto, and opened their correspondence columns so that the pro and anti Stanley factions could hammer away at one another.

A diamond-studded snuff box from the Queen and an audience with Victoria herself helped to sooth Stanley's bruised feelings. So did the award in October of the Victoria Medal of the Royal Geographical Society when, at the presen-

'Stanley's return to America – his reception at the Lotos Club, New York' – contemporary magazine picture

tation, Rawlinson who was the President, apologized for his previous remarks. Partly mollified, Stanley sailed for America the following month intending to make a nation-wide speaking tour at $500 each for sixty lectures, taking with him as stage props various samples of African cloth, African drums and spears, and the American flag said to have been carried at Ujiji.

But Stanley's dénouement was not yet over. America, unlike England, was not a fanatical spectator of the African game. Recovering from the effects of their civil war the Americans found the African adventure distant and trivial, and rather pompously British. Unfortunately for Stanley he arrived in America still showing the scars of his Brighton fiasco, and when he stood up to lecture his American audiences he bored them dreadfully, and they told him so. Trying to be scholarly, he was plain dull. Critics complained of his 'sing song doleful monotone' and his inability to marshal his arguments. 'Mr Stanley has utterly mistaken the necessities of the platform', wrote the man from the *New York Herald* itself.

> His map of Central Africa is not used, and the specimens of cloths which he brings on the stage are quite as useless, for he does not know how to make his hearers interested in them by making them illustrative of his subject. He overlooks the personal and the peculiar, and treats only of the geographical and the commonplace. All this is unnecessary, and it would be cruel to Mr Stanley not to say so.

The cruelty of course was in mocking Stanley so directly. But Bennett of the *Herald* still took a proprietorial view of Stanley, and he was piqued that his former employee had arranged the independent lecture tour. After an initially favourable reception, the African explorer was such a failure that he cancelled his engagement after the third lecture, and returned to England.

The robustness of American criticism brought home more clearly the fact that there was little time left for the non-specialist in African exploration. The opportunities of the amateur traveller were rapidly diminishing in Africa as the blank spaces were filled in, and new, more exacting, sciences arose. It was a trend which Burton saw very clearly. He wrote:

> The Anglo-African traveller in this section of the nineteenth Century is an over worked professional. Formerly the reading public was satisfied with dry details of mere discovery, was delighted with a few longitudes, latitudes and altitudes. Of late in this as in all other pursuits the standard has been raised. Whilst marching so many miles per diem and watching a certain number of hours per noctem the traveller who is in fact his own general, adjutant, quarter master, and commissariat officer, is expected to survey and observe, to record meteorology and trigonometry, to shoot and stuff birds and beasts, to collect geological specimens and theories, to gather political and commercial information, beginning of course with cotton; to advance the infant study of anthropology, to keep accounts, to sketch, to indite a copious, legible journal – notes are not now deemed sufficient – and to forward

long reports which shall prevent the Royal Geographical Society napping through its evenings.

Burton recalled that before he left for East Africa one 'ardent gentleman' wrote asking him to collect beetles and another sent 'recipes for preserving the tenantry of shells'.

The hard fact, too, was that African exploration was getting far more expensive. It had always been severe on a private purse, and one bone of contention between Speke and Burton had been the heavy debt incurred for porterage. Now, however, even Government-assisted expeditions were running into difficulty. Despite its £5,000 grant Livingstone's Zambesi trip lost him most of his private funds, and twenty years later Stanley needed £20,000 simply to put his second Congo task force into the field. These spiralling costs obliged hopeful explorers to modify their itineraries just when the lure of exploration was losing some of its glamour. A host of minor travels and support expeditions were beginning to follow in the tracks of the genuine trail-blazers and softened the impact of their achievements. It was no longer a daunting task to arrange a small-scale trip to Africa, and sometimes it was difficult to distinguish between the true explorer and a globe-trotting sportsman to whom Africa was merely an alternative to the Himalayas or Caucasus. The popularity of these trips was proved by the demand for the explorer's manual, *The Art of Travel*, written by Francis Galton, the Secretary to the Royal Geographical Society. The book, first published in 1855, ran through eight editions by 1893 and Burton himself took a copy to East Africa with him. It gave step-by-step instructions on how to prepare and conduct an expedition in all its details, from resilvering a sextant mirror to 'Savages, Management of'. Galton, a cousin of Charles Darwin, had himself trekked in South West Africa, and with Samuel Baker (followed by Cumming) as his most quoted pundit, it was inevitable that much of his advice had a strongly African flavour. There were helpful instructions on how best to filter muddy water in reed pens, the edibility of cake made from squashed gnats by the natives of the Shire River, and, for the Saharan traveller a recipe for replacing tent pegs by heavy weights buried two feet down in soft sand.

The increased popularity of African travel had the effect of putting a preservative gloss on the heroic aspect of the surviving Victorian lions. More and more travellers sought their opinions or read up their books before setting out themselves for Africa; and the public interest gained momentum with the new imperialist policies of governments. Sir Samuel Baker, after serving four years on the Upper Nile with the rank of an Egyptian pasha and a commission to suppress the slave trade, had retired to south Devon. From his large granite Gothic mansion, with its thatched summer-house to imitate an East African tribal hut, he wrote long letters to *The Times* advocating a bold policy in the

Sudan. As he was considered the outstanding Nile expert his opinions carried great weight. Richard Burton, after turning down an offer of £5,000 from Gordon to work for him, was belatedly awarded a K.C.M.G. towards the end of his life. He even mellowed sufficiently to give civil answers to the letters which hopeful explorers sent him at Trieste, where he spent his last years as British consul. Stanley of course was still in his late prime. Prematurely grey-haired from his exertions, he too was involved in river politics for a foreign power, serving King Leopold on the Congo.

Only Grant remained a comparatively minor figure. Although he was for a long time a council member of the Royal Geographical Society and served in the Intelligence Department of Lord Napier's Abyssinia expedition of 1868, he never became a truly popular hero. His policy of self-effacement almost seemed to be deliberate, for even after his death his family turned down a suggestion that his name should be added to the Speke obelisk. Nor, when the Royal Geographical Society transferred its premises, was he included on the frieze of illustrious explorers surmounting the panels of their new lecture hall in Kensington Gore. To the public as a whole the problem of the Nile source had really become passé almost as soon as it was solved, for neither Speke nor Grant was ever selected for Madame Tussaud's show; and when Lady Burton was asked to select a suitable costume for her husband's wax effigy, she chose to depict him as an Arab traveller. There he joined Livingstone, Stanley and Pasha Baker in the final pantheon of Victorian heroes.

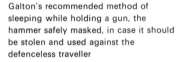

Galton's recommended method of sleeping while holding a gun, the hammer safely masked, in case it should be stolen and used against the defenceless traveller

Crisis in the Congo

CHAPTER TEN

Leopold II, King of the Belgians, was a very tall, rather pale man with the strained air of someone who suffered from chronic ill-health. This impression was reinforced by a slight stoop, a slow and deliberate manner of speaking, and a noticeable limp. His awkwardness, however, was misleading. Energetic and ambitious, he was to be notorious for a long series of love affairs with various mistresses and for the skill and determination with which he expanded his own, and Belgium's fortunes overseas. As a young man he had brought back from Greece a block of Acropolis marble and presented it to the Belgian Prime Minister, Frère-Oban. On it was inscribed 'Belgium must have colonies'. At forty years old, Leopold had been on the throne for a decade when he manoeuvred himself brilliantly into becoming the reigning genius of the African adventure.

His stratagem was a unique international conference held at the Palace in Brussels on 12–14 September 1876. The advertised purpose of the conference was to discuss Africa with regard to its future exploration, its 'civilizing', and the suppression of the remnants of the slave trade. The delegates to the conference were not official Government representatives, but academics, travellers, and men of note acting in a private capacity. Nevertheless, it was clear that they were also men of unusual influence. There were, for instance, no less than five presidents or vice-presidents of national geographical societies at the conference. Important delegations arrived from Great Britain, Germany, Austria-Hungary, France, and of course, from Belgium. But Italy and Russia sent only one representative each; and despite their own African colonies, Spain, Portugal, and Turkey did not send any at all. The most notable omission, though, was Africa. Not a single African country was represented at the conference for the very good reason that they were not asked. They were, it was tacitly felt, insufficiently civilized themselves to go about civilizing their neighbours. Even Egypt, the most industrially advanced of the African countries, had a gravely suspect record in the behaviour of its pashas. Besides, there was a nagging suspicion among the Brussels delegates that there were already too many countries involved in African affairs, and one reason why Leopold had called the conference was to sort out the confusion.

Leopold II, King of the Belgians

England's obsession with the Nile sources had rather blinded her to the fact that she was no longer alone in the field. Not only did she have serious rivals in African exploration, but in some cases she was actually lagging behind them. In North Africa, France was using her explorers to behave in an unashamedly colonial fashion. In 1830 she had openly moved against Algiers and, having expelled the Bey, who fled with his private fortune, established a French presence on the Barbary Coast. From there she was expanding both laterally along the Coast and southward into the Sahara. She had enlarged her Senegal Colony until it lapped against Gambia, and she held strategic bases in Dahomey. Farther south along the Atlantic coast Portugal was awakening from her African lethargy to quarrel over the ownership of the mouth of the Congo, and thinking of exploring inland more energetically. On the opposite perimeter of the continent Italian exploring parties had been probing into Ethiopia and along the tributaries of the Blue Nile. Across an enormous sweep of tropical Africa a large and active invasion of explorer-missionaries from almost every European nation was in full swing. Almost everywhere England was being challenged in regions to which she had once laid exclusive claim.

Nothing illustrated the anachronism of the British attitude more clearly than the contrast between their own delegation to the Brussels conference and the delegation which arrived from Germany. The British sent a blue ribbon party of ten men who reflected the traditional balance between commercial, philanthropic and academic interests in Africa plus the usual leavening of gentleman-travellers. It included Sir Bartle Frere who had been closely associated with the Abolitionist Movement; Sir Rutherford Alcock and Major General Sir

245

Henry Rawlinson, the President and Vice-President of the Royal Geographical Society; and William McKinnon who had substantial financial interests in Africa. In addition, there was the well-mannered James Augustus Grant, now a lieutenant-colonel and of course a man whose whole African career had been associated so far with the Nile sources. Rather more up to date was Commander Lovett Cameron, recently returned from his successful trans-continental journey which had started out in the tracks of David Livingstone. In sum, the delegation was imposing and splendid, but it was also slightly out of touch with new trends in Africa. Even Cameron could not have been called anything but a highly talented amateur.

Matched alongside them was a German delegation which, though only half as big, was made of far heavier metal. Led by the famous Chinese traveller and geologist Baron von Richthofen, it comprised three of the greatest names in contemporary African exploration: Dr Schweinfurth, Nachtigal, and Rohlfs. Taken together, they had spent longer in unknown Africa than the English, and had not merely been mapping the land and sketching its natives and fauna, but they had made expert studies of its languages, history, anthropology, geology, and botany. Schweinfurth in particular was a highly trained and dedicated scholar who represented the finest of the new generation of scientific travellers cast in the mould of Humboldt and Ritter, the pioneers of the new meticulous approach to geography.

The irony of the situation was that it was very largely the British who had introduced German travellers to Africa in the first place. Ever since the African Association paid to send Hornemann from Göttingen University into the Fezzan, it had been recognized that German scholars had particular success in travelling in Muslim Africa. The most illustrious example had been a remarkable young Arabist from the University of Berlin by the name of Heinrich Barth. While the Nile seekers were still preparing their great quest in East Africa, young Barth had been operating in disguise for almost five years in some of the most dangerous parts of the Sudan. Once again, it had been the British who had sent him there, though luck also played its part as Barth had initially been sent only as assistant to an Englishman, James Richardson. The purpose of the mission was to make one last attempt to open up commercial links with the states of the middle Niger and then carry on diagonally across Africa to emerge in Zanzibar. But Richardson died soon after reaching Lake Chad, and it was left to Barth to carry on his work.

Typically he gave it a more scientific slant. For month after month he travelled slowly across an immense area of the Sudan, including the kingdoms of Sokoto, Chad and Songhai, and he spent six months in Timbuctoo itself to obtain more accurate details about the city and its importance. As adept at languages as Richard Burton himself, Barth had passed himself off as an itinerant Muslim scholar so cleverly that in the end Sudanese villagers would come to ask for his blessing. By the time Barth re-emerged at Tripoli in 1855 he had explored the Sudan in such fine detail that his narrative alone ran to five thick volumes and he had sufficient notes to plan a monumental vocabulary of Sudanese languages. This he was never able to finish, dying a Professor at

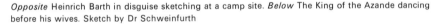

Opposite Heinrich Barth in disguise sketching at a camp site. *Below* The King of the Azande dancing before his wives. Sketch by Dr Schweinfurth

Berlin University at the remarkably early age of forty-four and regarded by many as the model explorer in Africa.

Georg Schweinfurth, the second member of the delegation after von Richthofen, had penetrated up the western Nile territories into the country of the Niam-niam (the Azande), an unpleasant race who filed their teeth to short points and practised ritual cannibalism. He had even been forced to accompany them on slave-catching expeditions. A first rank botanist and ethnographer, Schweinfurth was the first man to have confirmed the existence of the Central African pygmies, and had successfully bought one from the cannibal king in exchange for a small dog. The German had hoped to bring the pygmy back to Europe as living proof, but unfortunately his prize died on the return journey. Of his two colleagues, Gustav Nachtigal had served as physician to the Bey of Tunis and taken an embassy of gifts from the King of Prussia to the Sultan of Bornou; while the slightly sinister figure of Gerhart Rohlfs showed the more romantic side to the German view of Africa. Forty-five years old and an ex-sergeant of the Foreign Legion, Rohlfs was a lone traveller who had been attacked, beaten, robbed, and left for dead several times in his wanderings through the North African desert. As a result his left arm was now shorter than the right. He could no longer close the fingers of his right hand; and he carried a bullet scar in his thigh. Married to Schweinfurth's niece, Rohlfs had an important function at the Brussels conference for he was a confidante of Bismarck and seemed to the German public to be the standard bearer of their African dream.

The Conference opened on the serious and high-minded note which it was to maintain. The delegates were greeted by their Chairman and honorary host, King Leopold himself. Urbane, well travelled (as a young man he had toured in Europe, Asia and America), King Leopold was by his own admission deeply interested in geography and philanthropy. He had called the Conference, he told the delegates, 'to open to civilization the only part of our globe which it has not yet penetrated and to pierce the clouds which envelop entire populations'. He went on:

> It seems to me that Belgium, a central and neutral country, would be a good place for such a meeting, and this is what has encouraged me to call you all here in this small Conference which I have such great satisfaction in opening today. Have I any need to say that in calling you to Brussels, I have not been guided by selfish views. No, gentlemen, if Belgium is small she is happy and satisfied with her lot; I have no other ambition than to serve her well.

His exemplary behaviour quickly scotched the rumour that all he was really interested in was to found a Belgian penal colony in Africa; and even to the most cynical observers it appeared that although some of the decisions taken by the Conference were a little unrealistic, none of them was actually dangerous.

The basic premise was simple enough: that Africa should become another America in the degree of European influence. It was Leopold himself who suggested in his opening speech that the instrument of European intervention should be a string of 'civilizing stations' erected across Africa. These *stations civilisatrices* were to be beacons shining in the darkness. Established first on the coast of Africa and then inland, they would provide bases for exploration, centres for research programmes, and physical obstacles in the routes of the slave traders.

In the comfortable salons of the Brussels Palace, the Conference laid down precise guidelines for the operation of each *station*. They were to be unarmed and run by a handpicked commandant. Under him would be a staff of five or six Europeans, some of them scientists, others artisans who could demonstrate their practical skills to the natives. Each *station* was to contain observatories and laboratories, small museums and libraries devoted to local affairs. Their staffs would keep weather records, conduct soil tests, and compile dictionaries of local languages. Above all they would serve as advance bases for the explorers. No longer would it be necessary to suffer the hardships of a Livingstone or a Caillié. Each *station* would have a full inventory of explorers' necessities, from fresh clothing and trade goods to repair shops for their scientific instruments. There would be a map collection and an infirmary with all the modern medicines. Here the explorer could stock up on supplies, rest and recuperate, and seek sanctuary if ever he was sick or in danger. Of course the whole idea was gloriously impractical and absurd, but even such an experienced traveller as Rohlfs applauded the royal initiative. Carried away by the heady optimism of the Conference, he declared that nothing like it had yet been seen in Africa and that the *stations* would surpass even the role hitherto played by the English mission stations and consulates.

Bomby the Akka, drawn by Schweinfurth. One of the earliest sketches of a pygmy by a trained scientist

To finance this immense undertaking – which was no less than the systematic exploration of Africa – the Conference proposed that national committees should be established in every member country. Each national committee would be composed of local dignitaries. Their task would be to raise funds, select and equip expeditions, and to send their representatives to a Grand Central Committee in Brussels. Here would be the nerve centre of the entire international movement, and Belgium, King Leopold assured the Conference, was delighted that his country should be the host of such an illustrious venture.

Within a year it was done. The International Association, as it called itself, was in existence. There were national committees in every country which had sent delegates to the Conference, and in some, like Spain and Holland, which had not. The list of local patrons was dazzlingly royal. It included the King of Sweden, the Archduke of Austria, and Grand Duke Constantine of Russia. The German Emperor donated 25,000 marks to thé project. France's Committee included both de Lesseps, the man who had built the Suez Canal, and the editor Hachette.

Only the British response proved to be less than entirely satisfactory. The first full assembly of the new International Association, meeting in 1877, heard that for reasons of its Charter the Royal Geographical Society had been barred from acting as the National Committee for the United Kingdom. Moreover, in view of their unique position in Africa, the British felt that they would prefer to collaborate with, but not become part of, the International Association. Under the patronage of the Prince of Wales, they had set up a special African Exploration Fund (virtually administered by the Council of the Royal Geographical Society) and were looking into ways of helping the International Association's programme.

British coolness did little to dampen the ardour of the first Assembly of the Association, though it helped to strengthen Leopold's hand by removing from its Councils the most experienced nation in African affairs. Over the King's muted objections he was re-elected by a unanimous vote to a second term as President of the Association. It was a reasonable enough appointment as he had contributed generously to the Association's funds from his own purse and was readily available at its Brussels Headquarters. Indeed the advantages of close financial and geographical involvement in the Association's Head Offices were now becoming apparent. Enthusiasm among the member nations had been great, but cash donations were small. Money, when it was raised, was being earmarked for national expeditions and not being sent to Brussels. In Germany there had even been the creation of two geographical societies, one to collaborate with Brussels, the other to pursue specific German exploration in Africa. The only victor in this schizophrenic affair was Leopold and his Belgian Committee. His own national Committee became more and more synonymous with the International Association, and because he paid most of the Association's bills it was natural that he should have the greatest voice in its activities. Thus, one year after calling the original Brussels Conference, Belgium, which had scarcely had a single African explorer of any note to her name, now stood at the forefront of Europe's co-operative exploration of Africa. At least as valuable was the handsome asset of international moral approval which King Leopold was now about to put to good use.

The Association's Assembly now decided to put into action their scheme for a belt of *stations civilisatrices* across the width of Africa from one ocean to the other. The line that they chose was roughly Livingstone's old route from Zanzibar. The first *station* was to be near Ujiji on Lake Tanganyika, and the second at Nyangwe on the Lualaba. Later on it was proposed to build a third *station* in the little known territory of a South Congo king named Muato-yamvo, whom Lovett Cameron had encountered and who was chiefly remarkable for having a set of eye-teeth that curved out like a boar's tusks beyond his lips. Once these *stations* were established across Central Africa, the Assembly envisaged feeder routes reaching out north to the Nile, west to the Congo, and southwards to the Zambesi. Fleets of steam boats would move over these waterways and across the great lakes – Gordon Pasha's men were already planning to move up the Nile from Egypt and put boats on Lake Albert, knitting all Africa within a single vast system of civilized communication. Everywhere the Association's new flag, a yellow star on a blue background, would be the symbol for prosperity and enlightenment.

The International Association shipped a new brand of explorer out to Africa: the amateurs who knew nothing whatsoever about the realities of tropical life but who trusted to the sagacity of the organization they served. Inevitably most of them were Belgians, though there were also Germans, British, Swedes, Italians, Danes and French. They represented the advent of the international explorers to Africa and their experiences revealed the difficulties of running exploration by committee.

The Great Experimental Elephant Expedition was a case in point. For years people had been advocating the use of elephants on African expeditions to replace native porters. It was argued that elephants would prove to be more reliable and would repay their initial purchase price within a year because a single elephant could carry the equivalent of fifteen porter loads. Pundits quoted the example of Hannibal's trans-Alpine elephant corps and, much more recently, Lord Napier's use of elephants in the Magdala campaign. Previously it had been considered too expensive to fit out a special ship to carry trained elephants from India across to Africa for the purpose. But now, with King Leopold's cash available, the Belgians bought four elephants from the Bombay Government and landed them at Dar es Salaam, complete with their Indian mahouts and attendants. On 2 July 1879 they set out into the interior with three of the elephants carrying special 'elephant cases' of equipment, and the fourth, the same animal which had carried H.R.H. the Prince of Wales during his recent visit to India, bearing a howdah in which sat two Europeans beneath a large Belgian flag.

At first the procession made a triumphal progress, the Africans turning out to gaze in amazement at so extraordinary a spectacle. Even the African wild life was astonished: the men in the howdah had a chance to take pot shots at stationary giraffe apparently rooted to the spot by the novelty of the situation. The leader of the elephant force was an Irishman named Carter who had been specially brought over for the task, and he was delighted to observe that the animals seemed quite unaffected by tsetse fly, though bitten until the blood streamed down their flanks. At river crossings the elephants sported in the water and, in one place where the current ran too strongly for men to do the job, a she-elephant towed across a string of donkeys by holding their lead rope in her trunk. But the drawbacks to elephant travel in Africa soon became clear. The African paths simply could not bear the weight of the huge beasts, and crumbled away beneath their feet. Again and again the animals fell down or became mired in boggy ground, sinking up to the roots of their tails. When this happened they had to be unloaded and then coaxed free to the accompaniment of much roaring and trumpeting. One badly entangled elephant had to be towed out backwards by the other animals dragging on a chain. All the loading and unloading of equipment wasted time and energy, and when the elephants grew cautious and took to testing the roadway with their trunks before they would proceed, progress slowed to a crawl. Finally the big bull elephant known as 'Old Musty' showed signs of bad temper. He began cutting off the trail on detours of his own, and more time was wasted in recapturing him. Eventually he had to be shackled with heavy spiked iron bracelets and chains, and this reduced the speed of the column still further. The porters, the *pagazis*, resented having to chop a path for the elephants through the thick bush, and by the time the column was any distance inland they were arriving at camp five hours ahead of the animals.

'Old Musty' was the first elephant to die. His mahout found him one morning stretched on the ground. Carter's assistant cut up the body to see what had killed the animal but could find nothing wrong. He did note, however, that whereas the elephant had been sleek and fat when he started from Dar es Salaam, the corpse was now so thin that the flanks had fallen in and the backbone stood six or seven inches up from the flesh. It was the same with two of the other animals who died shortly afterwards. They had literally been worked to death. Instead of carrying a normal load of seven hundred pounds they had been overburdened with fifteen hundred pounds; and the long climb up from the coast, coupled with an inadequate diet, had undermined their health. By the time the column reached Lake Tanganyika only one animal survived, carefully nursed by the expedition.

The Elephant Experiment limped on for a time in the minds of its more ardent enthusiasts. It was suggested that on the next attempt it would be better if a gang of elephant catchers came over from India to capture young African elephants. Then they could be taken to a stockade in Zanzibar and trained to their work by two or three skilled Indian animals brought in for the purpose. For Carter the experiment ended tragically. Coming back down to the coast with an English companion, he was trapped in a village by a war party of Mirambo's men. Apparently by a misunderstanding Carter was shot while negotiating with the raiders. His companion killed fifteen attackers with his automatic rifle, and, seizing Carter's weapon, killed several more before he too was cut down.

This bloodstained calamity was a sign of the increasing chaos which was gripping the central lakes region. The whole area was in a state of flux brought on by rumours of King Mtesa's death and by inter-tribal bickering. Few of the Association's novices survived for long in this turmoil. Those officers who did not die of fever, soon lost all sense of purpose. Of the four Belgian officers with the first expedition, twó died at Zanzibar, one of dysentery on his way inland, and the fourth returned home. Only one *station* was built, at Karema, a hundred and twenty miles south of Ujiji, and it became little more than a fortified village. Forgetting the intention of being an unarmed beacon of civilization, it became the most heavily protected stockade in central Africa. It was surrounded by a sophisticated ringwork of glacis, trenches and counter scarps carefully designed by Belgian engineer officers, who were doing the job they had originally been trained to do.

Yet exploration in the traditional style was still possible in East Africa. During the time the Association was grinding to a halt there, the British had found themselves a new hero. He was Joseph Thomson, a young Scots geologist from Edinburgh University. He went out to East Africa in 1878 with an expedition led by a professional geographer and rowing enthusiast, Keith Johnston, who had been assistant curator in the Royal Geographical Society's map room. Johnston was trained to the German school of geography and would doubtless have introduced its more methodical imprint. But he died of fever soon after the expedition entered East Africa, and it was Thomson who took command. As with Barth who had turned out so well in similar circumstances, Thomson proved to be a natural leader. Though only twenty years old, he successfully explored the unknown region between Dar es Salaam and Lake Nyassa, discovering Lake Rukwa in the process. But the real measure of his success was that when he reappeared on the coast he had not lost a single man from his column. Moreover, he had been so frugal that there was enough money left over from the African Committee's initial grant to vote him a special gift of £250 and send Livingstone's former servant Chuma, who had acted as overseer on the expedition, a suitably inscribed first-class sword together with a silver medal. A second-class sword and medal were presented to the second overseer, and the hundred and fifty *pagazis* each received a bronze medal and a certificate of conduct bearing the Consular Seal.

The aloofness of the British, their demonstration of the correct way of doing things in East Africa, and the innumerable disasters suffered by the International Association expeditions, were beginning to sap the vigour of the Association, when its saviour appeared from the heart of Africa itself. It was, once again, the brisk H. M. Stanley, and he would be the pillar on which the international effort was to stand.

When the original Conference had met in 1876, Stanley had been somewhere in the middle of Africa, between Lake Tanganyika and Nyangwe, sending back stirring letters describing his progress. Almost a year later he had reappeared at the mouth of Congo, and immediately King Leopold had grasped the significance of his achievement. Without delay the King tried to hire Stanley, and the explorer was met at Marseille's railway station by two commissioners from the Association – shrewdly, one was an American – with a proposal that he should work for the Association. But Stanley was exhausted, emotionally as well as physically, and suffering from the effects of malnutrition. He also hankered after full recognition by the British, though there was no question of his claiming the Congo for England as a result of his newspaper-sponsored expedition (though Bennett of the *New York Herald* and Arnold of *The Daily Telegraph* both had rivers named after them). What Stanley had in mind was for the British to send him out again to the Congo as their agent in order to claim the whole river, and he dropped some very broad hints to this effect. In a letter to *The Daily Telegraph* he wrote:

> I feel convinced that the question of this mighty waterway will become a political one in time. As yet, however, no European power seems to have put forth the right of control . . . I could prove to you that the Power possessing the Congo, despite the cataracts, would absorb to itself the trade of the whole of the enormous basin behind. This river is and will be the grand highway of commerce to West Central Africa.

In a sense Stanley was quite right, but England missed her chance.

For several months Stanley waited. He visited continental spas to recruit his health, made speeches, and received a shower of geographical medals and citations. But the offer from the British never came, and finally he turned to pick up Leopold's invitation. Early in November 1878 he travelled to the Royal Palace at Brussels and met a specially convened panel of powerful merchants and financiers from Germany, France, England, Belgium and Holland. They met, like the 1876 Conference, at King Leopold's direct suggestion, and they proposed nothing less than the full-scale commercial penetration of the Congo. Cross-examining the explorer about navigation hazards on the river, the size of the bribes the river's bank chiefs would demand, and the potential for trade along the entire basin, they voted themselves into a syndicate calling itself the 'Comité d'Etudes du Haut Congo'.

For all its splendidly high sounding name, the new organisation's motives were unequivocally mercantile. Though the Comité declared that parts of its funds would go to scientific and philanthropic research projects in the Congo, the basic reason for its activities was to make money. It openly proposed to buy or lease river bank sites from the native chiefs in order to build trading posts and factories. Where necessary to protect its own interests or gain special advantage, the Comité announced itself prepared to buy up whole lengths of the river from the native inhabitants if it meant excluding other European rivals. The bankers and traders wanted to open up the entire Congo basin to a commerce which four years later, it was calculated, should return them eighteen times their original investment every single year. The idea was so attractive that the various members of the syndicate were prepared to put up £20,000 to get this project started on the spot, and they appointed Stanley to overall command of assembling the necessary personnel and equipment.

As always, King Leopold's role was crucial. Once again he had engineered the initial meeting, and once more he emerged from it as the dominant figure. From the Comité he accepted the position of honorary president and arranged that its chief executive post should go to his right-hand-man, Colonel Strauch of the Belgian Army. It was no accident that Strauch was already general secretary of the existing International Association and that the new Comité shared the same headquarters in Brussels. In effect, Leopold now controlled both wings of the international European approach to Central Africa, and managed to confuse the commercial and philanthropic distinctions still farther by arranging that the Comité should operate under the blue and yellow flag of the Association itself.

Leopold's brilliance as a diplomat now had to be matched by Stanley's expertise in the field. Even with the backing of a million gold francs, which was the Comité's official capital, it was obvious that he had an almost superhuman task. The crux of his problem was to force open the gates of the Congo by breaking past the great series of lower falls which barred direct access to the middle basin of the river. These lower falls ranked among the most daunting obstacles in Africa, a series of thirty-two treacherous rapids which rivalled the cataracts of the Nile for their difficulty. The river hurled itself through a narrow trench which it had slashed across the rugged Crystal Mountains, a trench barely a quarter of a mile wide in places but extending some two hundred miles in length. Here Stanley's two closest companions, Frank Pocock and the boy Kalulu, had both been killed on his previous trip, and here he had finally been forced to abandon the *Lady Alice*. Now he was faced with the immeasurably more difficult task of tackling the river from its downstream end and finding a way around the falls. The solution he proposed was to try to build a road around the falls, transport sectionalized steamers over this road, and then relaunch the boats for the run up to the middle Congo and its great inland embayment at Stanley Pool. Many observers and trained engineers considered the task impossible, even with the resources which Leopold and the Comité put at Stanley's command.

The resources in material alone cost the Comité 120,000 gold francs. Eighty tons of stores in 2,000 packing cases were shipped out to the mouth of the Congo in June 1879; clothing, tents, portable huts in galvanized iron, and road carts. With them went the new Congo River Fleet – the miniature side-wheeled paddleboat *En Avant*, 6 tons weight and 43 feet long; 3 screw-driven launches, *Royal*, *Espérance*, and *Jeune Afrique*; and the *Belgique*, a twin-screw steel steamer. The *Royal* was a special gift to the expedition by His Majesty the King of the Belgians. Built of mahogany to a lifeboat design by White of Cowes, she was fitted with a mahogany cabin, plate glass windows, rich fittings, and blue silk hangings. Together with a small wooden whale boat and two steel lighters, the vessels were expected to form a chain of communication stretching from the sea, deep into the interior highlands of Africa.

Meanwhile Stanley had gone first to Zanzibar to recruit *pagazis* from among the families and friends of his original Congo veterans. With the agreement of the Sultan he brought away sixty-eight Zanzibaris, three-quarters of whom had travelled across Africa with him before. Now he took them aboard the chartered steamer *Albion* by way of the Red Sea and the Suez Canal. At Aden he was intercepted by a telegram from Strauch to tell him that the Dutch merchants in the Comité syndicate had gone bankrupt. One of the principals had fled to America; another had tried to commit suicide. Strauch himself came down to Gibraltar to tell Stanley that Europe was buzzing with rumours that the new Congo venture had sinister colonial purposes. He hastened to reassure Stanley that though the original Comité was in ruins and its subscribers had asked for their money to be returned, King Leopold maintained his philanthropic interest. All that was left of the original Comité was the Brussels Secretariat and

The flotilla of the International Expedition at Banana Point near the mouth of the Congo

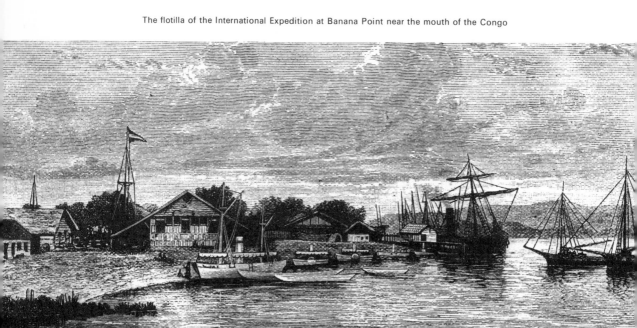

En Avant on the Congo

those officers connected with the International Association. But King Leopold, said Strauch, intended to use this foundation to build a new international organization to the same high ideals. In the meantime he sent Stanley an entirely new set of interim, and secret, instructions. They suggested the foundation of a new Congo state to be called Congoland. Stanley was to proceed with his original programme for opening up the river, but the outcome was to be a confederation of Negro tribes, led by their chiefs and advised by the white men at the *stations*. Each tribe and its *station* would be a little republic on its own, and through the intermediary of the *station* managers they would acknowledge the authority of a director general of *stations*, and beyond him, of the Belgian King.

How much of this scheme was the work of King Leopold and how much of it was concocted by Strauch, it is difficult to tell. But clearly the new arrangement had a much more political slant than the old merchant Comité. From being mere trading posts, the Congo *stations* were now intended as bases for political control. For a second time, King Leopold's position had been greatly strengthened by the withdrawal of his partners, and he was using his financial control and his central position in Brussels to strengthen his grip on the Congo. As for Stanley's role in all this, it was evident that he was quite out of his depth in the politics of the affair. He clung to the comforting notion that his task was basically a practical one. He was going back to the Congo to open up the river and build *stations* for the good of the Congo natives. He was so isolated from the main events that during the next two years he continued to address his field

257

H·M·
STANLEY
1893

reports to the Comité in Brussels, though by November 1879 the Comité had been formally dissolved. In its place existed the Association Internationale du Congo, a front organization whose only effective members were King Leopold and Colonel Strauch.

Stanley reached the trading town of Banana at the mouth of the Congo on 14 August 1879. There he found his river flotilla almost ready to proceed. A week was spent in correcting last minute faults in the boats and then, on the morning of the 21st, to the combined sound of their steam whistles, the little fleet set out upstream, making a brave show with their newly painted livery of grey hulls and gaily striped awnings fringed with red. Before long they entered upon a primeval scene which the members of the expedition would soon grow to detest for its alien monotony: a huge chocolate brown river slipping endlessly past the sheer impenetrable walls of dark green forest. The current ran at five knots so the boats had to keep close to the bank where the black, foetid earth of river alluvium was laced with the roots of the trees. Nothing moved or made a sound in this forest margin, and the clattering little flotilla with its asthmatic engines seemed utterly dwarfed in the immensity of the Congo. In Stanley's phrase, it seemed scarcely more than a flotilla of water-borne mosquitoes.

Up past the trading factories at Boma, the last European outpost on the Congo where some two years earlier Stanley had sent his despairing message for help, the fleet steamed towards its destination at the foot of the lower rapids. Several of the white members of the expedition – an American, two English, five Belgians, two Danish seamen and a Frenchman – were such novices to Africa that Stanley had to shoot a hippo to show them what the animal looked like. One of the Danes was so delighted that he climbed aboard the carcass to be able to write home about the experience. Fifty miles beyond Boma and the stretch called Hell's Cauldron, the expedition came to the head of navigation. There at the foot of the Yellala Falls they had to build their first and most important *station*. The place was called Vivi, and it was to become the pivot upon which the whole Congo operation turned. All reinforcements and supplies going upstream had to pass through Vivi because it was the last point for vessels from the sea. Equally, all products coming down the river would be handled there. It was the break of shipment between the tidal river and the huge detour which Stanley proposed to build around the lower falls of the Congo. Vivi was to be entrepôt, storehouse, outpost, and a showpiece for the outside world. It was also to be the grand prototype of Stanley's *stations* on the Congo.

Several days were spent in haggling with the local headmen over the purchase of a suitable site. Stanley wanted permission to build houses and make roads, and to exercise a trading factor's rights over any hitherto unoccupied lands

Stanley in the uniform of the Belgian Free State. Painting by Lady Stanley within a twenty-square-mile area of Vivi. For this he paid £32 down in cloth and a rental of £2 per month. The price, he pointed out, showed that the natives obviously knew about European trading practices for they had bargained shrewdly. Everything about them revealed regular contacts with the trading stations at the mouth of the river: they were armed with Tower muskets and their assortment of ceremonial dress ranged from an English red military tunic and a dark brown coat which had once belonged to a London club, to a banker's garb of black frock coat and silk hat.

The Vivi agreement was concluded on 24 September, and three months and twenty-four days later the *station* was complete. It was an incredible task. With the help of native labour, the summit of a 340-foot hill had been cleared of vegetation. A road had then been built up to the crest from the landing place on the river. While the more powerful boats of the flotilla ran a shuttle service in supplies, the top of the hill had been levelled. Houses had been built for the European staff; the Zanzibari lines, stables, repair shops, and storerooms had all been constructed and painted. The main headquarters building was a two storey chalet built of thick planks with a wine cellar beneath it. In the central plaza a garden had been constructed. To obtain suitable soil for it, Stanley had paid the natives of Vivi to bring up the rich dark river alluvium, 2,000 tons of it, carried up in boxes and checked for correct weight by Zanzibari policemen at the head of the road. In this garden Stanley had planted mangoes, oranges and lime plants brought from Zanzibar, as well as a variety of European vegetables. On 25 January 1880, to mark the completion of Vivi Station, he held a banquet for his European staff and the local headman. The order of his toasts indicated the nature of his priorities. They were to Leopold; then to Queen Victoria and the President of the United States; and finally to the 'Contributors to the support of the expedition'.

Stanley was now ready to tackle the heart of his Congo master plan: to open up the road around the lower falls and haul over it two complete steamers, their boilers and machinery, and sufficient equipment to establish the *stations* up as far as Stanley Pool. It was a task worthy of the Pharoahs, and indeed the immense effort of dragging the steamers over the land had a biblical flavour. In advance went a scouting party to mark out the line of the road with bamboo canes, from which fluttered strips of cloth. The bamboo canes were linked by a long cord, and on each side of this cord a pioneer corps of Zanzibaris and local labourers cleared a swathe through the vegetation, and levelled the ground with hoes and spades. Then they marched back to the *Royal* which, because she could not be dismantled into sections, rested entire on a great steel wagon specially built for the purpose. Harnessing themselves to enormous hawsers, the labourers dragged the *Royal* over the crude roadway as far as they had built it. Back again to collect the *En Avant*, and back twice more to pick

Left Hauling a boat up the Nyongena hill. *Right* The interior of Vivi Station

up supply carts, the hauliers travelled five times over each section of the road to shift the great mass of equipment forward. At first it was relatively easy work over a rolling plateau, but then they came to a series of ravines which had to be filled laboriously with earth to make causeways; a forest of hardwood through which men with axes had to hack a nine-foot passage; and a succession of deep valleys into which the ponderous, top heavy wagons were cautiously lowered and then dragged up the opposite slope with immense toil. At times the gradient was one in four against them, and huge pulleys were lashed to trees so that the files of porters could heave on cables against the purchase to creep the wagons up the hillside, while picked attendants risked their lives to place chocks behind the wheels. For fifty-two miles this prodigious labour continued, past native villages and over areas which crawled with spitting snakes. Each sack of food had to be carried up from Vivi by relays of porters, and Stanley calculated that by the time the expedition relaunched on the river, it had marched and countermarched a grand total of 2,352 English miles to achieve its object.

The strain on the European personnel was tremendous. The great adventure turned into a back-breaking nightmare which began every day at 6 am and, with a noontime break, finally ended at dusk. Every one of the dozen or so white men fell sick of fevers and gastric disorders. Stanley himself very nearly

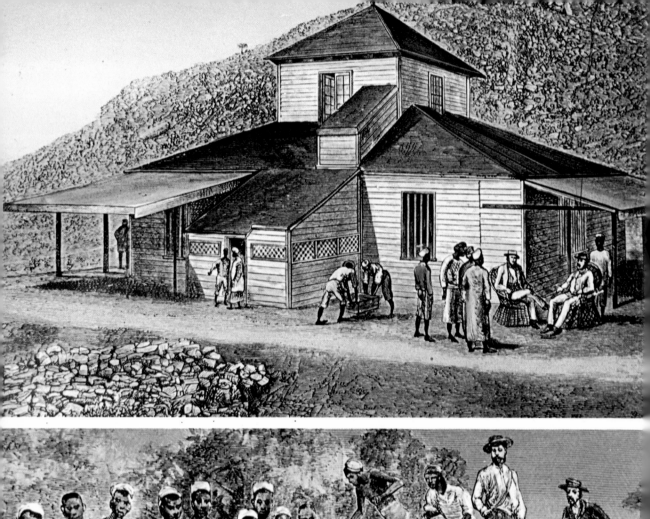

died of a particularly bad attack of fever. Several of his colleagues became disenchanted with the project and returned home. One or two died. One committed suicide. The Brussels Secretariat steadily sent out replacements and, after careful research by Colonel Strauch, even dispatched a score of donkeys from Teneriffe in the hopes of speeding up the progress into Africa. Those white men who managed to survive gradually acquired the skills of their trade. They learned to build their roads along the hippo trails because the giant animals always picked the easiest gradient, and the young army engineers gained a lifetime's experience in the blasting of stubborn rock faces. From the admiring natives Stanley acquired his nickname 'Bula Mutari', the 'Breaker of Rocks', and a British Consul who came up from Banana to look at the progress reported favourably back to the Royal Geographical Society that Stanley's energy would make the Congo 'the highroad from Western to Central Africa'.

But all this was not fast enough for King Leopold. Via Colonel Strauch, he kept bombarding Stanley with letters to speed up his progress. In addition to Stanley's other problems, he had to fend off a stream of questions and directives, all aimed at prodding him forward. He was told that the Brussels Bureau had learned that a French expedition was moving inland from Gabon, and threatening to bypass Stanley and establish their own *station* on the Congo ahead of him.

The first positive confirmation that Stanley received of this move came on 7 November 1880 when his expedition was still only two-thirds past the cataracts and encamped on a small stream, the Bula river. It was a Sunday morning and Stanley was resting in camp surrounded by the stranded hulks of his boats. One of his natives came running up with a sheet of paper which he thrust into Stanley's hand. On the paper, written in pencil, were the words 'Le Comte Savorgnan de Brazza, *Enseigne de Vaisseau*'. According to the native messenger, a tall white man was approaching from the interior who described himself a 'Francess' and carried a gun which fired many times. An hour later Savorgnan de Brazza himself appeared. Looking haggard but well turned-out in helmet, blue naval coat and his legs encased in leather gaiters, he marched into Stanley's camp at the head of fifteen men. Most of them were Gabonese sailors, armed with Winchester repeating rifles.

The meeting between Stanley and de Brazza was the third of the epic encounters between the explorers in Africa. It followed the famous Livingstone–Stanley meeting at Ujiji, and the rendezvous at Gondokoro where Samuel Baker had met Speke and Grant coming downstream from the Nile sources. Yet the de Brazza–Stanley confrontation was not quite like either of these earlier episodes. It had neither the salvationist quality of Ujiji, nor the camaraderie of Gondokoro. Instead, it was cool, unexpected, and sharpened by a slight edge of tension between the two men. Stanley was later to write that

Stanley's colour lecture slides: *above* the commandant's house at Vivi Station which even had its own wine cellar; *below* novice explorers celebrate on a dead hippo their interview was hampered by his own abominable French and de Brazza's poor command of English. But almost any of Stanley's Belgian assistants could have successfully acted as an interpreter, and the truth of the matter was that both men were very close-mouthed because they were, in the final analysis, rivals. Stanley must have been chagrined to see the small fast-moving French party marching out of an area which until recently had been regarded as Stanley's exclusive territory. The position was reversed from the days when he himself had thrust briskly through to rescue Livingstone. It was now de Brazza who could point to the huge ridge of mountain still lying across Stanley's path and say to him, 'It will take you six months to pass that mountain with those wagons. Your force is too weak altogether for such work as you are engaged in.' After more than a year toiling past the cataracts, Stanley was so out of touch with the political reality that until de Brazza actually strode into his camp, he had scarcely heard of the man by reputation, let alone imagined to meet him in the Congo.

Yet Pierre Paul François Camil Savorgnan de Brazza was France's best known African explorer. Though an Italian aristocrat by birth, he was totally enamoured of everything French. Sponsored by a French admiral he had joined the French navy as a cadet and later taken French citizenship. He believed deeply in the glory of France and considered Africa to be the ideal area

'Stanley was resting in camp surrounded by the stranded hulks of his boats . . . ,

De Brazza on the march with his marines

for the expansion of French culture. While Stanley was crossing the continent in 1875 with the *Lady Alice*, de Brazza had gone on a French expedition up the Oguwe river in Gabon. Emptying into the Atlantic north of the Congo, the Oguwe was a much shorter river than the Congo, but its feeder streams curved round until they interlocked with the tributaries of the middle Congo. On his first attempt de Brazza had actually reached the Alima-Congo watershed but was too exhausted to continue, and he had turned back without proceeding down the opposite slope and reaching the Congo. Had he done so he might have beaten Stanley in the discovery of Stanley Pool.

Returning to Europe, de Brazza begged the French Government to send him to Africa again to complete his mission, but met with a lukewarm response. Ironically it was the French National Committee of the International Association, supported by Gambetta, which eventually sponsored him to return to found two civilizing stations, helped by a grant from the French Government. Sailing back to Gabon, he arrived six months behind Stanley's international armada, but quickly closed the gap by the speed with which he advanced into the interior. Pausing only long enough to mark out his first *station*, Franceville, on a strategic confluence of the Oguwe, de Brazza moved by rapid marches over the watershed and down into the Congo basin. He travelled light, with only a sergeant and a squad of ten Senegalese marines. Along his route he contacted the local chiefs and, in exchange for small gifts, persuaded them to acknowledge French influence in the area. Reaching Stanley Pool he contacted the most important native leader in the area, who styled himself the Makoko, and persuaded him to place his tribal land under French protection. In a splendidly theatrical ceremony de Brazza handed him a French tricolour and proposed to 'bury war'. A hole was dug in the ground into which de Brazza flung a handful of cartridges. One native threw in some gunpowder, another a gunflint, and on the spot a tree was planted as a symbol of peace and plenty. As the Makoko claimed a nine-mile stretch of the right bank of the river, this treaty effectively placed a political clamp on one side of the Congo, while similar agreements with Ubangi chiefs on the Congo itself completed the political barrier. Leaving his Senegalese sergeant and two marines at the village of Ncouna, de Brazza then proceeded downriver to meet Stanley and his toiling pioneers.

De Brazza handled the meeting very shrewdly. During the two days he was at Stanley's camp he never once mentioned the treaty he had made with the Makoko, which ceded Congo territory directly to France. Relations between Stanley and de Brazza remained polite rather than cordial. De Brazza had every need to conceal his precise activities because his treaty had yet to be ratified by the French Government. Stanley, on the other hand, was too

Opposite 'Burying War'. *Above* Stanley directing a boat to be carried to the river

absorbed by the labour of his great enterprise, or perhaps too naïve, to suspect the French explorer of deception. At any rate, he overlooked the clear warning in one of Strauch's earlier letters that 'rivals whom we cannot disregard threaten, in fact, to forestall us on the upper Congo. Monsieur de Brazza will try to follow the Alima down to its junction with the Congo where he hopes to arrive before us. We have no time to lose.' To Stanley it must have seemed just another spur to prod him forward; but in fact de Brazza had already forced his hand.

This realization came long after de Brazza had gone on his way to Vivi. Stanley, having completed his road and relaunched the boats, was reconnoitering on foot along the north shore of Stanley Pool. He was at a native village, talking with its chief, when he saw an extraordinary sight. Marching towards him through the village were two Negroes dressed in French navy shirts and hats, one of them carrying high a tricolour on a staff. At the head of the little group strode a tall Senegalese sergeant, part Negro, part Moor, dressed in the costume of a French naval sergeant with the stripes of a non-commissioned officer on his sleeve. Marching boldly up to Stanley, the Negro sergeant addressed him in excellent French and handed him a note to read. It was a formal notification, signed by de Brazza, that the territory had already been claimed in the name of France.

Sergeant Malamine Kamara

The sergeant was Malamine Kamara, and among the African explorers he was remarkable not least because he was an African himself. It was true that there had been African-born explorers before him, men like Chuma and Susi, but they had always acted in the capacity of assistants to the explorers. Malamine Kamara, however, had been given his own command. It was nothing but a leaky hut in an African village, a flagpole and a large tricolour, and two black soldiers; but the sergeant discharged his duties with a fierce and unswerving loyalty. 'Sergeant Malamine is provisionally appointed head of the French Station at Ncouna. He will guard this post until the day he is relieved by the permanent head', ran the official letter of instruction left by de Brazza. Because Malamine could not read, he showed this letter to his European visitors but always made it clear that he would allow no trespass from anyone except a Frenchman. The power he wielded over his Congolese villagers was extraordinary. They regarded him as a great chief (he took to wearing his hair in the local style of plaits arranged like ribs on a melon) and an intruding Baptist missionary was nearly lynched by an angry crowd when he incautiously attempted to enter the village without permission. The mob was stopped just in time by the arrival of Malamine who coolly explained that he and the villagers merely wished 'to guard the flag of France'. Stanley, who was a good judge of men of action, had no hesitation in pronouncing his opinion of Malamine: 'A very short acquaintance with the sergeant,' he wrote, 'proved to me that he was a very superior man . . .'

The presence of Malamine and his dogged guardianship of Stanley Pool effectively removed the Congo question from the shadows where King Leopold would have preferred it to remain. Stanley was finally able to take his steamers into the Pool and establish a *station* on the south shore at Leopoldville. But until Malamine was placated it was clear that he could blockade the river with his native auxiliaries and Winchester rifles. To his credit, Stanley was loth to try a direct confrontation, and so the battle ground shifted from the Congo to the Conference rooms of Europe where the whole question was nervously discussed.

Meanwhile in France de Brazza had not been wasting his time. Convinced that Stanley was merely plotting a Belgian coup in the Congo, he began to undermine his rival's position. He revived those slurs against Stanley which claimed that he was a man of violence, too quick to pull a trigger. According to de Brazza the lower falls of the Congo were an impenetrable obstacle and it would cost far too much to build and maintain a roadway around them. Instead he suggested that the Oguwe was the easiest corridor into Stanley Pool and that the middle basin should therefore become the concern of France. Drumming up French public opinion behind him, de Brazza talked in glowing terms of the untapped riches of the Congo and the vast potential which lay awaiting a French initiative. To try to silence him King Leopold invited him to Brussels and offered him a job superintending the construction of a railway around the falls. But de Brazza would have none of it. He continued his campaign until Stanley himself arrived in Paris to refute the charges in public.

Leopold now realized that the whole matter was getting out of hand, and was beside himself with anxiety over a public confrontation between Stanley and de Brazza. 'What can be done to make Stanley keep quiet?' he wrote to Strauch, as Stanley began his counter-attack in the press. But Stanley could no longer be manipulated. He accepted an invitation to speak to a grand banquet on 20 October 1882. It was to be given by an old circle of his admirers from his first trip, the Stanley Club, and organized by the Paris correspondent of his old newspaper, the *New York Herald*. The event had all the anticipation and excitement of another 'Nile Duel'. People came to see a head-on clash, perhaps as sensational as the Burton–Speke feud at Bath. When his turn came to address the dinner guests, Stanley launched into a rebuttal of all that had been said against him and accused de Brazza of double dealing. He had duped the Makoko, said Stanley, because no African chief really understood what was meant by ceding his territory, least of all in exchange for a few trifling gifts and a French flag. De Brazza had introduced 'immoral diplomacy into a virgin continent', whereas he, Stanley, had no political ambitions whatever. Even as he was speaking de Brazza entered the banquetting hall and was invited to sit beside the United States Minister. When Stanley had finished, de Brazza rose and took Stanley's hand. His speech, which he had already written out and translated into English, was short and to the point. He praised Stanley's efforts in Africa, and he openly acknowledged his debt to Stanley's example. He continued:

> But the flags which I distributed everywhere as a symbol of friendship are borne from tribe to tribe and proclaim that a new era has begun for these populations. Gentlemen, I am French and a naval officer, and I drink to the civilization of Africa by the simultaneous efforts of all nations, each under its own flag.

De Brazza's public unrepentance meant only one thing: he knew that he had won. On 30 November, the French Parliament ratified the cessation of the *stations* given her by the Congo chiefs. The whole question of Central Africa was no longer a matter for the explorers alone, it was now openly acknowledged that it involved the territorial ambitions of the European Powers. The era of pure exploration was at an end, and the 'scramble for Africa' was now to take precedence.

Stanley watching the phalanx dance by Mazamboni warriors

Conclusion

CHAPTER ELEVEN

So it was de Brazza and Kamara, respectively an Italian and a Senegalese working for France, and Stanley, a Welshman working for the King of Belgium,* who finally brought down the curtain on the old style of African exploration. Their activities on the Congo forced the Great Powers in 1884 to hold a general Conference at Berlin to put the whole African question into perspective. Clearly it was no longer possible to allow European travellers to go exploring at will in Africa if they were liable to stake out national claims to large areas and these in turn led to international arguments. The official Conference agenda considered the problems of the Congo's navigation and what should constitute effective annexation of African territory; but the behind-the-scenes negotiations of the Powers were at least as crucial. The term 'spheres of influence' began to be bandied about and Africa was carved into portions as the rival Powers each took its share. In the main, the continent was parcelled out on the basis of previous exploring activity, so the efforts of the explorers had their reward. But there was also some difficulty in drawing precise boundary lines through areas that were still largely unknown, so there followed a slightly ludicrous stampede as national exploring parties over the next few years went dashing off to Africa to pick up the last few crumbs of land. Armed with bundles of flags to hand out to the chiefs, they set up the national outposts which the Conference had proposed should be the mark of 'effective occupation'. By 1892 over four-fifths of the continent was under foreign control, though by and large these late-comers obtained only the more desolate and useless parts of Africa. The choicer parts had already been claimed.

The Congo itself, one of the most valuable areas of all, had a most curious history. Despite its being a prime cause of the Conference, the grand delegations came to Berlin with only the vaguest suggestions as to a solution of the Congo problem. They were far more certain of what they did not want to see happen to the Congo than of any alternative to erect in its place. France and

---

* In 1882 Malamine Kamara received the Medaille Militaire for 'exceptional services; having stayed faithful as guardian of our flag at Brazzaville until relieved from his post'. Stanley finished up an M.P. and living in Surrey.

272

England were highly suspicious of one another, and each was determined to keep the other out. They were both fearful of German 'land hunger', though Germany had no historical reason to lay claim to the river basin. Portugal, already branded with a sour reputation for allowing slavery to continue in her colonies, further forfeited her position by entering into prior negotiations with England. By an extraordinary process of compromise – almost of oversight – the Congo was allowed to slide even more firmly into King Leopold's grasp. As always, he outmanoeuvred his opponents. Before the Conference opened, he obtained the support of the United States which entertained the mistaken idea that the King proposed to establish a number of Negro Congo states on the model of newly created Liberia. Elsewhere the King's lobbyists won friends and allies by administering his well-tried mixture of philanthropy and free enterprise. The missionary interests, who wielded considerable advisory power, were attracted by the avowedly humanitarian aims of the King's Association Internationale du Congo. The merchants liked its doctrine of free trade along the river. Most important of all, the Association's agents led by Stanley, whose prestige was enormous though he was only at Berlin officially as an American adviser, were able to find support from among the powerful national delegations who despaired of finding any other solution than to let the Congo remain 'internationalized' under the altruistic-sounding Association. Thus in February 1885 the Conference officially placed the Congo under the guardianship of the International Association, symbolized by the person of its royal President. The Belgian Parliament insisted that the whole matter was to be the King's own affair and let him proceed with it as he liked. Five months later, Stanley's successor at Banana was able to hold a small ceremony proclaiming King Leopold the 'Sovereign of the Congo Independent State', and in effect he became ruler of a personal fief of more than a million square miles of Africa. It was the richest single prize in the entire African adventure and demonstrated that African affairs had positively been transferred from the explorers in the field to the council chambers of Europe.

Caricature of de Brazza

The year 1884 also marked an important change in Africa itself for it was the year in which King Mtesa finally died. His death had been prematurely announced several times before and had called forth at least one solemn obituary in the columns of the British Press. Certainly by the time of his death Mtesa had come to seem almost a familiar figure to British public opinion, and the East African kingdom he ruled was now vastly changed from the days when Speke and Grant had visited his court and found it full of sycophantic nobles who considered the Ganda monarch the greatest lord on earth. Now there were regular visits by missionaries and engineers; there was a scheme to build a railway inland from the coast; and small steamers were appearing in ever-increasing numbers on the rivers and waterways of East Africa. The old tribal chiefdoms had been usurped or broken down by warrior captains like Mirambo. To the north men like Gordon and the American Chaillé-Long were trying to extend the Egyptian Khedive's influence and rule. Farther south, where Sparrman and Cornwallis Harris had once filled their collecting boxes and hunted big game, the Diamond Rush was over and the Gold Rush just beginning. With much of her mystery being stripped away and the poverty exposed beneath, Africa was no longer being called the Dark Continent but the 'Hapless Continent' and the 'Expiring Continent'. In geographical terms there were still large areas left to be explored – in the Sahara, along the upper Congo tributaries and elsewhere – and expeditions would soon be leaving to investigate these regions, but there would be very few discoveries of real grandeur. The basic geography of Africa had been laid bare and, what mattered for the explorers themselves, the essential elements of the African adventure were all well established. In future there would be little that was really new. Even the Fashoda incident, when the French officer Marchand moved across Africa by forced marches to the Nile and met Kitchener's steamers on the river, only followed the pattern already set by Stanley versus de Brazza on the Congo. And here again the outcome was decided, not in Africa, but in Europe when the French Government finally ordered Marchand to withdraw.

Indeed, looking back over the four centuries of the African adventure, it is remarkable how very early one can distinguish many of its characteristic features. There is a striking similarity to the successes as well as the failures of her explorers and travellers. The story of the Denham–Clapperton feud, for example, was repeated with an almost theatrical precision in the Burton–Speke quarrel in East Africa, right down to the innuendo of homosexuality levelled against one of the protagonists in each case. The festering resentment which poisoned both expeditions might have led an observer to suppose that two-man expeditions were impractical in Africa. But the Lander brothers and the later Speke–Grant partnership demonstrate that the trouble was not from the size of the team, but from the nature of its members. The lesson of the feuding expeditions in Africa is that very different types of men could be attracted to the continent and, once there, lapse into the most violent disagreements with one another.

In like fashion the same types of explorer-traveller appear again and again in the story of the African adventure. Speke was not only very similar to Denham in the somewhat priggish view of his own destiny, but he also echoed Captain Laing in the manner in which he proposed to carry out his African journeys and put them to good use later on. In a sense all three – Speke, Denham, and Laing – transposed their orthodox English careers to Africa as a short-cut to advancement and, while in Africa, behaved much as they would have done in army circles in England. By the same token Mungo Park can be

Punch's view of Stanley captioned 'H.M. Stanley. Portrait of the Explorer looking out for M. de Brazza. "I'll let him know if he Con-go on like this!"'

matched alongside H. M. Stanley as two of the most outstandingly successful men in African exploration who both rose from humble beginnings by virtue of very similar talents. Despite a gap of almost two hundred years and the advances of technique which had taken place, the same driving ambition and iron will carried them forward. On their two river-borne ventures of the Congo and the Niger, the parallels are unmistakable. Willing to make enormous personal sacrifices, both Park and Stanley were prepared to cajole and organize mercilessly, to drive their men forward and, when all else failed, to push themselves to the last pitch of exhaustion. Had Mungo Park been better armed or with a larger crew when he set off on his last voyage down the Niger, the outcome might well have been as spectacular as Stanley's bold thrust down the Congo from Nyangwe to the ocean.

Indeed the temptation is to classify too neatly all the African adventurers into their groups – the army officers, the hunting enthusiasts, the methodical Germans, and so forth. But the patterns are distorted by the presence of individualists with whom it is difficult to draw any close comparisons. It is asking too much, for instance, to seek another man quite like David Livingstone among the front rank African explorers, which is one reason why he retained his own particular charisma. Strangely enough, Richard Burton, who seemed in his own day to be unique, really shared many characteristics with James Bruce who was equally flamboyant and just as disposed to shock and amaze his contemporaries. On the other hand a Caillié or a Ledyard are more difficult to place, for they fall outside any of the easy divisions of the African travellers.

One genuine curiosity, though, of the African story, is the extraordinary number of Scotsmen who were involved. The list includes Mungo Park, Bruce, Oudney, Clapperton, Laing, Livingstone, Paterson, Grant, Lovett Cameron, Gordon Cumming, and Joseph Thomson. Indeed more than half the British travellers of note turn out to be Scotsmen and, as time went on, the travellers themselves were quick to point out their Scots ancestry and their links with their countrymen previously in Africa. On closer examination, however, the Scots travellers conform rather more significantly to the broad social divisions than to their national origin. The haughty James Bruce had little in common, apart from nationality, with the mild Doctor Oudney, whereas his aristocratic eccentricity matches well with the antics of Roualeyn Gordon Cumming, second son of the Laird of Altyre. In fact the Scottishness of the travellers appears as an overlay on their social background. As far as their fitness for Africa was concerned, Mungo Park and David Livingstone should be seen as lower middle class first, and lowland Scots second. Like their other country-men, their Scottishness was really more an encouragement to wander abroad to see a wider world and accept the outside challenge, which might have been found as well in Canada or Australia as in Africa.

The truth of the matter is that the whole African adventure shows that there was no such stereotype as the ideal African explorer. This is one of the story's great attractions, for it throws up such an army of characters and incidents. Almost anyone could try his hand in Africa provided that he had a strong constitution and was prepared to undergo some prior training. This was more than a question of walking barefoot on hunting trips like Speke or eating strange diets beforehand. The real need was to immerse oneself completely in the foreign culture, not necessarily to pass oneself off as a native – which was seldom really practical – but simply to avoid giving offence and in order to extract as much information as possible, despite the barrier of a foreign language. As it happened, this degree of preparation was really only possible for journeys in Muslim Africa, whose culture was sufficiently well known to be copied. Yet Arab culture extended so far into Africa that it was surprising that this technique was not practised more often. The proficiency of men like Hornemann and Barth contrasts strongly with the much more amateur ventures of Laing and Clapperton, and is reflected in the quality of their reports out of Africa. The difference is brought out even more sharply with Burton and Speke in East Africa where, as Burton maliciously pointed out, there was something ridiculous in the fact that Speke could not communicate with villagers or guides except through his interpreter Bombay, while Burton, the Arabist, was quite content to stay in the villages picking up a mass of geographical and anthropological information from Arab traders.

As for good health, it was essential that a traveller was able to resist African diseases and sicknesses of all sorts. Without doubt Africa was immensely hard on a man's constitution. When Livingstone set out on his last trip he was in his mid-fifties; yet his years in Africa made him look more like a man in his seventies. Mungo Park's quite extraordinary resilience to malaria and dysentery helps to explain his far greater success compared with his predecessors in West Africa. It was far more important that a man should be able to weather bouts of fever than that he should be a good shot or an experienced navigator capable of tracing a precise route across country. Livingstone managed to show how much could be accomplished by sheer will power – his own remedy for sickness was to keep on taking as much exercise as possible – but death by sickness cut short a large number of promising African careers, from Captain Clapperton at Sokoto to the Italian adventurer Belzoni, once a professional strong man in a circus, who had scarcely stepped ashore in West Africa, intending to traverse the continent, before he fell dead of fever.

Of equal importance to robust health in the field was the traveller's good fortune in finding himself reliable native helpers. It is difficult to undervalue the enormous contribution to the African adventure made by men like Bombay, Stanley's 'Uledi the Coxswain', Livingstone's Susi and Chuma, Isaaco, who helped Park and then recovered news of his death, and the Arab sheik, Hatitia, who saw a succession of British travellers into the North African desert. These are the prominent names in a large corps of African helpers and assistants who made a vital contribution to the opening up of their own continent. The African adventure was at least as dangerous and novel for them as for the Europeans. To a man like Isaaco the upper Niger kingdoms were almost as strange and foreign as they were to Park, and the mortality among Stanley's Zanzibaris during his Congo adventures showed that Africans, as much as Europeans, were sacrificed to the hazards of Africa. Often the white travellers complained about their native assistants, their drunkenness, their thievery and laziness; but to almost every expedition they were essential. Not only did the Africans carry most of the expedition equipment inland, but they served as the travellers' eyes and ears. On the tact and advice of native servants depended the fragile relationship between white visitor and native chief, and in rough or dangerous country it was the native assistant who scouted ahead. In short, Africa could not have been explored without the help of the Africans.

The help given to an explorer by his patrons back in Europe also made a great difference to the outcome of his African expedition. The letters of men like Livingstone and Hornemann show how much the explorer's spirits were buoyed up if he knew he had intelligent and concerned sponsorship at home, to whom he could report his endeavours and ask approval. But in the very opposite sense – with a Denham or a Major Houghton – the over-close watch-dog of a patron could so easily become a burden. The traveller was cursed with the necessity of preparing useless reports and crippled by inane or conflicting instructions, or – particularly in Denham's case – he might even begin to lean too much on the home authority and seek advice where advice was not really necessary. The records of the African travellers show that their flawless patron was a sympathetic and well-meaning sponsor, sufficiently generous to despatch the explorer in some style and send succour when required, but not so inquisi-

Speke's Faithfuls

Speke's Faithfuls.

277

tive or busy as to meddle in his affairs once he was safely launched, only to sit back and await his successful return.

It is strange how little the basic conditions of African travel changed over the span of the African adventure. There was really very little to choose between the daily routine of, say, Major Houghton or a well-equipped explorer like Georg Schweinfurth a hundred and fifty years later. The day usually began with a light breakfast, generally of coffee and local bread, and there followed the tedious process of loading up and organizing the column, making sure that every porter and pack animal had the correct load and that nothing had been stolen or left behind. In due course the party would be ready to move off, walking in the general direction of its destination but making any detours that were necessary to use fords and passes or to avoid difficult country. There was always plenty of time for the white man to make side-excursions in order to collect specimens or shoot for the pot, and still get back to catch up with the slow-moving column. Every village was guaranteed to punctuate the advance of the expedition as the men stopped to buy provisions, to gather information, or simply to amuse themselves. Speke was most chagrined in East Africa when his porters, including the steady-going Bombay refused to leave a native village and preferred to spend the evening having a riotous party which left the column with a terrific hang-over. Except in an emergency no one ever travelled after dark, for it was pointless as well as dangerous, and it was advisable to stop and humour every petty headman who wanted to palaver or show his importance. Every traveller eventually realized that African travel was not a matter to be rushed. Even the bustling Stanley, when he could afford the time on his second visit to the Congo, spent days in negotiations with Congo chiefs, and Joseph Thomson took as his slogan '*Chi va piano va sano, chi va sano va lontano*' – 'He who goes softly, goes safely, He who goes safely, goes far'.

One of the recurrent tendencies among the African travellers, as Alan Moorehead pointed out of the Nile explorers, was the manner in which they were irresistibly lured back to Africa, often in the face of their professional dislike of the continent. In *The White Nile*, Moorehead compares their behaviour to:

> . . . men who make a life at sea; having once committed themselves to its hazards, they feel impelled to go back again and again even if Africa kills them. At one time or another most of them rail against the country and its inhabitants, declaring them to be ugly, brutal, scheming debauched, and finally hopeless . . . All of them in their books claim that they are in Africa because they have a mission there; they want to resolve the geographical problems and they want to reform the country, to convert the untilled land into useful farms, to open up commerce, and to lift the natives out of their animism and savagery into a higher way of life. And yet one cannot help feeling that there is still another reason for their journeys: a fundamental restlessness, a simple absorbing curiosity in everything that is strange and new.

278

All this was very true of the Victorian explorers in Africa and also, in nearly ever case, of the African explorers from other centuries. What is equally notable is that the same fascination which caught up the explorers, reached out to embrace their families and acquaintances as well. The lure of Africa seemed almost to have been a contagious disease. It was not localized to a single individual but enveloped his contacts, until the African adventure swept whole families into its coils. The Livingstone family was a case in point. Not only did David Livingstone take along his wife and his brother Charles, with such disastrous results on the Zambesi expedition, but even when he was 'lost' in central Africa, it was his son, Oswell, who went on the rescue expedition to find him. Similarly one finds Samuel Baker's nephew, Julian, accompanying his uncle on an anti-slavery expedition, and Park's son going native in the Niger delta in the hopes of tracing what happened to his father. In fine, the African adventure was very liable to become a family affair, and the lure of Africa was not restricted to one man but likely to become his patrimony.

In much the same way the grand motives for exploration were also handed down from one generation to the next. From the Portuguese conquistadors in search of Prester John to David Livingstone, the same reasons impelled men to travel and explore the continent; and in three hundred years it can be said there was scarcely a new motive which had not been foreshadowed in some way. Naturally the emphasis and balance altered so that the Victorian evangelical

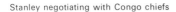

Stanley negotiating with Congo chiefs

missionaries came to Africa in a different mood from Da Gama's men-at-arms. Yet the Capuchins who followed Da Gama were as much missionaries to save the souls of what they felt to be schismatic Ethiopians, as the hardy pioneers of the Livingstone Missionary Society, named in the great man's honour, who pushed up the Congo in the late 1880's. Whether it was a desire to save souls, to trade, to acquire geographical knowledge, or simply to indulge one's curiosity, one intention seemed to grow out of the last, until the whole African adventure acquired a marked sense of unity as one phase of exploration passed into the next. Nowhere is this more clearly seen than in the path which African history took in relation to Livingstone's own dream of a Christianized continent. He intended to fight the evils of slavery, poverty, and ignorance with the 'two pioneers of civilization' as he called them: Christianity and commerce. Yet the inevitable result of his doctrines was that lucrative trade led to rivalry among the trading nations, and that this in turn brought claim and counter-claim by the trading nations until the disputes were solved by the outright annexation of the areas involved. Yet the mainstream of European involvement in Africa, which culminated in this scramble, goes even farther back. It can be traced to the days of the African Association when Joseph Banks, fearful of German interference, warned young Hornemann that he should not report his activities back to his old college friends at Göttingen, for fear of revealing valuable geographical secrets.

But in the last analysis it was Africa which was attractive for her own sake. The continent had an appeal that remained undimmed over the centuries. The African adventure took place while there were rival continents to lure the foot-loose travellers: Australia and the Americas were being opened for settlement; many parts of Asia were attracting scholars and adventurers; and even the stark physical challenge of the Polar regions was beginning to be met. Yet Africa was not quite like any of these. She offered a peculiar combination of attractions which no other continent could match. Her peoples rivalled Asia's for variety and colour. The sweep of her scenery was the equal of any other continent; and, as has been said, her wildlife was unparalleled in its quantity and diversity. Africa had a glamour, romantic and vivid, which made her the supreme continent for the enthusiastic visitor. It was a fact which from the 1800's onward was acknowledged by the shoals of artists and, later, photographers who went to Africa equipped with easels and tripods to record the visual splendours of the continent. When all else had been explored and reduced to the severe precision of maps and charts, Africa could still offer a panorama to excite and thrill the traveller. In the early days, when all this was new and strange, it was a rare quality which was almost intoxicating in its effect and accounted for the awe and wonder which, at its best, the African adventure aroused.

Illustration acknowledgments

Abbreviations used in the picture acknowledgments:
BM.: Reproduced by courtesy of the Trustees of the British Museum, London.
RGS.: The Royal Geographical Society, London.

10 Bibliothèque Nationale, Paris. Photo: BM.

14 From *Through the Dark Continent* by H. M. Stanley, London 1878. Photo: Derrick Witty.

15 From *The Congo* by H. M. Stanley, London 1885. RGS. Photo: Derrick Witty.

17 Photo: Colour Library International.

18 From *Sammlung alle Reisebeschreibungen*, 1749. RGS. Photo: Derrick Witty.

20–1 BM. (Manuscripts Add. 24065).

22 From *Journal of a Residence in Ashantee* by Joseph Dupuis, London 1824. Photo: Derrick Witty.

23 From *Missionary Travels and Researches in South Africa* by David Livingstone, London 1857. RGS. Photo: Derrick Witty.

24 BM. (Manuscripts Add. 5415A).

27 From *Scenes in Ethiopia* by John M. Bernatz, Munich-London 1852. RGS. Photo: Derrick Witty.

29 From *The Life of Tekla Haymanot*. BM. (Oriental 723). Photo: John Freeman Ltd.

30 From *The Life of Tekla Haymanot*. BM. (Oriental 723). Photos: John Freeman Ltd.

32 From *Shoa Mission* by R. Kirk, 1841–2. RGS. Photos: Derrick Witty.

35 Map by Tom Stalker-Miller.
Inset from *Livro do Estado da India Oriental* by P. Barretto de Resende, 1646. BM. (Manuscripts Sloane 197).

36 From *A Voyage to Abyssinia and Travels into the Interior of that Country* by Henry Salt, London 1814. RGS. Photo: Derrick Witty.

43 From *The Life of Tekla Haymanot*. BM. (Oriental 723). Photos: John Freeman Ltd.

45 From *The Life of Tekla Haymanot*. BM. (Oriental 723). Photo: John Freeman Ltd.

47 From *Historia Aethiopica* by Hiob Ludolf, Frankfort 1681. BM. (Printed books 583.k. 13, 14). Photo: John Freeman Ltd.

49 Horniman Museum, London. Photo: Derrick Witty.

51 From *A New History of Ethiopia* by Hiob Ludolf, London 1682. BM. (Printed books 1471.k.13). Photo: John Freeman Ltd.

52 From *Narrative of Ten Years Residence in Tripoli in Africa* by Richard Tully. RGS. Photo: Derrick Witty.

55 From *Petits Voyages* by J.-I. and J.-T. de Bry. BM. (Printed books G.6610).

56–7 BM. (Map Room CXVII No. 100). Photo: John Freeman Ltd.
Inset Museum für Völkerkunde, Vienna.

58 *Left* From *Nauwkeurige Beschryving van de Guinese Gond-tand-en-Slavekust* by Willem Bosman, Amsterdam 1709. BM. (Printed books 10095.dd.12).
Right From *A Relation of a voyage made in the years 1695–7 on the Coasts of Africa* by Sieur Froger, London 1698. BM. (Printed books 980.c.26). Photos: John Freeman Ltd.

60 From *Mission from Cape Coast Castle to Ashantee* by Edward Bowdich, London 1819. The Royal Commonwealth Society, London. Photo: Derrick Witty.

62 From *Thirty Drafts of Guinea* by William Smith, London 1749. BM. Photo: John Freeman Ltd.

64 From *Costume Antico e Moderno* by Giulio Ferrario, Milan 1815. BM. (Printed books 141.G.1). Photo: John Freeman Ltd.

67 Map by Tom Stalker-Miller.

68–9 From *Eben-ezer* by William Okeley, London 1675. BM. (Printed books 12202.aa.30). Photo: John Freeman Ltd.

71 *Left* From *Barbarian Cruelty* by Thomas Troughton, London 1751. BM. (Printed books 790.b.39).
Right From *Travels* by Thomas Shaw, Oxford 1738. BM. (Printed books G.11.145). Photos: John Freeman Ltd.

72–3 From *Histoire du Royaume d'Alger* by Langier de Tassy, Amsterdam 1725. RGS. Photo: Derrick Witty.

74 From *Esterretninger om Marokos og Fes* by Georg Höst, Kiobenhaven 1779. BM. (Printed books 454.d.8). Photo: John Freeman Ltd.

77 BM. (Print Room Crace Collection XXIX No. 10). Photo: John Freeman Ltd.

80 From *A New and Complete Collection of Voyages and Travels* by John Hamilton Moore, London 1780. BM. (Printed books 10003.f.2). Photo: John Freeman Ltd.

84 From *Travels in Western Africa* by William Gray and Staff Surgeon Dochard, London 1825. Photo: Derrick Witty.

85 From *Travels in Western Africa* by William Gray and Staff Surgeon Dochard, London 1825. Photo: Derrick Witty.

86 From *Travels in the Timanee, Kooranko and Soolima Countries in Western Africa* by Alexander Gordon Laing, London 1825. Photo: Derrick Witty.

88 From *Travels in Africa* by Mungo Park, London 1816. BM. (Printed books 12202.aa.30). Photo: John Freeman Ltd.

89 From *Travels in Africa* by Mungo Park, London 1816. BM. (Printed books 12202.aa.30). Photo: John Freeman Ltd.

91 From *Travels in the Interior Districts of Africa* by Mungo Park, London 1799. RGS. Photo: Derrick Witty.

92 From *Travels in the Interior Districts of Africa* by Mungo Park, London 1799. RGS. Photo: Derrick Witty.

93 From *Fragmens d'un Voyage en Afrique* by S. M. X. Golberry, Paris 1802. BM. (Printed books 978.k.14). Photo: John Freeman Ltd.

94 From *Travels in the Timanee, Kooranko and Soolima Countries in Western Africa* by Alexander Gordon Laing, London 1825. Photo: Derrick Witty.

97 National Portrait Gallery, London.

99 From *Travels in the Interior of Africa by Mungo Park* edited by John Campbell, Edinburgh 1816. BM. (Printed books C.108.bbb.27). Photo: John Freeman Ltd.

100–1 From *A Narrative of Travels in Northern Africa* by G. F. Lyon, London 1821. RGS. Photo: Derrick Witty.

104 From *A Narrative of Travels in Northern Africa* by G. F. Lyon, London 1821. Photo: Derrick Witty.

105 The Royal Society, London. Photo: Derrick Witty.

107 From *Travels in Abyssinia* by James Bruce, bound with other chap books of 1810–40. BM. (Printed books 12330.aa.60). Photo: John Freeman Ltd.

109 *Above left* Scottish National Portrait Gallery, Edinburgh. Photo: Tom Scott. *Below* RGS. Photo: Derrick Witty.

110 From *Scenes in Ethiopia* by John M. Bernatz, Munich-London 1852. RGS. Photos: Derrick Witty.

112 From *A Narrative of Travels in Northern Africa* by G. F. Lyon, London 1821. Photo: Derrick Witty.

114 RGS. Photo: Derrick Witty.

115 National Portrait Gallery, London.

118 Public Record Office (Safe Room 21:36:2). Crown copyright. By permission of the Controller of H.M. Stationery Office.

120 From *Narrative of Travels and Discoveries in Northern and Central Africa* by Dixon Denham and Hugh Clapperton, London 1826. Photo: Derrick Witty.

122 From *A Narrative of Travels in Northern Africa* by G. F. Lyon, London 1821. RGS. Photo: Derrick Witty.

124 RGS. Photo: Derrick Witty.

126 From *A Narrative of Travels in Northern Africa* by G. F. Lyon, London 1821. RGS. Photo: Derrick Witty.

129 From *Nouvelle Bibliothèque des Voyages* by Auguste Duponchel, Paris 1841. BM. (Printed books 1424.e.5). Photo: John Freeman Ltd.

131 From *Nouvelle Bibliothèque des Voyages* by Auguste Duponchel, Paris 1841. BM. (Printed books 1424.e.5). Photo: John Freeman Ltd.

133 From *Journal of an expedition to explore the course and termination of the Niger* by Richard and John Lander, London 1833. RGS. Photo: Derrick Witty.

135 BM. (Map Room Royal CXVII No. 116F). Photo: John Freeman Ltd.

136 From *African Scenery and Animals* by Samuel Daniell, London 1805. BM. (Printed books 458.h.14). Photos: John Freeman Ltd.

138 Africana Museum, Johannesburg.

139 Africana Museum, Johannesburg.

140 Africana Museum, Johannesburg.

142 From *Travels in the Interior of Southern Africa* by William Burchell. Photo: Derrick Witty.

143 Africana Museum, Johannesburg.

145 Africana Museum, Johannesburg.

146 From *African Scenery and Animals* by Samuel Daniell, London 1805. BM. (Printed books 458.h.14). Photo: John Freeman Ltd.

149 Mansell Collection, London.

150 From *Narrative of a Journey to the Zoolu Country* by A. F. Gardiner, London 1836. Photo: Derrick Witty.

151 From *Narrative of a Journey to the Zoolu Country* by A. F. Gardiner, London 1836. Photo: Derrick Witty.

154–5 Map by Tom Stalker-Miller. *Insets* from *Wild Sports of Southern Africa* by W. Cornwallis Harris, London 1841. Photos: Derrick Witty.

156 From *Narrative of a Journey to the Zoolu Country* by A. F. Gardiner, London 1836. Photo: Derrick Witty.

157 From *Narrative of a Journey to the Zoolu Country* by A. F. Gardiner, London 1836. Photos: Derrick Witty.

158–9 Africana Museum, Johannesburg.

163 From *Wild Sports of Southern Africa* by W. Cornwallis Harris, London 1841. Photo: Derrick Witty.

165 From *Voyages de C. P. Thunberg au Japon par le Cap de Bonne Espérance*, Paris An IV (1796). BM. (Printed books G.2815). Photo: John Freeman Ltd.

166 From *A Narrative of four journeys into the country of the Hottentots and Caffraria* by William Paterson, London 1789. BM. (Printed books 455.b.11). Photo: John Freeman Ltd.

169 From *Nouvelle Bibliothèque des Voyages* by Auguste Duponchel, Paris 1841. BM. (Printed books 1424.e.5). Photo: John Freeman Ltd.

170 From *Wild Sports of Southern Africa* by W. Cornwallis Harris, London 1841. Photo: Derrick Witty.

171 From *Wild Sports of Southern Africa* by W. Cornwallis Harris, London 1841. BM. (Printed books 10095.ee.23). Photo: Derrick Witty.

172 From *Voyage de M. le Vaillant dans l'Intérieur de l'Afrique par le Cap de Bonne-Espérence*, Paris 1790. BM. (Printed books G.2573–6). Photo: John Freeman Ltd.

173 *Above* Victoria and Albert Museum, London. Photo: Derrick Witty.

Below From *Travels in the Interior of Southern Africa* by William Burchell, London 1822. Photo: Derrick Witty.

174 *Above* From *Wild Sports of Southern Africa* by W. Cornwallis Harris, London 1841. BM. (Printed books 10095.ee.23). Photo: John Freeman Ltd. *Below* RGS. Photo: Derrick Witty.

175 From *Wild Sports of Southern Africa* by W. Cornwallis Harris, London 1841. BM. (Printed books 10095.ee.23). Photo: John Freeman Ltd.

181 Africana Museum, Johannesburg.

182 From *Wild Sports of Southern Africa* by W. Cornwallis Harris, London 1841. BM. (Printed books 10095.ee.23). Photo: John Freeman Ltd.

183 Africana Museum, Johannesburg.

185 From *Wild Sports of Southern Africa* by W. Cornwallis Harris, London 1841. BM. (Printed books 10095.ee.23). Photo: John Freeman Ltd.

187 From *Five Years of a Hunter's Life in the Far Interior of South Africa* by R. G. Cumming, London 1850. BM. (Printed books 010095.g.46). Photo: John Freeman Ltd.

189 From *The Lion Hunter of South Africa* by R. G. Cumming, London 1856. BM. (Printed books 7905.c.9). Photo: John Freeman Ltd.

191 RGS. Photo: Derrick Witty.

192 From *Heroes of North African Discovery* by N. D'Anvers, London 1877. Photo: Derrick Witty.

195 RGS. Photo: Derrick Witty.

196 From *Missionary Travels and Researches in South Africa* by David Livingstone, London 1857. RGS. Photo: Derrick Witty.

198 From *Life and Explorations of Dr Livingstone*. Adam & Co., 1878. RGS. Photo: Derrick Witty.

201 Mansell Collection, London.

202 Mansell Collection, London.

205 Mansell Collection, London.

207 From *Stanley's Emin Pasha Expedition* by A. J. Wanters, London 1890. RGS. Photo: Derrick Witty.

208 From *Through the Dark Continent* by H.M. Stanley, London 1878. Photo: Derrick Witty.

209 Richard Stanley Collection.

210 From *Through the Dark Continent* by H. M. Stanley, London 1878. Photo: Derrick Witty.

211 From *Through the Dark Continent* by H. M. Stanley, London 1878. Photo: Derrick Witty.

212 Map by Tom Stalker-Miller.

213 *Above* Mansell Collection, London. *Below* United Society for the Propagation of the Gospel, London. Photo: Derrick Witty.

215 Mansell Collection, London.

217 Peter Speke Collection. Photo: Bolwell Studio.

219 Mansell Collection, London.

220 From *Lake Regions of Central Africa* by Richard F. Burton, London 1860. RGS. Photo: Derrick Witty.

221 RGS. Photo: Derrick Witty.

224 Rodney Searight Collection. Photo: Derrick Witty.

228 RGS.

231 V. E. Baker Collection. Photo: Derrick Witty.

232 From *The Albert N'yanza* by S. W. Baker, London 1866. Photos: Derrick Witty.

233 From *Journal of the Discovery of the Source of the Nile* by J. H. Speke, London and Edinburgh 1863. RGS. Photo: Derrick Witty.

235 From *Journal of the Discovery of the Source of the Nile* by J. H. Speke, London and Edinburgh 1863. RGS. Photos: Derrick Witty.

240 Mansell Collection, London.

243 From *The Art of Travel* by Francis Galton, London 1860. BM. (Printed books 10002.a.3). Photo: John Freeman Ltd.

245 From *Pictorial Edition of the Life and Discoveries of David Livingstone* edited by J. Ewing Ritchie. RGS. Photo: Derrick Witty.

246 From *Travels and Discoveries in North and Central Africa* by Heinrich Barth, London 1857. RGS. Photo: Derrick Witty.

247 From *The Heart of Africa* by G. Schweinfurth, London 1873. RGS. Photo: Derrick Witty.

249 From *The Heart of Africa* by G. Schweinfurth, London 1873. RGS. Photo: Derrick Witty.

256 From *The Congo* by H. M. Stanley, London 1885. Photo: Derrick Witty.

257 From *The Congo* by H. M. Stanley, London 1885. Photo: Derrick Witty.

258 Richard Stanley Collection. Photo: Derrick Witty.

261 From *The Congo* by H. M. Stanley, London 1885. Photos: Derrick Witty.

262 Richard Stanley Collection.

264 From *The Congo* by H. M. Stanley, London 1885. Photo: Derrick Witty.

265 From *Conférences et Lettres de P. Savorgnan de Brazza* edited by N. Ney, Paris 1887. BM. (Printed books 10096.gg.6). Photo: John Freeman Ltd.

266 From *Conférences et Lettres de P. Savorgnan de Brazza* edited by N. Ney, Paris 1887. BM. (Printed books 10096.gg.6). Photo: John Freeman Ltd.

267 Richard Stanley Collection.

268 From *Conférences et Lettres de P. Savorgnan de Brazza* edited by N. Ney, Paris 1887. BM. (Printed books 10096.gg.6). Photo: John Freeman Ltd.

270–1 Richard Stanley Collection.

273 From *L'Uomo che dono un impero* by F. Savorgnan di Brazza, Firenze 1945. BM. (Printed books 10665.ff.79.) Photo: John Freeman Ltd.

274 Mansell Collection, London.

277 From *Journal of Discovery of the Source of the Nile* by J. H. Speke, London and Edinburgh 1863. RGS. Photo: Derrick Witty.

279 From *The Congo* by H. M. Stanley, London 1885. Photo: Derrick Witty.

We would like to thank Hamish Hamilton Limited for allowing us to quote from *The White Nile* by Alan Moorhead on page 278.

Index

Figures in **bold** type indicate pages with colour illustrations; figures in *italics* indicate pages with monochrome illustrations.

Abdullady (Clapperton's Arab servant), 119
Aborigines Commission, 135
Abuna (Ethiopian archbishop), 28
Aden, 256
African Association, 75 *et seq.*; committee members, 76; 80, 82, 83, 87; dissolved, 105; 106, 112, 117, 246, 280
African fever (malaria), 196
Africander, Andries, *175*, 178, 184
Ahmad ibn Ibrahim El Ghazi *see* El Gran
Albert Nyanza (Baker), 237
Albert, Prince, 200, 220, 236
Albion, 256
Alburka, 133
Alcock, Sir Rutherford, 245
Algeria, 70
Algiers, 54, 69, 70, *72–3*, 107, 245
Alima river, 265, 267
Alvarez, Father Francisco, 31; impression of Ethiopia, 34, 36; demonstrates church ritual for Negus, 39, 40; 41, 42
America, 79, 241
Anderson, Alexander, 95, 98, 132
Anderson, Alice (Mrs Mungo Park), 95, 98
Anglo-American Expedition for the Discovery of the Nile and Congo Sources, 203, 206
Antilope lunata, 176
Arabs, effect of their invasion of North Africa, 19; 22, 69, 70, 81, 124, 201, 206, 208, 276
Archbell, Reverend, 141, 145
Arnold, Edwin, 203, 254
Art of Travel, The (Galton), 242, *243*
Aruwimi river, 209
Association for Promoting the Discovery of the Interior Parts of Africa *see* African Association
Association Internationale du Congo, 259, 273
Astley, Thomas, 53, 55, 63, 88, 134
Athenaeum, The, 222
Austria-Hungary, 244
Axum, 41
Az Zanj, 19
Azande, king dancing, *247*; tribe, 248

Badagry, 130
Bahrnagast (Ethiopian provincial governor), 30, 31, 33, 34
Baines, Thomas, 174, 199
Baker, Lady Florence, *231*, *232*, 233
Baker, Sir Samuel, 14, 15, 189; background and character, 190, 216, 217, 218, 230, 231; 191; on firearms and 'the Baby', 193, 230; *219*, 220, *231*, *232*, 233, 235, 237, 238, 242, 243
Balugani, Luigi, 108
Bamangwato, 188
Bambuk, 60; King, 86
Banana, Point, *256*; 259, 273
Banks, Sir Joseph, 75 *et seq.*; background, 75; 82, 89; dealings with Mungo Park, 95; 102, 103, **105**; death, 105; 106, 111, 280
Bantu tribe, migration, *137*; comparison with Boers, 137; 146
Barbary, Coast, 54, 66, 245; torture scene, 64, *68–9*; 70, 71, 74, 77, 78, 80
Barker, Frederick, 203
Barolong tribe, 147
Barotse tribe, 137
Barth, Heinrich, 15, *246*, 247, 276
Bashaw, the (ruler of Tripoli), 114, 116, 117, 123, 127
Bastaards, 137
Basuto tribe, 137
Basutoland, 137
Bath, 229
Bathurst, Lord, 112, 113, 116, 119, 121, 123, 124
Battersea Dogs' Home, 204
Battles, Veg Kop, 144, *145*; Blaauwkrantz, *158–9*; Blood River, 162, 163
Beaufoy, Henry, 76, 78, 79, 81, 83, 85, 86, 94, 105
Bechuana tribe, lion hunting, 154; 180
Bechuanaland, 176
Bedouin, 70, 79, 129
Behemoth (hippopotamus), 170
Belgique, 256
Belgium, 244, 249, 250, 254
Belgrave Square, London, 219
Belzoni (Italian explorer), 276
Ben Ali, 82, 83
Benin, bronze **57**; 58, 66, 125
Bennett, Gordon, 201, 203, 241, 254
Berbers, 11, 66
Berlin, 272
Biafra, 53; King, 59
Bight of Benin, 15, 132, 207
Bismarck, 248

Black Shield regiment, 157, 160
Blackwood, John, 226, 228, 236, 237
Blackwood's Magazine, 222, 223, 226, 229
Blaquiere (French trader), 54
Blood river, 164
Blue Nile *see under* Nile
Blumenbach, Professor, 102, 103
Boers, 135 *et seq.*; house, *136*; returning from hunting, *136*; comparison with Bantu, 137; trekkers on the march, *138*; 141, 143; battle of Veg Kop, 144, *145*; resting, **146**; defeat Matabele, 147; forces split, 148; double cross Dingaan, 153; massacred, 160, 161; revenge, 162; massacre Zulus, 162, 164; farmers, 168, 171, 176, 179; ivory hunters, 177, 179; *178*, 181
Boma, 214, 259
Bombay, Sidy, 194, 196, **217**, 226, 228, 235, 276, 278
Bondou, King, 85, 90
Bornou, 103, 104, 112, 113
Bornou Mission, 113; feud, 116, 117, 118, 119, 121, 123
Boswell, 108
Botha trekkie, 141; mauled by Matabele, 142
Brak of Maka, 59
Brazza, Comte P.P.F.C. Savorgnan de, 263; meeting with Stanley, 263–4, 266–7; background, 264–5; *265*; 'burying war', 266; slanders Stanley, 268; Stanley hits back, 269; 272, *273*
Brighton, 239, 241
British, 134, 250, 253, 254
British Association, 229, 239
British Government, 130, 133
British Museum, 176
Bruce, James, 78; background, 106; *107*; equipment, 107–8; in Ethiopia, 108; ridiculed in London, 108, 111; **109**; death, 111; 113, 114, 117, 133, 223, 225, 275
Brussels, 244, 245, 249, 250, 254, 269
Brüe, André, 58, 59, 74
Buffalo regiment, 152
Buffon (French naturalist), 108, 170
Bula river, 263
Bumbireh natives, 204
Burchell, William, *173*; specimens, 173, 176; wagon, *173*; *175*, 177
Burckhardt, Johan Ludwig, 104
Burlington House, London, 236
Burton, Lady, 229, 243

Burton, Sir Richard, background and personality, 190, 191, 216, 217, 218, 223, 225; **193**, 194; on Speke, 197, 223, 266–7, 230; on Stanley, 205; expedition with Speke, 220, 221; **224**; Nile duel, 225–9, 242; described by Rigby, 228; 236, 237, 238; on African exploration, 241; 243, 247, 275, 276
Bushmen, 146, 168, 188
Bussa Falls, 14, 98, 132

Cabeata (Ethiopian court functionary), 37, 38
Caillié, René, 15, 128; in disguise, *129*; 133, 275
Cairo, 11, 79, 80, 81, 82, 83, 102, 103, 128, 207, 236
Caledon river, 147
Cambridge, 75, 150, 238
Camden, Earl of, 98
cameleopard (giraffe), 23, 184
camels, importance in North Africa, 19; **122**
Cameron, Commander Lovett, 207, 245, 250
Camp Life (Grant), 237
Cape Coast Castle, 61, *62*
Cape Colony *see* Cape Province
Cape Corse, 65
Cape of Good Hope, 165
Cape Province (Cape Colony), 147, 165, 167, 172, 173, 184
Cape Town, 134, *135*, 150, 167, 168, 172, 178
Carron Iron Company, 107, 111
Carter (leader of Experimental Elephant Expedition), 251, 252
Carthage, 16, 18
Carthaginians, 18
Cashna, 104
Castra Nova, 16
Central Africa, 205, 206; map *212*; 239, 251, 269
Cervantes, 69
Ceylon, 190, 216
Chad, 247
Chaillé-Long (American explorer), 274
Chaka Zulu (Dingaan's brother), 137, 138, 148
Charles V, King, 12
Chinese, 22, 191
Chronos temple, 18
Chuma (Livingstone's native attendant), 200, 253, 268, 276
Church Missionary Society, 148, 150
Cilliers, Sarel (Boer leader), 141, 143, 144, 148, 161, 164
Clapperton, Lieutenant Hugh, 112, 113, **114**, 116, 117, 118; accusation of homosexuality,

119; dies of dysentery, 121;
124, 125, 130, 131, 276
Clarendon, Lord, 220
Clinker, 130
Cohors Breucorum, 16
Colonial Office, 112, 113, 117,
121
Comité d'Etudes du Haut
Congo, 254, 255, 256, 259
commando, 145, 146, 147, 162;
Flug (Flight) Commando, 162
Compagnon (French explorer),
60
Congo, river, 13, 192, 194, 203,
207, 210, 251, 254, 266, 267,
268, 274; cataracts, 13, 255;
basin, 206, 255; tribes, 208–9;
current, 211; River Fleet,
256; plans for Congoland,
257; wealth, 269, 272;
Leopold wins the Congo,
273; Stanley negotiating with
Congo chiefs, *279*
Cook, Captain James, 75, 77,
78, 79, 111, 167
Coptic Church, 28
Crocodile, 211
Crystal Mountains, 255
Cumming, Roualeyn Gordon,
186; description, 187; *187*,
188, *189*; exhibits at Great
Exhibition, 189; 242, 275

Da Covilham, Pedro, 39, 40
Da Gama, Christoval, 42, 43;
meeting with Sabla Vengel,
44–5; first battle with El
Gran, 46–7; insults El Gran,
48; tortured, 49, 50; executed,
50
Da Gama, Estevam, 42
Da Gama, Vasco, 19, 42
Da Lima, Rodrigo, 31, 33, 34,
36, 37, 38, 40, 41, 53, 66
D'Abreu, Jorge, 31, 41
Dahomey, 63, 152, 245; King,
63–5
Daily Telegraph, The, 203, 222,
236, 239, 254
Damel of Kayor, 58, 59, 74
Dappers (Calvinist trekkers),
142
Dar es Salaam, 251, 253
De Kaap (Cape Town), 134
Debaroa, 42
Delagoa Bay, 134
Demba (Park's servant), 90, 93
Denham, Major Dixon, 112,
113, **115**, 116; on Oudney,
117; 119; death, 121; 274,
277
Derby, Earl of, 239
Devonshire, Duchess of, 95
Devra Damo, *36*
Dickson, William, 89, 94
Dingaan (Zulu Chief), 137, 138;
the politian, 139; love of
novelties, 139, 141, 147, 148;
dancing dress of his harem,
150; *151*; plans Boers'
defeat, 152–3; his house, *156*;

massacre of Boers, 160–1;
fugitive and death, 164
Disa longicornis, 165
Dowlish Wake, 229
Drakensberg mountains, 148
Dutch, traders, 55, 74; in Cape
Town, 134; 175
Dutch Reformed Church, 141
Dutchman's Graveyard, 62
dysentery, Hornemann's death
from, 104; Clapperton dies of,
121

East Africa, map of North-east
Africa, *35*; 222, 225, 273
East India Company, 177
Edinburgh, 89, 113, 121
Egypt, 28, 103, 107, 244
El Gran, invades Ethiopia, 42;
43, 44; insults Da Gama, 48;
defeats Portuguese, 50;
death, 49, 51
El Maghrib, 11
eland, **174**, 180
Elephant regiment, 152
elephants, *58*; myths about, 61,
170; feasting on, *221*; Great
Experimental Elephant
Expedition, 251–2; 'Old
Musty', 252
Elgin, Lord, 229
Elizabeth I, Queen, 12
Embellybelli, *157*
En Avant, 256, *257*, 260
Endeavour, 75
England, 167, 186, 191, 223,
225, 236, 241, 254
English, traders, 55, 74
Espérance, 256
Ethiopia, 26, 27, 28, *32*;
comparison with Portugal,
33; map, *35*; invaded by
Muslims, 42; Muslims
expelled, 51; 53, 66, 78, 107,
108, 111, 139, 245
Ethiopian Christianity, 27, 28,
34
explorers, motives for going to
Africa, 15, 16; on the march,
19; equipment, 193; in East
Africa, 220; outfits, 235–6;
newspapers and articles, 236;
note-takers and authors, 237;
as speakers, 238; cost of
exploring, 242; efforts
rewarded, 272; Scottish
explorers, 275

Fashoda incident, 274
Fernando Po, 121, 133
Fezzan, 103, 247
Florence, 108
Fountain of Life, 25
France, 244, 245, 254
Franceville, 265
French Government, 127, 265,
274
French, traders, 55, 74
French Senegal, 58, 245
French Senegal Company, 58
Frere, Sir Bartle, 245

Frère-Oban (Belgian Prime
Minister), 224
Fuli tribe, 59, 63, 74
Furious, 229

Gabon, 263, 265
Galawedos, 42, 44, 47, 50, 51
Galton, Francis, 242, 243
Gambia river, 60, 61, 83, 84,
87, 90, 93, 98, 245
Ganda, 227, 234, 235, 273
Garamante tribe, 16
Gardiner, Allen (missionary at
Port Natal), 148; his paintings
of Dingaan and his women,
150, **151**
Germany, 244, 245, 250, 254
Geographical Society of Paris,
128, 130
George III, King, 167
George, IV, King, 114
Geranium, Nova Species, *167*
Gibbon (historian), 77
giraffes, 22, 184, *185*
gnus, **155**, 169
Gold Coast, 16, 53, 65
Gondokoro, *192*, 230, *231*, 233,
263
Good Words, 222
Gordon, 243, 251, 274
Goree, 83, 95
gorilla, 22, 184
Gran *see* El Gran
Grant, James Augustus,
background and personality,
190, 216, 217, 218, 238; 191,
193, 194, 195, **217**, 227, 229,
230, *231*, 232, *233*, 234, *235*,
236, 237, 239, 240, 243; at
Brussels conference, 245
Great Exhibition 1851, 189
Great Experimental Elephant
Expedition, 251, 252
Great Trek, 137, 142, 147, 178
Greeks, 16; early traders, 27
Griqua tribe, 147, 168, 185
Griqualand, 137
Guinea, 12; new coastal
settlement, **56–7**; *58*
Gum Coast, 53

Hachette (French editor), 250
Harar, 48
Harris, Captain William
Cornwallis, 177, 178, 179,
180, 181; meeting with
Umzilikazi, 182–3; *184*, *185*,
186, *187*, 189
hartebeest, **170**
Hassan ibn Mohammed al
Wezaz al Fazi *see* Leo
Africanus
Hatitia (Arab Sheik), 277
Hell's Cauldron, 259
Herodotus, 13, 16
Herrador (Spanish Consul in
Tripoli), 125
hippopotamuses, method of
killing, 61; myths about, 170;
187; capsizing Livingstone,
213, shot by Stanley, 259, **264**

Hlomo Ambata *see* Place of the
Skull
Holland, 249, 254
Hornemann, Frederick, 102–4,
246, 276, 277, 280
Hottentots, 134, 136, 141, 146,
178, 184, 188
Houghton, Major Daniel, 83,
84, 85; reports that Niger
flows eastward, 85; death, 86;
90, 104, 277, 278
Houghton, Mrs, 87
Hudson, Sir Jeffrey (Charles II's
court dwarf), 70
Humboldt (Scientific explorer),
246
Hunter (surgeon), 77

Ibo river pirates, 132; canoe,
133
Ihlangu Inhlope *see* White
Shield regiment
Ihlangu Umnyama *see* Black
Shield regiment
Illustrated London News, 222,
237
impi (Zulu guild regiment), 139,
151; dancing display, 152;
file past Dingaan, *157*; 161,
162, 181, 184
In Salah, 125
Incomi river, 162
India, 186, 190, 216, 222, 223,
252
Indian Army, 177, 216, 228
induna (Zulu officer), 137, 139,
147, 152, 156, 160, 161, 162
Inkisi, 211
International Association,
established, 249; first
Assembly, 250; 253; Stanley
given command, 255; links
with Comité, 255, 257
International Conference 12–14
September 1876, participating
countries, 224; Leopold's
address, 248; plans *stations
civilisatrices*, 249; proposes
national committees, 249;
International Association
established, 249
Isaaco (Park's guide), 96, 98,
276, 277
Islam, 12, 25, 26, 33, 42, 54, 190
Italy, 244, 245
Ivory Coast, 53, 63

James Fort, 61, 62
Jeune Afrique, 256
Jews, 27
Jobson, Richard, 60, 61
John Bull, 222
Johnson (Park's servant), 90, 93
Johnson, Dr, 106, 111
Johnston, Keith, 253
Joliba, 98, 102
Joloff tribe, 62, 63, 65
Jomard (French geographer),
130

Kabaka *see* Mtesa

Index

Kaffir Wars, 137, 146
Kalahari, 172, 176, 186, 190
Kalipi (Umzilikazi's senior
 general), 143, 144, 145, 181,
 184
Kalulu (Stanley's native
 attendant), 211; his death,
 211; 214, 255
Kamara, Sergeant Malamine,
 267, *268*
Kamrasi (King of Nyoro), 231,
 232, 234, 235, 237
Kano, 120
Karema, 253
Karroo, 134, 176
Kensington Gardens, London,
 229
Kensington Gore, London, 243
Khartoum, 230, 236
King Solomon, 27, 42
Kirk (consul at Zanzibar), 201
Kitchener, 274
Kolobeng, 188
Koran, 128, 129
Koranna tribe, 145, 147
Kruger, Paul, 141
Kruger trekkie, 141
Kuruman, 179, 199

Lady Alice, 13, 203, 204, 207,
 209, 210, 214, 255
Laidley, Dr, 83, 84, 86, 88, 90
Laing, Emma *see* Warrington,
 Emma
Laing, Major Gordon, 121, 122,
 124; sets out for Timbuctoo,
 124; mutilated by Tuaregs,
 125–6; murdered by Tuaregs,
 127; 128, 129, 133, 222, 274,
 276
Lake Albert, 230, 251
Lake Bangweolo, 201
Lake Chad, 22, 120, 247
Lake Mweru, 201, 202
*Lake Regions of Central Africa,
 The* (Burton), 226
Lake Tana, 42, 51, 108
Lake Tanganyika, 19, 195, 225,
 227, 229, 250, 252, 254
Lake Victoria, 204, 205, 214,
 225, 226, 227, 229
Lalibela, 28, 41
Lamarck (French zoologist), 173
Lamb, Bullfinch, 63, 64
Lander, John, 130, *131*, 132,
 133
Lander, Richard, 130, *131*, 132,
 133, 203
Le Vaillant, *169*, 171; 'giraffe
 camp', *172*; cures giraffe
 skin, 173
Ledyard, John, background and
 previous adventures, 78–9;
 81; death, 82; 102, 103, 275
Leo Africanus, 66
Leo X, Pope (Giovanni de
 Medici), 66
Leopold II, King, 243;
 organizes International
 Conference, 244; *245*, 246;
 addresses Conference, 248;

249; elected president of
 International Association,
 250; approaches Stanley, 254;
 255, 256; strengthens grip on
 Congo, 257; 259, 263, 268;
 offers de Brazza a job, 269;
 wins the Congo, 273
Leopoldville, 268
Lepcis Magna, 17, 19
Lesseps, de, 250
Levant, 104
Liebenberg, Behrend, 142
Liebenberg trekkie, 141;
 attacked by Matabele, 142
Limpopo river, 147, 164, 184;
 valley, 188
Linnaeus, 165, 167
Lion's Head, 134
lions, *154*; myths about, 169;
 mauling Livingstone *196*
Livingstone, Charles, 197, 279
Livingstone, Dr David, 14, 15,
 19, 179, 186, 190, *191*, 193,
 194, *195*; on 'African fever',
 196; mauled by a lion, 14,
 196, 197; status as an
 explorer, 197; on his ox
 Sinbad, 197, *198*; character,
 199, 200, 214–5; letter writer,
 200, 201, 202; on travel, 197,
 200; *201*; death and funeral,
 202; 203, 204, 206, **213**, 214;
 with Stanley, *215*; 218, 222,
 229, 230, 236, 237; speech
 making, 238; 239, 240, 242,
 243, 246, 275, 276, 277, 279,
 280
Livingstone Falls, 211
Livingstone Missionary Society,
 280
Livingstone, Oswell, 279
Llandaff, Bishop of, 76, 77
Loanda, 190, 192
London, 75, 79, 80, 82, 83, 86,
 89, 108, 111, 119, 135, 167,
 211, 217, 239
London Missionary Society,
 199, 200
Long Street, Cape Town, 134
Lualaba river, 201, 207, 210,
 250
Lucas, Simon, 77, 78, 79, 80,
 81, 82, 83
Lyon, G. F., 111, 132

Ma Robert, 195
Madame Tussauds, 243
Makoko, the (Congo native
 leader), 266, 269
Makula, 207
Mandingo tribe, 63, 84;
 country, 123
Manoel, King, 31
Mansa Musa, Lord of Mali, *10*,
 11, 12, 13, 23, 25, 28
Marchand (French officer), 274
Maritz, Gerrit (Boer leader),
 138, 146, 147, 148, 161
Martyn, Lieutenant (officer on
 Park's second expedition), 96,
 98, 102

Mary I, Queen, 12
Masai tribe, 22
Mashonaland, 137, 186
Massassa ledge, 211
Massawa, 30, 31, 41, 43
Masson (George III's gardener),
 167, 168
Matabele tribe, 137; raiders,
 139; justice, *139*; warriors,
 140, **163**; battle technique
 against Boers, 142–3; battle
 of Veg Kop, 144, *145*;
 defeated at Mosega, 147;
 151, 156, 160, 162, 178, 179,
 182, 184, 185
Matabeleland, 137, 151, 178
matamores, 69
Matopo hills, 164
Mazamboni warriors, **270**–1
Mbelo natives, 212
McKinnon, William, 245
Mecca, 11, 12, 41, 69, 71, 190
Medina (Capital of Woolli), *84*,
 85; (Arabia), 190
Mediterranean, 54, 107
Mequinez, 69
Meritsane, *171*; river 179
Mesopotamia, 104
Mirambo, 206, 252, 274
Missionary Travels
 (Livingstone), *23*, 237
Moffat, Robert, 179, 199
Moore, Sir John, 219
Moorehead, Alan, 278
Moors, 54, 66; described by
 Thomas Salmon, 69;
 described by Thomas Shaw,
 70; 71; described by Ledyard,
 81; in London, 82; take
 Park prisoner, 91; camp, *92*
Morocco, 54, 66, 69, 71, 78,
 128; King, *71*, *74*
Mosega, 147, 179, 180
Mosheshe (King of the Basuto),
 137, 141
Motabhoy, Nasserwanji (Parsee
 manservant), 178, 183
Mount Soma, 123
Mountains of the Moon, 192,
 220
Mouri, 62
Mourzouk, 104, 116, 117;
 castle, **104**
M'Queen, James, 228, 229
Mtesa (Kabaka of Buganda),
 205, 232; his court, 234; *235*;
 253, 273
Muato-yamvo (Congo King),
 250
Mulai Ismail, Emperor, 71
Munchausen, Baron, 111
Murchison Falls, 220, 230
Murchison, Sir Roderick Impey,
 218; background, 219; *219*;
 220, 221, 223; Speke's ally
 in Nile duel, 227, 229
Murray (travel writer), 187, 188
Murray, John, 133, 237
Murray, Margaret (James
 Bruce's fiancée), 107, 108
Musa Mali *see* Mansa Musa

Muslims, invade Ethiopia, 42;
 burning churches, 49; 51, 74,
 78, 91, 93, 276

Nachtigal, Gustav, 246, 248
Namaqualand, 172
Napoleon, 103
Narrative . . . (Denham), 121
Natal, 138, 148, 156, 162
Ncouna, 266, 268
Negus, the (ruler of Ethiopia),
 27; participates in mass
 baptism, 28, *30*, 40; 31;
 reception of Da Lima's
 embassy, 37–8; *39*, 40, 41, 42,
 108, 139; *see also* Galawedos
 and Prester John
New York Herald, 201, 203,
 239; criticism of Stanley, 241;
 254, 269
Niam-niam *see* Azande tribe
Niger river, 66, 84, 85, 90, 93,
 94, 95, 96, 98, 102, 113, 120,
 121, 123, 124, 125, 130, 132,
 133, 207, 247
Nile, source, 16, 107, 190, 192,
 207, 216, 220, 222, 223, 225,
 227, 229, 230, 234, 245;
 river, 18, 213, 227, 251, 274;
 Blue Nile, Bruce at source,
 107, 108; falls, 211; Upper
 Nile, 242
Nimrod (sporting journalist),
 114; nimrods (big game
 hunters), 177, 179, 186, 187
North Africa, map, *67*; coast,
 54; 74
Nyangwe, 201, 206, 207, 250,
 254
Nyongena hill, *261*
Nyoro, 231, 233, 237

Oguwe river, 265, 268
Oliphant, Laurence, 229
Orange river, 137, 141, 169, 179
Oswell, William Cotton, 186
Oudney, Walter, 113, 116;
 described by Denham, 117;
 death 120; 121, 275
Owen, Reverend Francis, 150,
 151; describes Zulu dancing
 display, 152; 153, 156, 160;
 description of massacre of
 Boers, 161; 162
Oxford, 75, 223, 225

Pall Mall Gazette, 239
Palmerston, 220
Panda (Dingaan's half-brother),
 164
Paris, 108, 173, 269
Park, Mungo, 14, 87, *88*, *89*;
 description, 90; sets off on
 first trip, 90; *91*; prisoner of
 the Moors, 91–3; reaches
 Niger river, 94; feted in
 London, 94; account of
 journey, 95; second trip,
 95–6; **97**; theories on his
 death, 98, *99*, 102; 112, 132,
 222, 274, 275, 276, 277

Pasha of Tripoli, 80
Pasha of Zebid, 50
Paterson, William, 167, 275
Pearl, 195
Pelagonium ('geranium'), *166*, 167
Pellow, Thomas, 66, 68, 70, 78
Pepper Coast, 53, 54, 63
Petra, 104
Phillip II, King, 12
Pillars of Hercules, 16
Pindar, Peter (satyrist), 111
Place of the Elephant *see* Umgungundhlovu
Place of the Skull, 160
Pliny, 12, 23
Pocock, Edward, 203
Pocock, Frank, memorial, *14*; 203, 207, *208*, 211; Stanley on his death, 212, 214; 255
Port Natal, 148, 162
Portugal, 244, 245
Portuguese, 23; search for kingdom of Prester John, 26; Da Lima's embassy to Ethiopia 1520, 30 *et seq.*; nobleman, *35*; rescue force led by Christoval da Gama 1541, 43 *et seq.*; expelled from Ethiopia, 51; traders, 54, 55, **57**
Potgieter, Hendrik, 143, 145, 147, 162
Potgieter trekkie, 141
Present State of All Nations (Thomas Salmon), 69
Prester John, 23, *24*; his legendary kingdom, 25–6; 28, 30, 31, 33, 34, 48, 51, 53, 66; *see also* Negus, the
Pretorius, Andreus, 162
Punch, 236, *274*
pygmies, 207, 209, 248, *249*

Quarterly Journal of Science, 123
Queen of Sheba, 27, 42
Quoja tribe, 63

Rabat, 128
Rah Eesa, **32**
Ras Gedam, **32**
Rasselas (Johnson), 111
Rawlinson, Major General Sir Henry, 239, 241, 245
Red Sea, 16, 19, 27, 30, 31, 40, 256
Rennell, Major James, 16, 94
Resolution, 167
Retief, Piet (Boer leader), 138, 148, 151, 152, 153, 156, 160, 164
Rhenoste river, 143
rhinoceroses, *14*; myths about, 169, 171, 172; 'white rhino', 173; 184
Rhodes, Cecil, 164
Richardson (W. C. Harris's companion), 177, 178
Richardson, James, 247
Richthofen, Baron von, 246
Rigby, Christopher, *228*

Ritter (geographer), 246
Robinson Crusoe, 15
Rohlfs, Gerhardt, 246, 248, 249
Romans, 16, 18; early traders, 27
Rome, 28
Rossetti (Venetian consul in Cairo), 81, 82, 103
Rousseau, Baron (French consul in Tripoli), 127, 128
Royal, 256, 260
Royal African Company, 60, 63, 64
Royal Cornwall Gazette, 132
Royal Geographical Society, 105, 133, 190, 204, 216, 218; Baker addressing a meeting, *219*; 220, 221, 225, 227, 228, 229, 239, 242, 243, 245, 250, 263
Royal Navy, 112, 148, 194
Royal Society, 75, 108, 219
Ruanda, 23
Russell, Lord John, 220
Russia, 79, 244

Sabla Vengel (Ethiopian Queen Mother), 42, 44, 45, 46, 48, 50
Safeni (coxswain of *Lady Alice*), 214
Sahara, 12, 13, 16, 19, 22, 66, 68, 82, 104, 112; Saharan scene, **122**; 123, 128, 245, 274
St Andrews, 237
St Asaph, 190, 239
St Mary, 28, 30
St Thomas, 25
Sallee, 66
Sansanding, 96, 98
sassaby, **170**
Saturday Club, 76, 105
Savile Row, London, 218
Schweinfurth, Dr Georg, 246, 248, 278
Scot, George, 95, 98
Scotland, 111, 189, 217
Senegal river, 54
Seven Fountains District, 179
Shaw, Dr Thomas, 70, *71*
Shoa, 31, 33
Sierra Leone, 121, 128
Simon's Bay, 177
Sinbad, (Livingstone's ox), 197, *198*
Siyonkella (Basuto chief), 152, 153, 156
Slave Coast, 53
slaves, slavery, 55; slave ship, **56**–**7**; as source of informa-tion, 63; in North Africa, 66; atrocities, *68*–*9*; abolition and suppression, 135, 192, 203, 242; traders, 203, 215, 233
smallpox, 208
Smit trekkie, 141
Smith, Dr Andrew, 178
snakes, *14*; treatment of bites, 60
Society for the Protection of Aborigines, 204

Soho Square, London, 75, *77*, 83, 102, 219
Soir, Le, 239
Sokoto, 120, 121, 130, 131, 247
Solomon, King, *see* King Solomon
Somali natives, 222
Somaliland, 190, 221; Burton-Speke trip, 222
Songhai, 247
South Africa, map, *154*–*5*; plant life, 167; zoology, 169; 173, 178, 185, 187
Southampton, 202
Spain, 244, 249
Sparrman, Anders, 167, 168, 175
Speke, John Hanning, 189, 190, 191, 193, 194, 195, 196; described by Burton, 197, 223, 226–7, 230; background and personality, 216, 218, 222, 223; *217*; expedition with Burton, 220–22; Nile duel, 225–9, 242; described by Rigby, 228; described by M'Queen, 229; account of his death, 229; 230, *231*, *232*, *233*; and Mtesa, 234, *235*; 236, 237, 243, 274, 276, 278
Stanley, Sir Henry Morton, 13, 19; background and personality, 190, 191, 203; organizer, 194, 204; 195, 196, 201, *202*; first Congo expedition, 203 *et seq.*; criticized for treatment of natives, 204; *205*; and Mirambo, 205; deal with Tippu Tib, 206; negotiates cataracts, 211; Pocock's death, 212, 214; comparison with Livingstone, 214–5; 216, 217, 222, 230; 'Congo hat', 236; 237; press criticism, 238–41; in America, 241; cost of second Congo expedition, 242; 243, 253; approached by Leopold, 254; appointed leader of Inter-national Association's new Congo expedition, 255; *258*; sets off up the Congo, 259; builds Vivi Station, 259; labours of building road, 260–1; almost dies of fever, 263; 'Bula Mutari', 263; meeting with de Brazza, 263–4, 266–7; *267*; slandered by de Brazza, 268; hits back, 269; *270*–*1*; 275, 277, 278, *279*
Stanley Club, 269
Stanley Falls, 211
Stanley Pool, 255, 260, 265, 267, 268
stations civilisatrices, 249, 250, 251, 253, 257; Vivi Station, 259–60, *261*, **264**
Stewart, Commodore, 71
Stewart, James, 237

Stibbs (English explorer), 60
Strauch, Colonel, 255, 256, 257, 259, 263
Sudan, 18, 243, 247
Suez Canal, 250, 256
Susi (Livingstone's native attendant), 200, 268, 276
Swaziland, 164
Sydney, Lord, 78

Table Bay, 167
Table Mountain, 134, *135*, 165
Tanganyika territory, 200
Tangier, 70, 128
Tanit, temple of, 18
Taunton, 236
Tetuan, 54
Thaba Nchu, 141, 147
Thompson (English explorer), 60
Thomson, Joseph, 253, 278
Thunberg, Carl Peter, *165*, 167, 168, 175
Timbuctoo, 15, 66, 83, 86, 104, 121, 124, 125, 126, 127, 128, 130, 247
Times, The, 190, 222, 229, 236, 239, 242
Tippu Tib, 206; *207*, *208*
Tozer, 70
traders, in West Africa, 53, 54, 55, 61; in North Africa, 54; life in trade forts, 61–2; importance to exploration, 62; 63; 74
Trajan (Roman emperor), 16
Travels into the Interior Districts of Africa (Park), 90, *91*
tribes *see under* tribe name; diversity, 22; contact with traders, 62–3, 65; source of information, 63
Trieste, 243
Tripoli, 54, 78, 80, 83, 103, 111; ruins, **112**; 113, 114, 116, 121, 127, 247
Tsetse fly, 23, 251
Tuaregs, *10*, 13, 98; Ahaggar Tuareg attack Laing, 125; **126**; Berabich Tuareg murder Laing, 127; 128
Tuckey, Captain (Congo explorer), 210; 'Tuckey's Farthest', 210
Tunis, 70
Tunisia, 70
Turkey, 244
Turks, soldiers, 44, 47, 48, 50; described by Ledyard, 81
Tutsi tribe, 23
Twa tribe, 23

Ubangi chiefs, 266
Ujiji, 19, 201, 203, 221, 236, 239, 241, 250, 253, 263; 'Sea of Ujiji', 220, 225
Ukulima (Bugandan Queen Mother), 234, *235*
Uledi, the Coxswain, 276
Umgungundhlovu (Place of the Elephant), 138, 150, 151;

Index

layout, 153–4; 156
Umzilikazi (Matabele chief),
    description, 137–8; receiving
    visitors, *140*; 142, 143, 145;
    defeat of Mosega, 147; 151,
    156, 164, 178, 179, 180, 181,
    183; presents, 178, 182, 183;
    discipline in his kraal, 183;
    184, 185
United Service Club, 127, 226

Vaal river, 142; fording the
    river, *143*; 176, 181, 184
Veg Kop, 143; battle, 144, *145*;
    147, 162, 181
Victoria Falls, 22
Victoria, Queen, 200, 239, 260
Vivi Station, 259–60, *261*, **264**

Waganda tribe, canoes, 204
Wagenya natives, 207
Wales, 190
Wangwana tribe, canoes, 204
Warrington, Emma (Mrs
    Gordon Laing), 121, 122,
    124, 125, 126, 127, 130
Warrington, Hanmer (British
    consul in Tripoli), 114; his
    house, 116, **118**; 117; defends
    Clapperton, 119; and Gordon
    Laing, 121, 123, 124, 125,
    126; hounds French consul
    127, 128
Wavuma tribe, 205
Wedgwood (potter), 77
Wellington, Duke of, 113

West Africa, coast 53; map, *67*;
    74, 83
Westminster Abbey, *202*
Whiddah, 63
White Nile, The (Moorehead),
    278
White Shield regiment, 157,
    160, 164
Whitehall Place, London, 218
Wilberforce (abolishionist), 77
Wilge river, 143
Windus, John, 71
Wood, William (interpreter at
    Umgungundhlovu), 160
Woolli, 84

Yellala Falls, 259
York, Duke of, 61
Young, James 'Paraffin', 200,
    202

Zambesi, 22, 192, 194, 197,
    199, 236, 237, 251
Zanzibar, 19, 192, 194, 201,
    203, 207, 208, 214, 220, 221,
    228, 247, 252, 256
Zinga, cataract, 211; natives,
    214
Zulu tribe, 137, 138; Zulu
    woman of rank, **150**; 151;
    dancing display by warriors,
    152; importance of impis,
    152; 156; dance with oxen,
    157; Great dance at
    Embellybelli, *157*; massacre
    Boers, 160–1; defeated by
    Boers, 162, 164
Zululand, 137, 151